# 100 SOULS

## CHRONICLES OF THE WALKER & MCCALL FAMILIES OF PERRY, GEORGIA & DUBLIN, GEORGIA

*100 Souls: Chronicles of The Walker & McCall Families of Perry, Georgia & Dublin, Georgia*
Copyright © 2022 Maurice Allen, Jr., CG

Divine Alliance Publishing

All rights reserved. No part of this book may be reproduced (except for inclusion in reviews), disseminated or utilized in any form or by any means, electronic or mechanical, including photocopying, recording, or in any information storage and retrieval system, or the Internet/World Wide Web without written permission from the author or publisher.

Printed in the United States of America

*100 Souls: Chronicles of The Walker & McCall Families of Perry, Georgia & Dublin, Georgia*
Maurice Allen, Jr., CG

1. Title 2. Author 3. Ancestry

ISBN 13: 978-0-9861610-4-9

# 100 SOULS

## CHRONICLES OF
## THE WALKER & MCCALL FAMILIES
## OF PERRY, GEORGIA & DUBLIN, GEORGIA

MAURICE ALLEN, JR., CG

Divine Alliance Publishing

The pictorial presentation of four generations of the author, Maurice Allen, Jr. and his family, is an example of what many families can access and compile for themselves. There are fifteen people that are contained in the four generations of every person. Everyone has eight great-grandparents, four grandparents, and two parents. The individual is always included when counting generations. The author is shown bottom center, and his parents are pictured directly above him.

The left side is the paternal side of the author's family. His father's parents are pictured left-center. The far left pictures are the parents of the author's grandfather. The above left pictures are the parents of his grandmother.

The right side represents his maternal side. His mother's parents are pictured right-center. The upper right picture is the mother of his grandmother, and the top center is the mother of his grandfather. The search goes on for family members who may have photographs of his maternal great-grandfathers.

Mr. Allen chose as the background, the 1830 will of a Georgia slaveholder. She bequeathed an eight year-old boy named Hamlet, to her youngest daughter. He was the great-great-great-grandfather of the author.

# COLOR KEY

| | |
|---|---|
| **THE CHILDREN** | |
| **Ethel McCall Walker** | |
| **Milous Wilburn Walker, Jr.** | |
| **Mattie Walker** | |
| **Annie Walker** | |
| **Their PARENTS** | |
| **Milous Wilburn Walker** | |
| | **Louisa 'Lula' Rebecca McCall** |
| **Their GRANDPARENTS** | |
| **John Angus Walker** | **John Stanley** |
| **Emma Felder** | **Tena McCall** |
| **Their GREAT – GRANDPARENTS** | |
| **Alex Nixon (Emma's father)** | **(Tena's father) Hamlet McCall** |
| **Grace Felder (Emma's mother)** | **(Tena's mother) Patsey Yopp** |
| **Their GREAT – GREAT – GRANDPARENTS** | |
| | **(Hamlet's father) Will McCall** |
| | **(Hamlet's mother) Louisa** |
| | **(Patsey's mother) Peggy Yopp** |

**Explanation: The Color Key uses the first five colors of the color chart; Red, Blue, Yellow, Green, and Orange. ORANGE highlights names of family members such as aunts/uncles, sisters/brothers, (non-ancestors), and non-relatives who were a peripheral part of the family. Red, Blue, Yellow, and Green are used to represent your ancestors (ones who made it possible for you to exist, i.e. Mother/Father, grandM/grandF, GgM/GgF, etc.). RBYG are used alternately, each generation, to represent the Parents, gP, GgP, etc. While RED & YELLOW are the females, BLUE & GREEN highlight the male ancestors.**

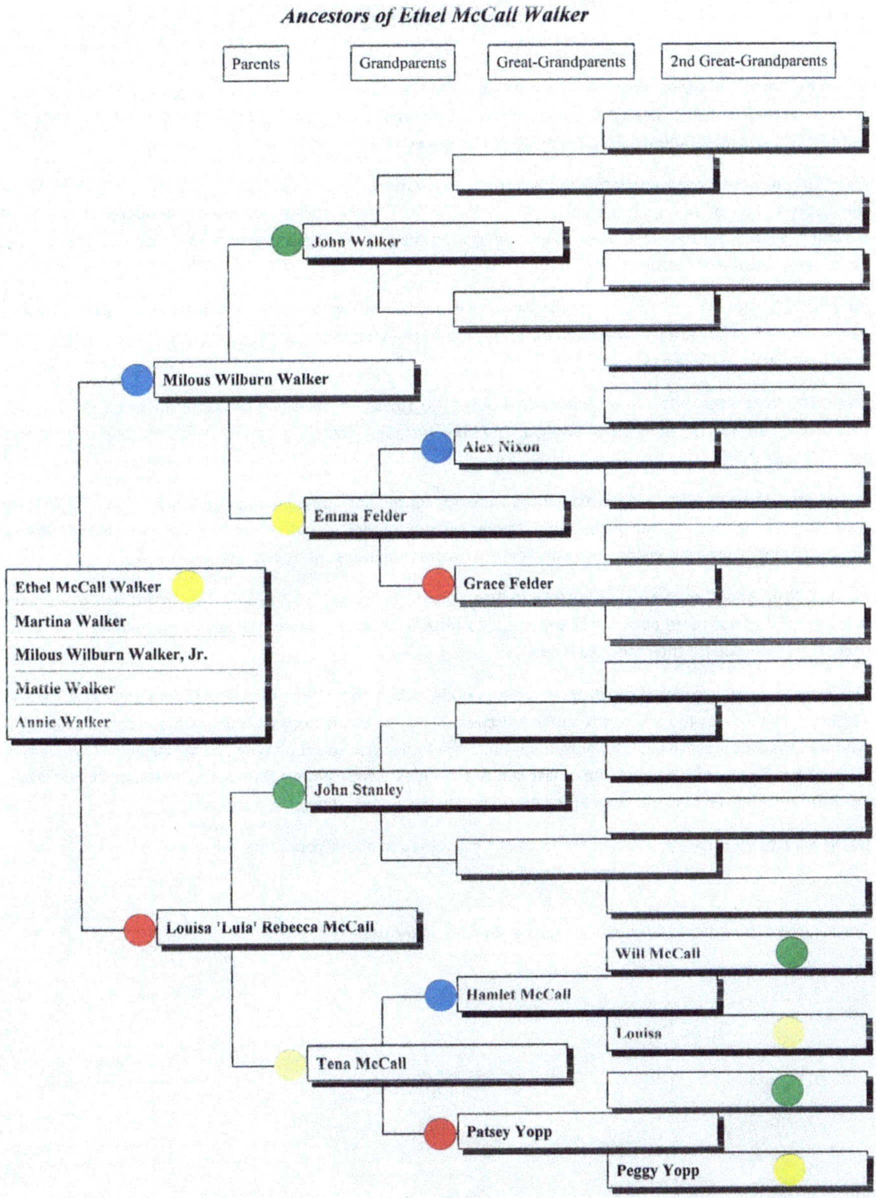
Ancestors of Ethel McCall Walker
Parents
Grandparents
Great-Grandparents
2nd Great-Grandparents
John Walker
Milous Wilburn Walker
Alex Nixon
Emma Felder
Grace Felder
Ethel McCall Walker
Martina Walker
Milous Wilburn Walker, Jr.
Mattie Walker
Annie Walker
John Stanley
Louisa 'Lula' Rebecca McCall
Will McCall
Hamlet McCall
Louisa
Tena McCall
Patsey Yopp
Peggy Yopp

# FOREWORD

When my cousin, Maurice Allen, Jr., asked me to write the foreword for his book **"100 Souls"** I was honored and also apprehensive to take on this task. However, by reading **"100 Souls"**, I have a better understanding of our family's accomplishments, despite the obstacles placed in their way.

Therefore, have you ever wondered and wanted to know more about your family's history? Many of us know the backgrounds of our grandparents. But, what do we know about our great-grandparents and their parents? Where did they live? How many siblings did they have? There are so many questions many of us have, regarding our ancestors.

Your family's ancestry and legacy are important to every family. Yet, if you are of any nationality other than a descendant of enslaved men and women, born here in the United States, you can trace your family's roots back to the actual village or town.

This is the reason the author has written the book: **"100 Souls"**. It takes you on a journey to tell the story of The Walker and McCall Families of Georgia. The book includes pictures of family members, and census data from 1870 to 1940.

Before the census of 1870, African Americans were not counted as human beings, only as property. Therefore, very little is known of our forbearer's family history before or after arriving in the United States. Unfortunately, African Americans can only refer to records vaguely kept by county courthouses.

Reading **"100 Souls"** is more than a story, telling of the Walker and McCall Families, and it will pique your curiosity to find out more about your own family's history. To assist you with finding more about your roots, there is a workbook for the reader to follow.

The book takes the reader through three time periods, called Chronicles: #1: 1830-1870, #2: 1871-1900 and #3: 1901-1940. Over the years, the author discussed a lot of this history with my father, Edgar De Allen III, who was the eldest brother of the author's father. My father was so proud when he was asked, 10 years ago, to write the foreword. Now, as the eldest son of the eldest son, I submit this writing in honor of my father, Edgar De Allen III, and my uncle, Maurice Allen, Sr. They are now among the ancestors.

By the way, there is always a good time to have a conversation about your family's history!

*Darnell Allen, retired Vice-President, Diversity, Equity and Inclusion*

Edgar D. Allen III
2-16-2013

# TABLE OF CONTENTS

**CHRONICLE I 1830 - 1870**

The Walker Family of Perry, Houston County, Georgia

SURNAMES

Walker

Felder

Nixon

Swift

**CHRONICLE II 1871 - 1900**

The McCall Family of Dublin, Laurens County, Georgia

SURNAMES

McCall

Yopp

Stanley

**CHRONICLE III 1901 - 1940**

The Walker – McCall Family Migration to Chicago, Cook County, Illinois

SURNAMES

Allen

Milhous

# *Chronicle I*

*…and man became a living soul.*
*Genesis 2:7*

100 souls ago, the father of the Walker/McCall family tree would be born on Friday, July 7, 1876. His parents, Emma Felder and John Walker, proudly named him, Milous Wilburn Walker. They were residents of Perry, Houston County, Georgia, and both John and Emma were native Georgians, who were born 36 and 28 years earlier, respectively. John worked in the harness shop and livery stable, while his wife, Emma, raised their children, kept house, and took in washing and ironing.

Emma would soon deliver her husband, John's eighth child, that summer. Emma's first daughter, Evaline, was not John's issue, but he dutifully gave her his surname out of love for both of them. Evaline was born three years before Emancipation, in 1862. Her mother, Emma, was about 15 years old. Now, Evaline was old enough to help her mother with the daily chores, which included taking care of her younger siblings.

The names of Emma and John's children were, Martha Grace (who was named after Emma's mother, Grace Felder), Augustus, Mary, John Jr., and Annie. Emma would especially watch Evaline, while she cared for her two year-old sister, Annie. The fourteen years between them was close enough to the age difference between Evaline and Emma to bring back fond memories of her early motherhood experience. Emma knew that Evaline would become a wonderful wife and mother, someday soon. In fact, she was very intuitive about the personalities of each of her children.

Gracie, at 12 years old, took instructions well. Yet, Emma noticed how well she could administer those same instructions. Gracie would make an excellent teacher. Now, Augustus, on the other hand, was Emma's 10 year-old handyman and jack-of-all-trades, who loved fixing and building things. Emma saw a very skilled tradesman in Gus.

Mary was quite young to be as organized as she was. The eye of her seven year-old mind could see a specific place for every moveable object in her immediate space. Emma recognized that she liked to maintain an orderly environment, just like any of the best housekeepers in Perry.

Emma named Little John after his father because he looked the most like him. She certainly realized by the time he was four years old that she named him well. Everything he saw his father do, Little John would try to do it. He was intently focused on being his Daddy's son, and John was a good example to follow. He made it easy for his young sons to look to him as an excellent example of manhood. Gus and Little John eagerly walked in John's footsteps. Not only was Little John his father's shadow, he was his pulse.

Baby Annie's affectionate ways tended toward caring and loving others rather than seeking any attention for herself. Whenever the children cried about anything, she approached them with a consoling pat on the back, as she embraced their necks. Emma watched the children when they would often play what they called "The Weeping Game" with Baby Annie. Each one would take turns and begin to pretentiously cry to invoke her aid. Annie would immediately, almost instinctively, make her way to each of them, first examining their hands for any sign of injury.

As she touched their hands to her face, she would kiss each hand, search their eyes until they stopped crying, and then she'd hug them for awhile. Another started to cry. She would make her rounds with each of the children until all were quieted. Emma sought to nurture her little caregiver to become the best nurse around. She smiled at the thought that her new baby would be a unique addition to the family. Even the children eagerly awaited the new arrival.

*Your wife shall be as a fruitful vine by the sides of your house:*
*your children like olive plants round about your table.*
*Psalm 128:3*

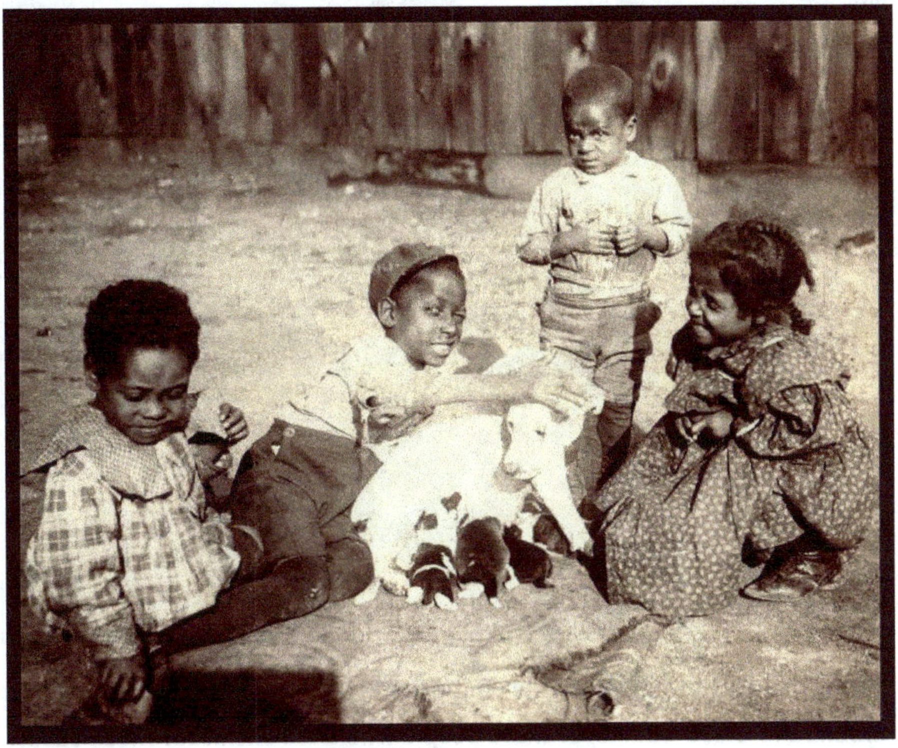

**Children Playing in the 1870s**

**This photograph and the scene on the next page, represent the activities around the 'slave' cabins, of those people who were enslaved. These cabins were actually located in South Carolina, and were used as staging areas before the transient laborers were taken to auction or market.**

**Woman On Wash Day w/ Children At Play**

ancestry

## 1870 United States Federal Census

| | |
|---|---|
| Name: | **John Walker** |
| Birth Year: | abt 1840 |
| Age in 1870: | 30 |
| Birthplace: | Georgia |
| Home in 1870: | Perry, Houston, Georgia |
| Race: | Black |
| Gender: | Male |
| Value of real estate: | |

Household Members:

| Name | Age |
|---|---|
| John Walker | 30 |
| Emma Walker | 22 |
| Evaline Walker | 10 |
| Martha Walker | 6 |
| Augustus Walker | 4 |
| Mary Walker | 1 |

**Source Citation:** Year: *1870*;
Census Place: *Perry, Houston, Georgia*; Roll: *M593_158*;
Page: *147A*; Image: *298*; Family History Library Film: *545657*.

ancestry

## 1870 United States Federal Census

| | |
|---|---|
| Name: | **Emma Walker** |
| Age in 1870: | 22 |
| Birth Year: | abt 1848 |
| Birthplace: | Georgia |
| Home in 1870: | Perry, Houston, Georgia |
| Race: | Black |
| Gender: | Female |
| Post Office: | Perry |
| Value of real estate: | |

Household Members:

| Name | Age |
|---|---|
| John Walker | 30 |
| Emma Walker | 22 |
| Evaline Walker | 10 |
| Martha Walker | 6 |
| Augustus Walker | 4 |
| Mary Walker | 1 |

**Source Citation:** Year: *1870*; Census Place: *Perry, Houston, Georgia*; Roll: *M593_158*; Page: *147A*; Image: *298*; Family History Library Film: *545657*.

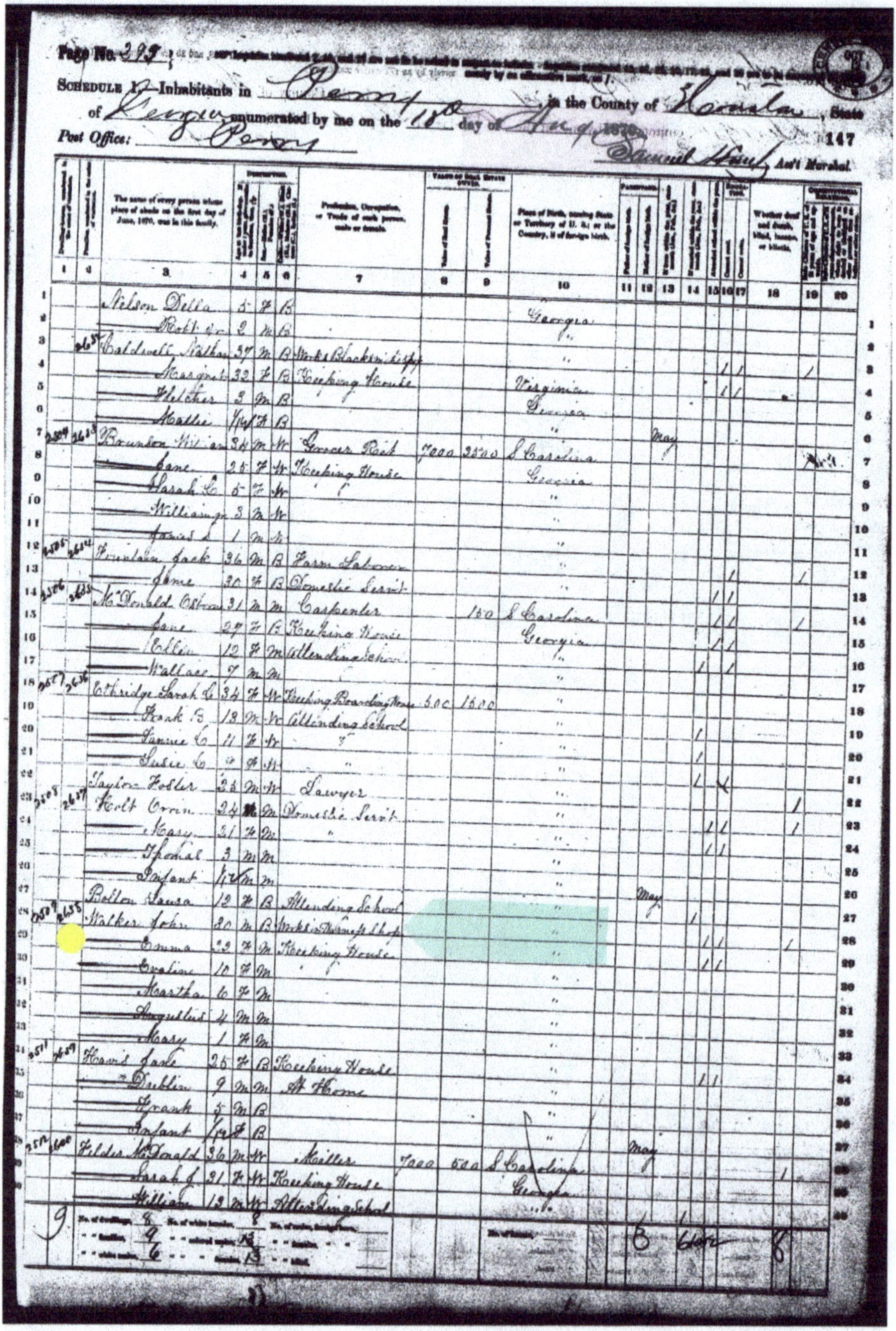

Page No. 299

SCHEDULE 1.—Inhabitants in Perry, in the County of Houston, State of Georgia, enumerated by me on the 18th day of Aug, 1870.

Post Office: Perry

Samuel Howl, Ass't Marshal. 147

| Line | 1 | 2 | 3 | 4 | 5 | 6 | 7 | 8 | 9 | 10 | 13 | 15 | 16 | 17 | 19 |
|---|---|---|---|---|---|---|---|---|---|---|---|---|---|---|---|
| 1 | | | Nelson Della | 5 | F | B | | | | | | | | | |
| 2 | | | Robt Jr | 2 | M | B | | | | Georgia | | | | | |
| 3 | | 2633 | Caldwell Nathan | 37 | M | B | Works Blacksmith Shop | | | " | | | | | |
| 4 | | | Margaret | 32 | F | B | Keeping House | | | " | | | 1 | 1 | 1 |
| 5 | | | Fletcher | 3 | M | B | | | | Virginia | | | 1 | 1 | |
| 6 | | | Mattie | 1/12 | F | B | | | | Georgia | | | | | |
| 7 | 2504 | 2633 | Brunson William | 34 | M | W | Grocer Reit | 7000 | 3500 | " | May | | | | |
| 8 | | | Jane | 25 | F | W | Keeping House | | | S Carolina | | | | | |
| 9 | | | Sarah E | 5 | F | W | " | | | Georgia | | | | | |
| 10 | | | William Jr | 3 | M | W | | | | " | | | | | |
| 11 | | | James L | 1 | M | W | | | | " | | | | | |
| 12 | 2505 | 2634 | Fountain Jack | 36 | M | B | Farm Laborer | | | " | | | | | |
| 13 | | | Jane | 30 | F | B | Domestic Servt | | | " | | | | 1 | 1 |
| 14 | 2506 | 2635 | McDonald Osborn | 31 | M | M | Carpenter | | | " | | | 1 | 1 | |
| 15 | | | Jane | 27 | F | B | Keeping House | | 150 | S Carolina | | | 1 | 1 | 1 |
| 16 | | | Ellen | 12 | F | M | Attending School | | | Georgia | | | 1 | 1 | |
| 17 | | | Wallace | 7 | M | M | | | | " | | 1 | | 1 | |
| 18 | 2507 | 2636 | Ethridge Sarah E | 34 | F | W | Keeping Boarding House | 500 | 1500 | " | | | | | |
| 19 | | | Frank B | 13 | M | W | Attending School | | | " | | | | | |
| 20 | | | Fannie C | 11 | F | W | " | | | " | | 1 | | | |
| 21 | | | Susie C | 9 | F | W | " | | | " | | 1 | | | |
| 22 | | | Taylor Foster | 35 | M | W | Lawyer | | | " | | 1 | | X | |
| 23 | 2508 | 2637 | Holt Orrin | 24 | M | M | Domestic Servt | | | " | | | | | 1 |
| 24 | | | Mary | 31 | F | M | " | | | " | | | 1 | 1 | 1 |
| 25 | | | Thomas | 3 | M | M | | | | " | | | 1 | 1 | |
| 26 | | | Infant | 1/12 | M | M | | | | " | | | | | |
| 27 | | | Bolton Laura | 12 | F | B | Attending School | | | " | May | | | | |
| 28 | 2509 | 2638 | Walker John | 30 | M | B | Works in Warnock Shop | | | " | | 1 | | | |
| 29 | | | Emma | 23 | F | M | Keeping House | | | " | | | 1 | 1 | 1 |
| 30 | | | Evaline | 10 | F | M | " | | | " | | | 1 | 1 | |
| 31 | | | Martha | 6 | F | M | | | | " | | | | | |
| 32 | | | Augustus | 4 | M | M | | | | " | | | | | |
| 33 | | | Mary | 1 | F | M | | | | " | | | | | |
| 34 | 2511 | 2639 | Harris Jane | 25 | F | B | Keeping House | | | " | | | | | |
| 35 | | | Dublin | 9 | M | M | At Home | | | " | | | 1 | 1 | |
| 36 | | | Frank | 5 | M | B | | | | " | | | | | |
| 37 | | | Infant | 1/12 | F | B | | | | " | | | | | |
| 38 | 2512 | 2640 | Felder McDonald | 36 | M | W | Miller | 7000 | 500 | " | May | | | | |
| 39 | | | Sarah J | 31 | F | W | Keeping House | | | S Carolina | | | | | 1 |
| 40 | | | William | 12 | M | W | Attending School | | | Georgia | | | | | |

9 — No. of dwellings, 8; No. of white females, 8; No. of families, 9; No. of colored males, 13; No. of white males, 6; No. of colored females, 13.

8   6   8

ancestry.com

## 1870 United States Federal Census

| | |
|---|---|
| Name: | **Jefferson Swift** |
| Age in 1870: | 41 |
| Birth Year: | abt 1829 |
| Birthplace: | Georgia |
| Home in 1870: | Perry, Houston, Georgia |
| Race: | Black |
| Gender: | Male |
| Post Office: | Perry |
| Value of real estate: | |

Household Members:

| Name | Age |
|---|---|
| Jefferson Swift | 41 |
| Lucinda Swift | 27 |
| William Swift | 15 |
| Sylvester Swift | 13 |

**Source Citation:** Year: *1870*; Census Place: *Perry, Houston, Georgia*; Roll: *M593_158*; Page: *144B*; Image: *293*; Family History Library Film: *545657*.

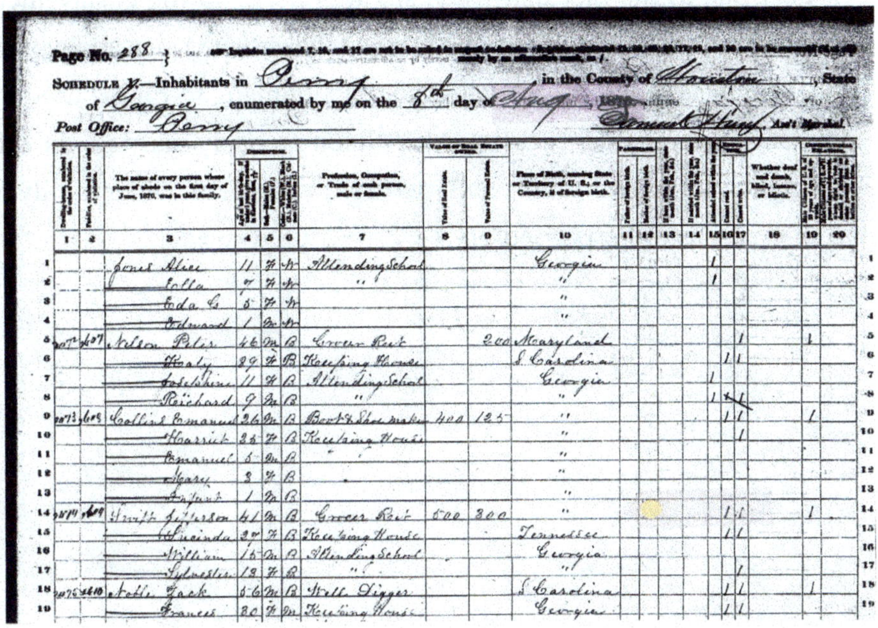

Page No. 288

Schedule 1.—Inhabitants in Perry, in the County of Houston, State of Georgia, enumerated by me on the 8th day of Aug, 1870. [illegible], Ass't Marshal.

Post Office: Perry

| | 1 | 2 | 3 | 4 | 5 | 6 | 7 | 8 | 9 | 10 | 11 | 12 | 13 | 14 | 15 | 16 | 17 | 18 | 19 | 20 | |
|---|---|---|---|---|---|---|---|---|---|---|---|---|---|---|---|---|---|---|---|---|---|
| | | | The name of every person whose place of abode on the first day of June, 1870, was in this family. | | | | Profession, Occupation, or Trade of each person, male or female. | | | Place of Birth, naming State or Territory of U. S.; or the Country, if of foreign birth. | | | | | | | | Whether deaf and dumb, blind, insane, or idiotic. | | | |
| 1 | | | Jones Alice | 11 | F | W | Attending School | | | Georgia | | | | | 1 | | | | | | 1 |
| 2 | | | Ella | 7 | F | W | " | | | " | | | | | 1 | | | | | | 2 |
| 3 | | | Eda G | 5 | F | W | | | | " | | | | | | | | | | | 3 |
| 4 | | | Edward | 1 | M | W | | | | " | | | | | | | | | | | 4 |
| 5 | 2072 | 607 | Nelson Peter | 46 | M | B | Grocer Ret | | 200 | Maryland | | | | | | | 1 | | 1 | | 5 |
| 6 | | | Hoaly | 29 | F | B | Keeping House | | | S Carolina | | | | | | 1 | 1 | | | | 6 |
| 7 | | | Josephine | 11 | F | B | Attending School | | | Georgia | | | | | 1 | | | | | | 7 |
| 8 | | | Richard | 9 | M | B | " | | | " | | | | | 1 | 1 | 1 | | | | 8 |
| 9 | 2073 | 608 | Collins Emanuel | 26 | M | B | Boot & Shoe maker | 400 | 125 | " | | | | | | 1 | 1 | | 1 | | 9 |
| 10 | | | Harriet | 35 | F | B | Keeping House | | | " | | | | | | | 1 | | | | 10 |
| 11 | | | Emanuel | 5 | M | B | | | | " | | | | | | | | | | | 11 |
| 12 | | | Mary | 3 | F | B | | | | " | | | | | | | | | | | 12 |
| 13 | | | Infant | 1 | M | B | | | | " | | | | | | | | | | | 13 |
| 14 | 2074 | 609 | Swift Jefferson | 41 | M | B | Grocer Ret | 500 | 300 | " | | | | | | 1 | 1 | | 1 | | 14 |
| 15 | | | Lucinda | 27 | F | B | Keeping House | | | Tennessee | | | | | | 1 | 1 | | | | 15 |
| 16 | | | William | 15 | M | B | Attending School | | | Georgia | | | | | | | | | | | 16 |
| 17 | | | Sylvester | 13 | F | B | " | | | " | | | | | | | 1 | | | | 17 |
| 18 | 2075 | 610 | Noble Zack | 56 | M | B | Well Digger | | | S Carolina | | | | | | 1 | 1 | | 1 | | 18 |
| 19 | | | Frances | 30 | F | M | Keeping House | | | Georgia | | | | | | 1 | 1 | | | | 19 |

Footnote: 1870 was the first U.S. Decennial census where any citizen of African ancestry was listed as a person, instead of being listed as property. Our ancestors, John and Emma Walker, were a young couple with a family, and they were living among people who were very significant in their lives. John's wife, Emma Felder Walker, would be widowed by him, and would marry Mr. Jefferson Swift in 1890. On her marriage record, Emma used her mother's maiden name as her own surname, instead of using her Walker surname from her marriage to John. Emma and Jefferson had likely been neighbors for awhile, before they were listed on the 1870 census.

On Emma's death certificate in 1922, her parents' names were provided by the informant, her daughter, Annie Williams. Her mother was Grace Felder, and her father was Alex Nixon. Both were also neighbors of the John Walker Family. Emma did not wear the Nixon surname of her father, probably due to the fact that when she was born, during enslavement, marriage was not legally recognized among the enslaved men and women (who were regarded as property and not fully human), so Emma used the name of the slaveholder (Felder). Alex Nixon probably married his wife, Amy, right after emancipation, and was listed with her and their family on the 1870 census of Perry, Georgia.

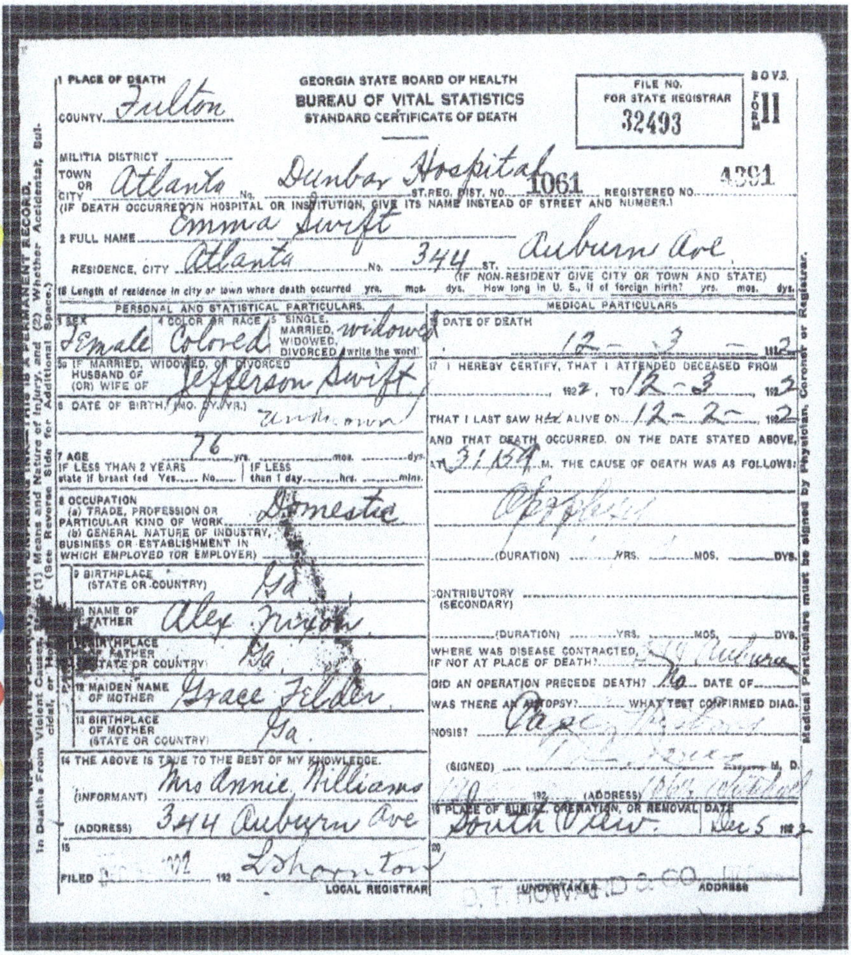

1 PLACE OF DEATH
COUNTY Fulton

GEORGIA STATE BOARD OF HEALTH
BUREAU OF VITAL STATISTICS
STANDARD CERTIFICATE OF DEATH

FILE NO. FOR STATE REGISTRAR 32493

BOVS FORM II

MILITIA DISTRICT
TOWN OR CITY Atlanta No. Dunbar Hospital ST. REG. DIST. NO. 1061 REGISTERED NO. 4391
(IF DEATH OCCURRED IN HOSPITAL OR INSTITUTION, GIVE ITS NAME INSTEAD OF STREET AND NUMBER.)

2 FULL NAME Emma Swift

RESIDENCE, CITY Atlanta No. 344 ST. Auburn Ave
(IF NON-RESIDENT GIVE CITY OR TOWN AND STATE)
18 Length of residence in city or town where death occurred yrs. mos. dys. How long in U. S., if of foreign birth? yrs. mos. dys.

PERSONAL AND STATISTICAL PARTICULARS

3 SEX Female
4 COLOR OR RACE Colored
5 SINGLE, MARRIED, WIDOWED, DIVORCED (write the word) widow
5a IF MARRIED, WIDOWED, OR DIVORCED HUSBAND OF (OR) WIFE OF Jefferson Swift
6 DATE OF BIRTH (MO. DY. YR.) Unknown
7 AGE 76 yrs. mos. dys.
IF LESS THAN 2 YEARS state if breast fed Yes No
IF LESS than 1 day hrs. mins.
8 OCCUPATION
(a) TRADE, PROFESSION OR PARTICULAR KIND OF WORK Domestic
(b) GENERAL NATURE OF INDUSTRY, BUSINESS OR ESTABLISHMENT IN WHICH EMPLOYED (OR EMPLOYER)
9 BIRTHPLACE (STATE OR COUNTRY) Ga
10 NAME OF FATHER Alex Nixon
11 BIRTHPLACE OF FATHER (STATE OR COUNTRY) Ga.
12 MAIDEN NAME OF MOTHER Grace Felder
13 BIRTHPLACE OF MOTHER (STATE OR COUNTRY) Ga.
14 THE ABOVE IS TRUE TO THE BEST OF MY KNOWLEDGE.
(INFORMANT) Mrs Annie Williams
(ADDRESS) 344 Auburn Ave
15
FILED [illegible] 1922 L Sharnton LOCAL REGISTRAR

MEDICAL PARTICULARS

16 DATE OF DEATH 12 - 3 - 1922
17 I HEREBY CERTIFY, THAT I ATTENDED DECEASED FROM 1922, TO 12 - 3 - 1922
THAT I LAST SAW HER ALIVE ON 12 - 2 - 1922
AND THAT DEATH OCCURRED, ON THE DATE STATED ABOVE, AT 3:15 P.M. THE CAUSE OF DEATH WAS AS FOLLOWS:
[illegible]
(DURATION) [illegible] YRS. [illegible] MOS. DYS.
CONTRIBUTORY (SECONDARY)
(DURATION) YRS. MOS. DYS.
WHERE WAS DISEASE CONTRACTED, IF NOT AT PLACE OF DEATH? 344 Auburn
DID AN OPERATION PRECEDE DEATH? No DATE OF
WAS THERE AN AUTOPSY? WHAT TEST CONFIRMED DIAGNOSIS? [illegible]
(SIGNED) [illegible] M. D.
192 (ADDRESS) [illegible]
19 PLACE OF BURIAL, CREMATION, OR REMOVAL South View DATE Dec 5 1922
20
UNDERTAKER D. T. HOWARD & CO. ADDRESS

ancestry.com

## 1870 United States Federal Census

| | |
|---|---|
| Name: | **Alex Nixon** |
| Birth Year: | abt 1810 |
| Age in 1870: | 60 |
| Birthplace: | Georgia |
| Home in 1870: | Perry, Houston, Georgia |
| Race: | Mulatto |
| Gender: | Male |
| Value of real estate: | |

Household Members:

| Name | Age |
|---|---|
| Alex Nixon | 60 |
| Amy Nixon | 40 |
| Julia Nixon | 11 |

**Source Citation:** Year: *1870*;
Census Place: *Perry, Houston, Georgia*; Roll: *M593_158*;
Page: *145A*; Image: *294*; Family History Library
Film: *545657*.

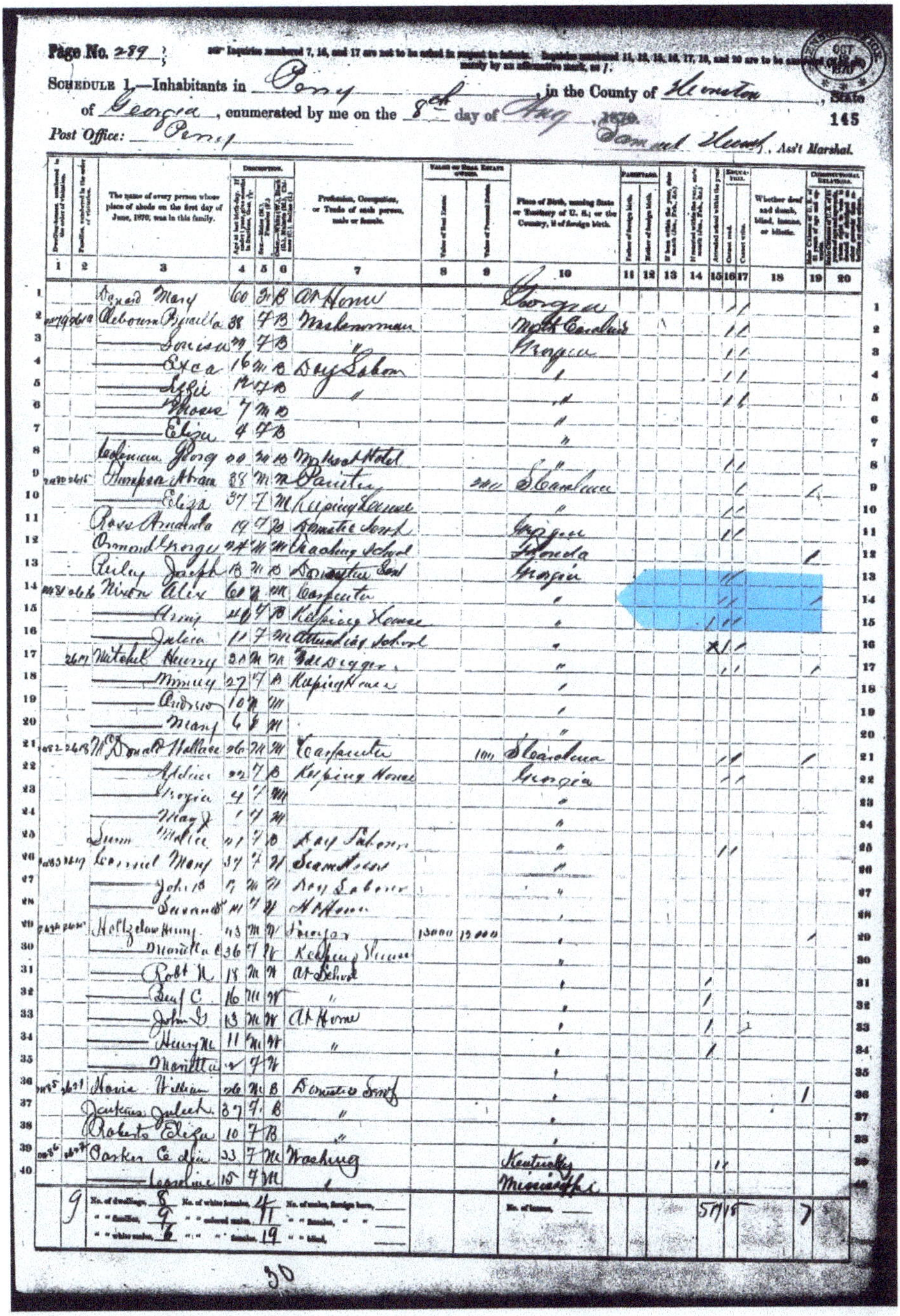

Page No. 289 ; ☞ Inquiries numbered 7, 16, and 17 are not to be asked in respect to infants. Inquiries numbered 11, 12, 15, 16, 17, 18, and 20 are to be answered (if at all) merely by an affirmative mark, as /.

SCHEDULE 1.—Inhabitants in Perry, in the County of Houston, State of Georgia, enumerated by me on the 8th day of Aug, 1870.

Post Office: Perry

Samuel Head, Ass't Marshal.

145

| Line | 1 | 2 | 3 Name | 4 Age | 5 Sex | 6 Color | 7 Profession, Occupation, or Trade | 8 Value of Real Estate | 9 Value of Personal Estate | 10 Place of Birth |
|---|---|---|---|---|---|---|---|---|---|---|
| 1 | | | Dyzaid Mary | 60 | F | B | At Home | | | Georgia |
| 2 | 279 | 261 | Osborn Priscilla | 38 | F | B | Washerwoman | | | North Carolina |
| 3 | | | —— Louisa | 19 | F | B | " | | | Georgia |
| 4 | | | —— Exca | 16 | M | B | Day Labor | | | " |
| 5 | | | —— Lizzie | 12 | F | B | " | | | " |
| 6 | | | —— Moses | 7 | M | B | | | | " |
| 7 | | | —— Eliza | 4 | F | B | | | | " |
| 8 | | | Lademan George | 00 | M | B | Wks at Hotel | | | " |
| 9 | 280 | 265 | Thompson Abram | 38 | M | M | Painter | | 200 | S Carolina |
| 10 | | | —— Eliza | 37 | F | M | Keeping House | | | " |
| 11 | | | Ross Amanda | 19 | F | B | Domestic Servt | | | Georgia |
| 12 | | | Ormond George | 24 | M | M | Teaching School | | | Florida |
| 13 | | | Riley Joseph | 13 | M | B | Domestic Servt | | | Georgia |
| 14 | 281 | 266 | Nixon Alex | 60 | M | M | Carpenter | | | " |
| 15 | | | —— Amy | 40 | F | B | Keeping House | | | " |
| 16 | | | —— Julia | 11 | F | M | Attending School | | | " |
| 17 | | 267 | Mitchel Henry | 30 | M | M | Well Digger | | | " |
| 18 | | | —— Minney | 27 | F | B | Keeping House | | | " |
| 19 | | | —— Andrew | 10 | M | M | | | | " |
| 20 | | | —— Mary | 6 | F | M | | | | " |
| 21 | 282 | 268 | McDonald Wallace | 26 | M | M | Carpenter | | 100 | S Carolina |
| 22 | | | —— Addie | 22 | F | B | Keeping House | | | Georgia |
| 23 | | | —— Georgia | 4 | F | M | | | | " |
| 24 | | | —— Mary J | 1 | F | M | | | | " |
| 25 | | | Dunn Mollie | 21 | F | B | Day Labor | | | " |
| 26 | 283 | 269 | Cornel Mary | 37 | F | W | Seamstress | | | " |
| 27 | | | —— John B | 17 | M | W | Day Labor | | | " |
| 28 | | | —— Susan E | 11 | F | W | At Home | | | " |
| 29 | 284 | 270 | Holtzclaw Henry | 43 | M | W | Lawyer | 13000 | 12000 | " |
| 30 | | | —— Marietta E | 36 | F | W | Keeping House | | | " |
| 31 | | | —— Robt N | 18 | M | W | At School | | | " |
| 32 | | | —— Benj C | 16 | M | W | " | | | " |
| 33 | | | —— John G | 13 | M | W | At Home | | | " |
| 34 | | | —— Henry M | 11 | M | W | " | | | " |
| 35 | | | —— Marietta | 2 | F | W | | | | " |
| 36 | 285 | 271 | Harris William | 26 | M | B | Domestic Servt | | | " |
| 37 | | | Jenkins Juliet | 37 | F | B | " | | | " |
| 38 | | | Roberts Eliza | 10 | F | B | " | | | " |
| 39 | 286 | 272 | Parker C Ann | 33 | F | M | Washing | | | Kentucky |
| 40 | | | —— Caroline | 15 | F | M | " | | | Mississippi |

9 — No. of dwellings, 8; No. of white females, 4; No. of males, foreign born, ——
" " families, 9; " " colored males, 11; " " females, " ——
" " white males, 6; " " " females, 19; " " blind, ——
No. of insane, ——

30

*Train up a child*
*in the way he should go:*
*and when he is old,*
*he will not depart from it."*

*Proverbs 22: 6*

# Milus Walker in household of John Walker, "United States Census, 1880"

| | |
|---|---|
| name : | Milus Walker |
| event: | Census |
| event date: | 1880 |
| event place: | Perry, Houston, Georgia, United States |
| gender: | Male |
| age: | 3 |
| marital status : | Single |
| occupation : | At Home |
| race or color (original) : | |
| ethnicity (standardized) : | American |
| relationship to head : | Son |
| birthplace : | Georgia, United States |
| birthdate : | 1877 |
| spouse's name : | |
| spouse's birthplace : | |
| father's name : | John Walker |
| father's birthplace : | Virginia, United States |
| mother's name : | Emma Walker |
| mother's birthplace : | Georgia, United States |
| page : | 427 |
| page character : | B |
| entry number : | 2524 |
| nara film number : | T9-0153 |
| gs film number : | 1254153 |
| digital folder number: | 004240146 |
| image number: | 00058 |

| | Household | Gender | Age | Birthplace |
|---|---|---|---|---|
| self | John Walker | M | 35 | Virginia, United States |
| wife | Emma Walker | F | 34 | Georgia, United States |
| daughter | Grace Walker | F | 13 | Georgia, United States |
| son | John Walker | M | 8 | Georgia, United States |
| daughter | Annie Walker | F | 6 | Georgia, United States |
| son | Milus Walker | M | 3 | Georgia, United States |
| daughter | Theodosia Walker | F | 0 | Georgia, United States |
| step daughter | Evilyn Walker | F | 18 | Georgia, United States |

**Citing this Record**

"United States Census, 1880," index and images, *FamilySearch* (https://familysearch.org/pal:/MM9.1.1/M8GH-477 : accessed 04 Dec 2012), Milus Walker in household of John Walker, Perry, Houston, Georgia, United States; citing sheet 427B, family 5, NARA microfilm publication T9-0153.

**100 Years - USA**

100 years ago, and three days before Milous Walker was born, the 13 original colonies that would become the United States of America, marked their freedom from British rule by adopting and signing the Declaration of Independence. Emma continued to do her chores that sunny, 4th of July Tuesday, while the townspeople of Perry enjoyed the festivities on America's centennial birthday.

She contemplated the life of her unborn baby that was due any day. How ironic it would be if Emma's baby was born on the 100th anniversary of the U.S.A. ...a new country that fought for its own "freedom", yet denied "freedom" to a people; Emma's people; her African ancestors, who were abducted to this country over 200 years before.

The birth of her ninth baby was at hand. Two of her unnamed babies had already died, and Emma pondered if her new baby would survive to adulthood. Would she have the opportunity to teach this child the significance of his being born during the celebration of an historic event? What a privilege to carry... Would her own experience of emancipation, just over ten years earlier, be a reality that she could share with each of her children? Come on children let's sing...

Milous would later learn from his mother the significance of his birth during the centennial birthday of the United States of America. Harboring anger about the subjected conditions of his parents' early lives, could have caused a deep-rooted bitterness within Milous' mind. Overcoming the irony of his birth to parents who, themselves, were born into an institution called "slavery" in this "free" country, would be just as significant a reality of life to young Milous Walker as any other historic event.

The toddler years of Milous Walker would present him with a baby sister, Theodosia, by the time he was three years old. This was Emma's tenth baby, and the last child she bore for John Walker. Milous' oldest brother, Augustus, and older sister, Mary, would die before he turned four years old. The 1870s were now over, having claimed the young lives of two more of Emma's children.

*When I was a child...*

*I Corinthians 13:11*

*From the rising of the sun…*
*Psalm 113:3*

The horizon of a new decade gradually divided the past pains felt by a mother of dying children, from the future expectation of fulfilled dreams through her surviving children. Evaline was a great help to Emma, as they diligently managed the housekeeping and laundry business. Gracie was now old enough to look after the younger girls, Annie and Dosie, while she learned about the washing and ironing from her mother and big sister.

Little John had the responsibility of teaching and taking care of his brother, Milous. Any toting and heavy work that had to be done around the house to help the women, they were ready for the tasks at hand. As Milous got older, he and Little John would spend time working around the harness shop with their father. John would have the boys groom the horses, feed and water them, and clean out the stalls. They took great pride in working with their father and learning his trade.

Emma's older brother, Solomon Felder, worked at the livery stable next to the harness shop. He was a wagoner. Solomon grew up with a great love for horses, and his nephews were very observant of the meticulous care and attention he lavished on the livestock. Little John and Milous would jump at every opportunity they had to ride with their Uncle Sol on errands and fares. He would especially load them on the wagon when he had to pick up bales of hay for the horses. This gave the brothers all the heavy lifting and hauling exercise they would need on any given work day.

The 1880s continued without much event. The U.S. population census that was taken in January of 1880, gave a total count of the number of people that lived in Houston (pronounced Howston) County since the last enumeration in 1870. It was a significant time for the Walker Family, since this was the second decennial census in which they were counted as people, and not property. John Walker was proud to be recognized for his contribution of six children to the population of Perry, Georgia, U.S.A. John's employment in the harness shop sufficiently sustained his moderately sized family, supplemented by the domestic work of his wife, and the compensation his sons received for their labor.

ancestry

## 1870 United States Federal Census

Name: **Solomon Felder**

Birth Year: abt 1845

Age in 1870: 25

Birthplace: Georgia

Home in 1870: Perry, Houston, Georgia

Race: Black

Gender: Male

Value of real estate:

Household Members:

| Name | Age |
|---|---|
| Solomon Felder | 25 |
| Henry Felder | 21 |

**Source Citation:** Year: *1870*;
Census Place: *Perry, Houston, Georgia*; Roll: *M593_158*;
Page: *142B*; Image: *289*; Family History Library
Film: *545657*.

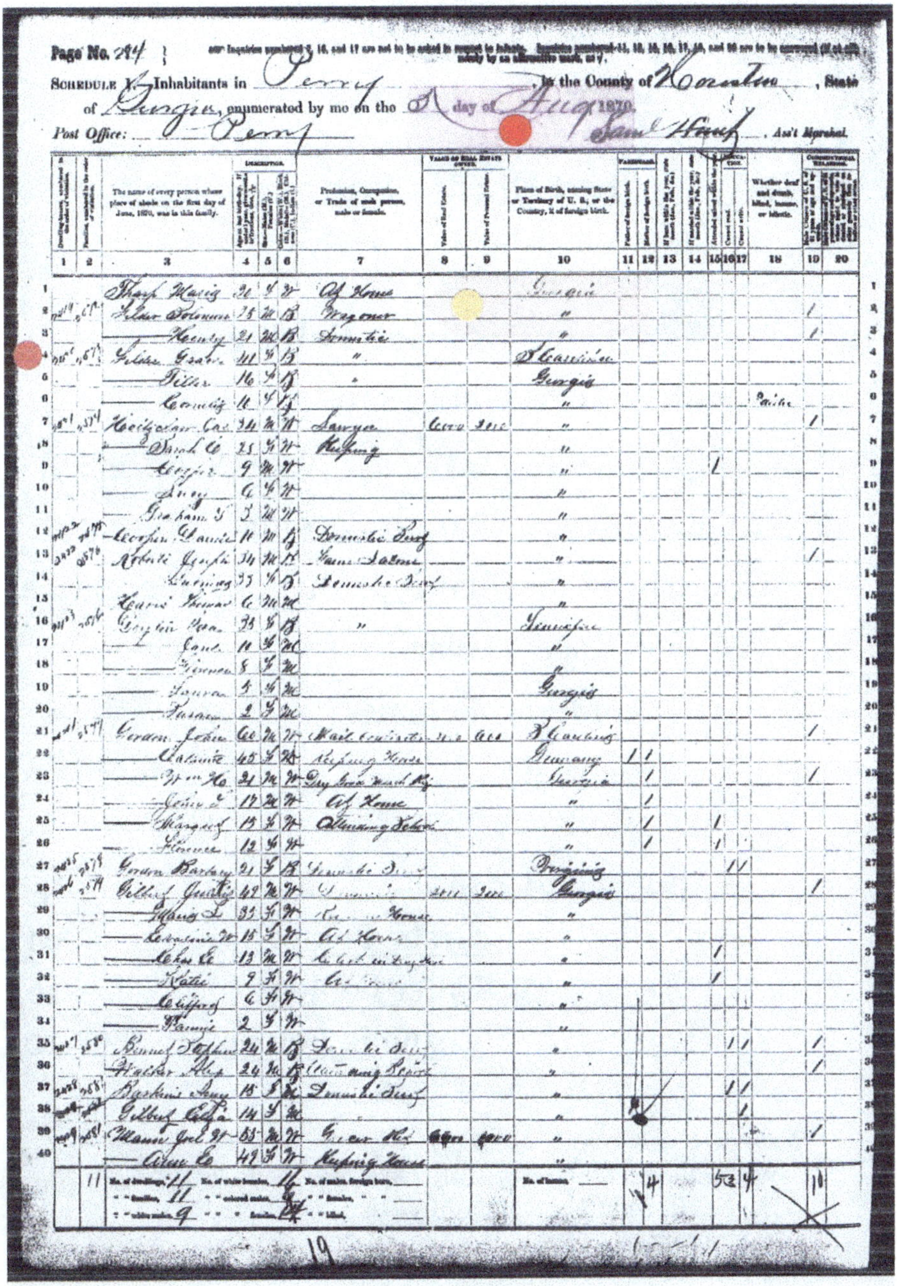

Page No. 284

Schedule 1.—Inhabitants in Perry, in the County of Houston, State of Georgia, enumerated by me on the 8 day of Aug 1870.

Post Office: Perry. Saml Hauf?, Ass't Marshal.

| Line | 1 | 2 | 3 | 4 | 5 | 6 | 7 | 8 | 9 | 10 | 11 | 12 | 15 | 16 | 17 | 18 | 19 |
|---|---|---|---|---|---|---|---|---|---|---|---|---|---|---|---|---|---|
| 1 | | | Tharp Marie? | 30 | F | W | At Home | | | Georgia | | | | | | | |
| 2 | 2419 | 2570? | Glover? Solomon | 35 | M | B | Wagoner | | | " | | | | | | | 1 |
| 3 | | | Henry | 21 | M | B | Domestic | | | " | | | | | | | 1 |
| 4 | 2420 | 2573 | Glover? Grace | 41 | F | B | " | | | N Carolina | | | | | | | |
| 5 | | | Tiller? | 16 | F | B | " | | | Georgia | | | | | | | |
| 6 | | | Cornelia | 11 | F | B | | | | " | | | | | | Idiotic? | |
| 7 | 2421 | 2574 | Houston? Cas | 34 | M | W | Lawyer | 6000 | 2000 | " | | | | | | | 1 |
| 8 | | | Sarah E | 25 | F | W | Keeping [house] | | | " | | | | | | | |
| 9 | | | George | 9 | M | W | | | | " | | | 1 | | | | |
| 10 | | | Lucy | 6 | F | W | | | | " | | | | | | | |
| 11 | | | Graham S | 3 | M | W | | | | " | | | | | | | |
| 12 | 2422 | 2575 | Cooper Daniel | 11 | M | B | Domestic Serv | | | " | | | | | | | |
| 13 | 2423 | 2576 | Roberts Joseph | 34 | M | B | Farm Laborer | | | " | | | | | | | 1 |
| 14 | | | Laurinda? | 33 | F | B | Domestic Serv | | | " | | | | | | | |
| 15 | | | Harris Thomas | 6 | M | M | | | | " | | | | | | | |
| 16 | 2423? | 2576? | Gaylor? Ann | 33 | F | B | " | | | Tennessee | | | | | | | |
| 17 | | | Jane | 11 | F | M | | | | " | | | | | | | |
| 18 | | | Florence | 8 | F | M | | | | " | | | | | | | |
| 19 | | | Laura | 5 | F | M | | | | Georgia | | | | | | | |
| 20 | | | Fanny | 2 | F | M | | | | " | | | | | | | |
| 21 | 2424? | 2577 | Gordon John | 60 | M | W | Mail Contractor | [illegible] | 400 | N Carolina | | | | | | | 1 |
| 22 | | | Catherine? | 45 | F | W | Keeping House | | | Germany | 1 | 1 | | | | | |
| 23 | | | Wm H | 21 | M | W | Dry Goods Merch Clerk? | | | Georgia | | 1 | | | | | 1 |
| 24 | | | John ? | 17 | M | W | At Home | | | " | | 1 | | | | | |
| 25 | | | Margaret | 15 | F | W | Attending School | | | " | | 1 | 1 | | | | |
| 26 | | | Florence | 12 | F | W | | | | " | | 1 | 1 | | | | |
| 27 | 2425 | 2578 | Gordon Barbary? | 21 | F | B | Domestic Serv | | | Virginia | | | | 1 | 1 | | |
| 28 | 2426 | 2579 | Gilbert Justis? | 49 | M | W | [illegible] | 2000 | 2000 | Georgia | | | | | | | 1 |
| 29 | | | Mary L | 35 | F | W | Keeping House | | | " | | | | | | | |
| 30 | | | Lavinia? W | 15 | F | W | At Home | | | " | | | | | | | |
| 31 | | | Chas E | 13 | M | W | Clerk in Drug Store? | | | " | | | 1 | | | | |
| 32 | | | Katie | 9 | F | W | At [illegible] | | | " | | | 1 | | | | |
| 33 | | | Clifford | 6 | F? | W | | | | " | | | | | | | |
| 34 | | | Fannie | 2 | F | W | | | | " | | | | | | | |
| 35 | 2427 | 2580 | Bennet Stephen | 24 | M | B | Domestic Serv | | | " | | | | 1 | 1 | | 1 |
| 36 | | | Walker Alex? | 24 | M | B | Carriage Repairer? | | | " | | | | | | | 1 |
| 37 | 2428 | 2581? | Barkins? Amy | 15 | F | B | Domestic Serv | | | " | | | | 1 | 1 | | |
| 38 | [illegible] | [illegible] | Gilbert Eliza | 14 | F | M | | | | " | | | | | 1 | | |
| 39 | 2429 | 2581 | Mann Joel W | 55 | M | W | Grocer Merchant? | 6000? | 2000? | " | | | | | | | 1 |
| 40 | | | Anne E | 49 | F | W | Keeping House | | | " | | | | | | | |

| | | |
|---|---|---|
| 11 | No. of dwellings, 11 | No. of white females, 16 | No. of males, foreign born, ___ |
| | No. of families, 11 | No. of colored males, 9 | No. of females, foreign born, ___ |
| | No. of white males, 9 | No. of colored females, 24 | No. of blind, ___ |

No. of insane, ___ | 4 | 53? | 4 | 10

19

ancestry.com

## 1870 United States Federal Census

| | |
|---|---|
| Name: | **Grace Felder** |
| Birth Year: | abt 1829 |
| Age in 1870: | 41 |
| Birthplace: | South Carolina |
| Home in 1870: | Perry, Houston, Georgia |
| Race: | Black |
| Gender: | Female |
| Value of real estate: | |

Household Members:

| Name | Age |
|---|---|
| Grace Felder | 41 |
| Tiller Felder | 16 |
| Cornelia Felder | 10 |

**Source Citation:** Year: *1870*;
Census Place: *Perry, Houston, Georgia*; Roll: *M593_158*;
Page: *142B*; Image: *289*; Family History Library
Film: *545657*.

*"A wise son
makes a glad father:"*

*Proverbs 10:1*

*"A wise son
hears his father's instruction:"*

*Proverbs 13:1*

## *"…but when I became a man…"*

## *I Corinthians 13:11*

As Milous approached his adolescent years, he closely observed his big brother's good example of young manhood. The five years between their ages were full of mutual respect and admiration. Their bond of brotherhood was fostered at home, and especially encouraged during their days spent at the harness shop with their father, and Uncle Solomon. Little John's rapidly changing stature caused him to lose his title. He would be called either John or Johnny, by many, and his dad was called Big John, to make the distinction between the two, whenever they were in the same space.

Big John would often catch himself looking proudly upon his sons. He anticipated what the future would hold for them. How many strong grandsons, and beautiful granddaughters would they present to him? Would they follow and improve on his footsteps? The best answer came straight from his heart. Whatever he could contribute to their lives, it would certainly be done… unconditionally.

**Sons watch their father shoe a horse**

ancestry

## 1880 United States Federal Census

| | |
|---|---|
| Name: | **Emma Walker** |
| Age: | 33 |
| Birth Year: | abt 1847 |
| Birthplace: | Georgia |
| Home in 1880: | Perry, Houston, Georgia |
| Race: | Black |
| Gender: | Female |
| Relation to Head of House: | Wife |
| Marital Status: | Married |
| Spouse's Name: | John Walker |
| Father's Birthplace: | Georgia |
| Mother's Birthplace: | Georgia |
| Neighbors: | |
| Occupation: | Keeping House |
| Cannot read/write: | |
| Blind: | |
| Deaf and dumb: | |
| Otherwise disabled: | |
| Idiotic or insane: | |

Household Members:

| Name | Age |
|---|---|
| John Walker | 38 |
| Emma Walker | 33 |
| Evelin Walker | 18 |
| Gracey Walker | 13 |
| Johny Walker | 8 |
| Anna Walker | 4 |
| Milas Walker | 3 |
| Theodocia Walker | 11m |

**Source Citation:** Year: *1880*; Census Place: *Perry, Houston, Georgia*; Roll: *153*; Family History Film: *1254153*; Page: *468A*; Enumeration District: *033*; Image: *0136*.

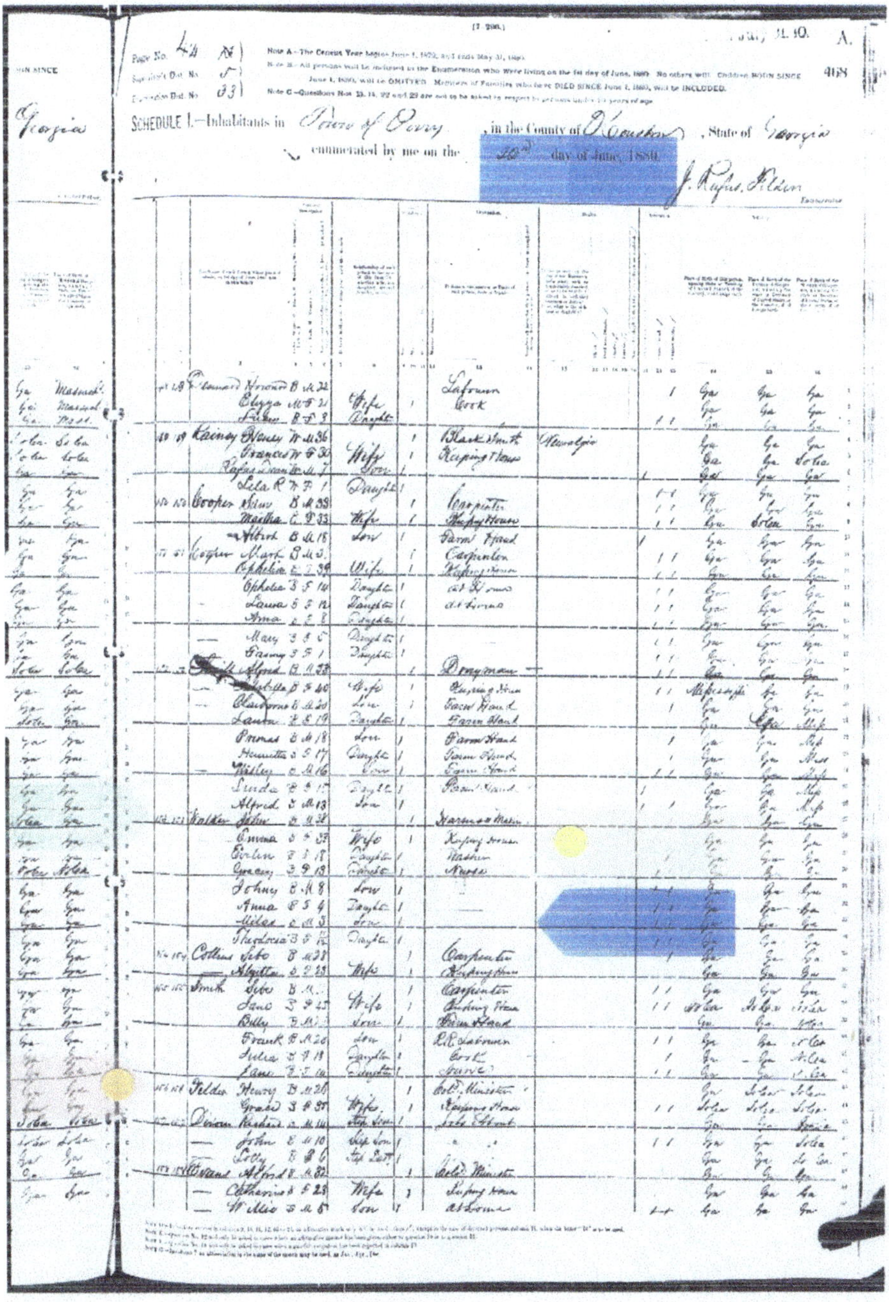

Page No. 44 (N)
Supervisor's Dist. No. 5
Enumeration Dist. No. 33

Note A.—The Census Year begins June 1, 1879, and ends May 31, 1880.
Note B.—All persons will be included in the Enumeration who were living on the 1st day of June, 1880. No others will. Children BORN SINCE June 1, 1880, will be OMITTED. Members of Families who have DIED SINCE June 1, 1880, will be INCLUDED.
Note C.—Questions Nos. 13, 14, 22 and 23 are not to be asked in respect to persons under 10 years of age.

SCHEDULE 1.—Inhabitants in Town of Perry, in the County of Houston, State of Georgia, enumerated by me on the 10th day of June, 1880.

J. Rufus Felder, Enumerator.

| Name | Color | Sex | Age | Relationship | Occupation | Birthplace | Father's birthplace | Mother's birthplace |
|---|---|---|---|---|---|---|---|---|
| Leonard, Howard | B | M | 22 | | Laborer | Ga | Ga | Ga |
| Eliza | M | F | 21 | Wife | Cook | Ga | Ga | Ga |
| [illegible] | B | F | 3 | Daughter | | Ga | Ga | Ga |
| Rainey, Henry | W | M | 36 | | Black Smith | Ga | Ga | Ga |
| Frances | W | F | 30 | Wife | Keeping House | Ga | Ga | So Ca |
| Rufus [illegible] | W | M | 7 | Son | | Ga | Ga | Ga |
| Lela R | W | F | 1 | Daughter | | Ga | Ga | Ga |
| Cooper, [illegible] | B | M | 33 | | Carpenter | Ga | Ga | Ga |
| Martha | [illegible] | F | 33 | Wife | Keeping House | Ga | So Ca | Ga |
| Albert | B | M | 18 | Son | Farm Hand | Ga | Ga | Ga |
| Cooper, Mark | B | M | [illegible] | | Carpenter | Ga | Ga | Ga |
| Ophelia | [illegible] | F | 39 | Wife | Keeping House | Ga | Ga | Ga |
| Ophelia | B | F | 14 | Daughter | At Home | Ga | Ga | Ga |
| Laura | B | F | 12 | Daughter | At Home | Ga | Ga | Ga |
| Anna | [illegible] | F | 8 | Daughter | | Ga | Ga | Ga |
| Mary | B | F | 5 | Daughter | | Ga | Ga | Ga |
| Fanny | B | F | 1 | Daughter | | Ga | Ga | Ga |
| [illegible], Alfred | B | M | 53 | | Drayman | Ga | Ga | Ga |
| [illegible] | B | F | 40 | Wife | Keeping House | Mississippi | Ga | Ga |
| Claiborne | B | M | 20 | Son | Farm Hand | Ga | Ga | Ga |
| Laura | B | F | 19 | Daughter | Farm Hand | Ga | Ala | Miss |
| Primas | B | M | 18 | Son | Farm Hand | Ga | Ga | Miss |
| Henrietta | B | F | 17 | Daughter | Farm Hand | Ga | Ga | Miss |
| Willey | B | M | 16 | Son | Farm Hand | Ga | Ga | Miss |
| Linda | B | F | 15 | Daughter | Farm Hand | Ga | Ga | Miss |
| Alfred | B | M | 13 | Son | | Ga | Ga | Miss |
| Walker, John | B | M | 38 | | Harness Maker | Ga | Ga | Ga |
| Emma | B | F | 37 | Wife | Keeping House | Ga | Ga | Ga |
| Evelin | B | F | 18 | Daughter | Washer | Ga | Ga | Ga |
| Gracey | B | F | 13 | Daughter | Nurse | Ga | Ga | Ga |
| Johny | B | M | 8 | Son | | Ga | Ga | Ga |
| Anna | B | F | 4 | Daughter | | Ga | Ga | Ga |
| Miles | B | M | 3 | Son | | Ga | Ga | Ga |
| Theodocia | B | F | [illegible] | Daughter | | Ga | Ga | Ga |
| Collins, Sebo | B | M | 38 | | Carpenter | Ga | Ga | Ga |
| Alzetta | B | F | 23 | Wife | Keeping House | Ga | Ga | Ga |
| Smith, Sebo | B | M | [illegible] | | Carpenter | Ga | Ga | Ga |
| Jane | B | F | 45 | Wife | Keeping House | So Ca | So Ca | So Ca |
| Billy | B | M | [illegible] | Son | Farm Hand | Ga | Ga | So Ca |
| Frank | B | M | 20 | Son | R.R. Laborer | Ga | Ga | N Ca |
| Julia | B | F | 18 | Daughter | Cook | Ga | Ga | N Ca |
| Jane | B | F | 16 | Daughter | Nurse | Ga | Ga | N Ca |
| Felder, Henry | B | M | 26 | | Col. Minister | Ga | So Ca | So Ca |
| Grace | B | F | 35 | Wife | Keeping House | So Ca | So Ca | So Ca |
| Dixon, Richard | B | M | 14 | Step Son | [illegible] | Ga | Ga | [illegible] |
| John | B | M | 10 | Step Son | | Ga | Ga | So Ca |
| Polly | B | F | 6 | Step Dau. | | Ga | Ga | So Ca |
| Evans, Alfred | B | M | 32 | | Col. Minister | Ga | Ga | Ga |
| Catherine | B | F | 23 | Wife | Keeping House | Ga | Ga | Ga |
| Willis | B | M | 5 | Son | At Home | Ga | Ga | Ga |

ancestry

## 1880 United States Federal Census

| | |
|---|---|
| Name: | **Emma Walker** |
| Age: | 34 |
| Birth Year: | abt 1846 |
| Birthplace: | Georgia |
| Home in 1880: | Upper Town, Houston, Georgia |
| Race: | Mulatto |
| Gender: | Female |
| Relation to Head of House: | Wife |
| Marital Status: | Married |
| Spouse's Name: | John Walker |
| Father's Birthplace: | Georgia |
| Mother's Birthplace: | South Carolina |
| Neighbors: | |
| Occupation: | Washes & Irons |
| Cannot read/write: | |
| Blind: | |
| Deaf and dumb: | |
| Otherwise disabled: | |
| Idiotic or insane: | |
| Household Members: | Name |
| | John Walker |
| | Emma Walker |
| | Grace Walker |
| | John Walker |
| | Annie Walker |
| | Milus Walker |
| | Theodosia Walker |
| | Evilyn Walker |

**Source Citation:** Year: *1880*; Census Place: *Upper Town, Houston, Georgia*; Roll: *153*; Family History Film: *1254153*; Page: *427B*; Enumeration District: *032*; Image: *0056*.

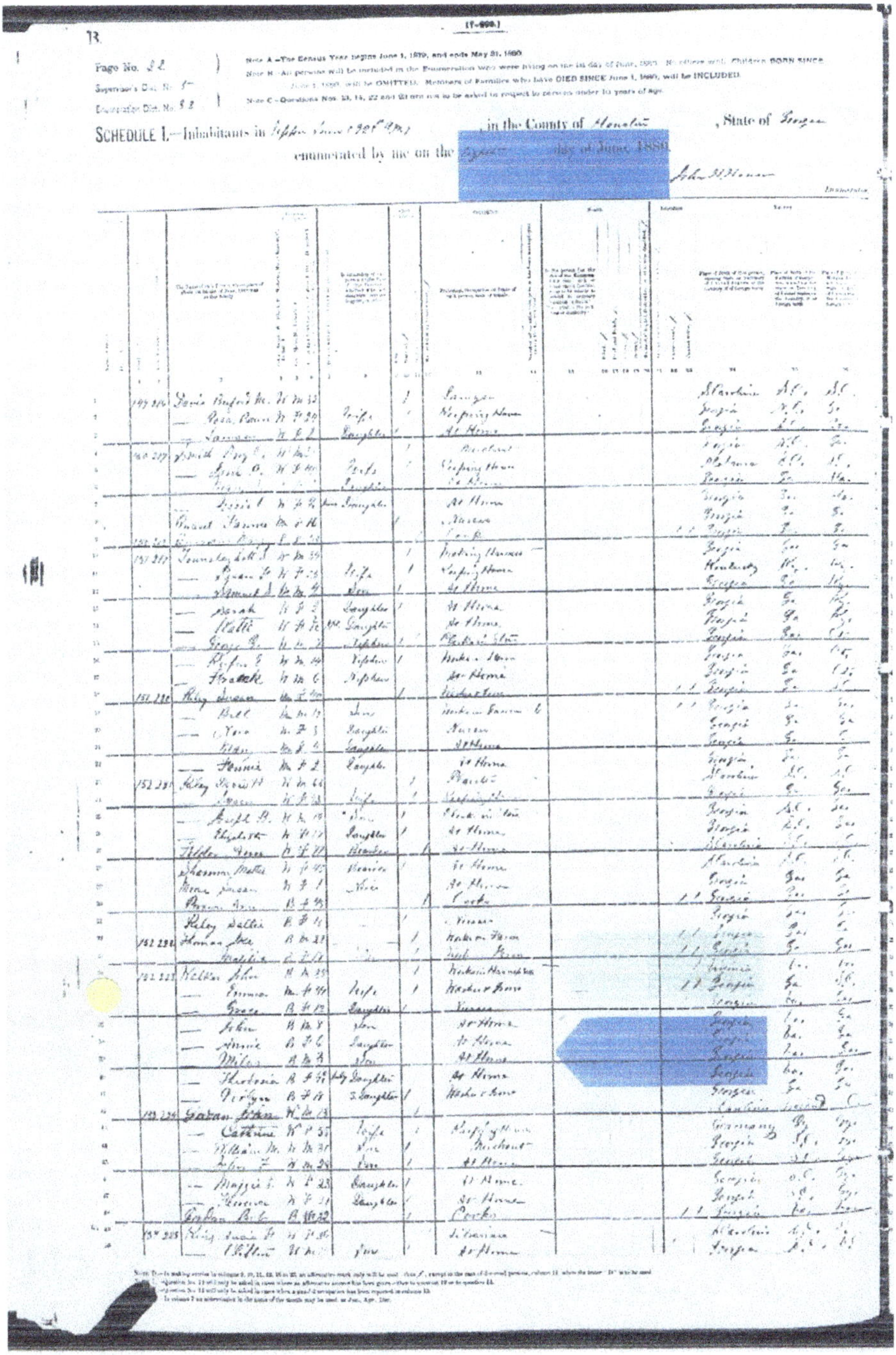

[7-399.]

B.

Page No. 22
Supervisor's Dist. No. 5
Enumeration Dist. No. 82

Note A.—The Census Year begins June 1, 1879, and ends May 31, 1880.
Note B.—All persons will be included in the Enumeration who were living on the 1st day of June, 1880. No others will. Children BORN SINCE June 1, 1880, will be OMITTED. Members of Families who have DIED SINCE June 1, 1880, will be INCLUDED.
Note C.—Questions Nos. 13, 14, 22 and 23 are not to be asked in respect to persons under 10 years of age.

SCHEDULE 1.—Inhabitants in [illegible], in the County of Houston, State of Georgia, enumerated by me on the [illegible] day of June, 1880.

[illegible], Enumerator.

| Dwelling / Family | Name | Color | Sex | Age | Relationship | Occupation | Place of birth | Father's birthplace | Mother's birthplace |
|---|---|---|---|---|---|---|---|---|---|
| 149 216 | Davis Buford M. | W | M | 33 | | Lawyer | S. Carolina | N.C. | S.C. |
| | — Rosa [illegible] | W | F | 24 | Wife | Keeping House | Georgia | N.C. | Ga. |
| | — [illegible] | W | F | 2 | Daughter | At Home | Georgia | [illegible] | Ga. |
| 150 217 | Smith [illegible] | W | M | [illegible] | | Merchant | Georgia | N.C. | Ga. |
| | — [illegible] | W | F | [illegible] | Wife | Keeping House | Alabama | S.C. | [illegible] |
| | — [illegible] | [illegible] | [illegible] | [illegible] | Daughter | At Home | Georgia | Ga. | Ala. |
| | — [illegible] | W | F | [illegible] | [illegible] Daughter | At Home | Georgia | Ga. | Ala. |
| | [illegible] | M | F | 14 | | Nurse | Georgia | Ga. | Ga. |
| 151 218 | [illegible] | [illegible] | F | [illegible] | | Cook | Georgia | Ga. | Ga. |
| 151 219 | Townsley [illegible] | W | M | 39 | | Making Harness | Georgia | Ga. | Ga. |
| | — [illegible] | W | F | 33 | Wife | Keeping House | Kentucky | Ky. | Ky. |
| | — [illegible] | W | M | 4 | Son | At Home | Georgia | Ga. | Ky. |
| | — Sarah | W | F | 2 | Daughter | At Home | Georgia | Ga. | Ky. |
| | — Hattie | W | F | [illegible] | [illegible] Daughter | At Home | Georgia | Ga. | Ky. |
| | — George [illegible] | W | M | [illegible] | Nephew | [illegible] | Georgia | Ga. | [illegible] |
| | — [illegible] | W | M | 14 | Nephew | [illegible] | Georgia | Ga. | [illegible] |
| | — Fratelle | W | M | 6 | Nephew | At Home | Georgia | Ga. | [illegible] |
| 151 220 | Riley Susan | M | F | 40 | | [illegible] | Georgia | Ga. | [illegible] |
| | — Bell | M | M | 19 | Son | Works on Farm | Georgia | Ga. | Ga. |
| | — Nora | M | F | 3 | Daughter | Nurse | Georgia | Ga. | Ga. |
| | — [illegible] | M | F | 4 | Daughter | At Home | Georgia | Ga. | Ga. |
| | — Fannie | M | F | 2 | Daughter | At Home | Georgia | Ga. | Ga. |
| 152 221 | Riley [illegible] | W | M | 66 | | [illegible] | S. Carolina | S.C. | S.C. |
| | — [illegible] | W | F | [illegible] | Wife | Keeping House | Georgia | Ga. | Ga. |
| | — [illegible] | W | M | 19 | Son | [illegible] | Georgia | S.C. | Ga. |
| | — Elizabeth | W | F | 17 | Daughter | At Home | Georgia | S.C. | Ga. |
| | Tilden [illegible] | W | F | [illegible] | Boarder | At Home | S. Carolina | S.C. | [illegible] |
| | Sherman Mattie | W | F | 45 | Boarder | At Home | S. Carolina | S.C. | S.C. |
| | [illegible] Susan | W | F | 1 | Niece | At Home | Georgia | Ga. | Ga. |
| | [illegible] | B | F | 43 | | Cook | Georgia | Ga. | [illegible] |
| | Riley Sallie | B | F | [illegible] | | Nurse | Georgia | Ga. | [illegible] |
| 152 222 | Thomas [illegible] | B | M | 22 | | Works on Farm | Georgia | Ga. | Ga. |
| | — Matilda | B | F | [illegible] | [illegible] | [illegible] | Georgia | Ga. | Ga. |
| 152 223 | Walker John | B | M | 35 | | [illegible] | Virginia | [illegible] | [illegible] |
| | — Emma | M | F | 34 | Wife | [illegible] | Georgia | Ga. | S.C. |
| | — Grace | B | F | 12 | Daughter | Nurse | Georgia | Ga. | Ga. |
| | — John | B | M | 8 | Son | At Home | Georgia | Ga. | Ga. |
| | — Annie | B | F | 6 | Daughter | At Home | Georgia | Ga. | Ga. |
| | — Miles | B | M | 3 | Son | At Home | Georgia | Ga. | Ga. |
| | — [illegible] | B | F | [illegible] | [illegible] Daughter | At Home | Georgia | Ga. | Ga. |
| | — [illegible] | B | F | 18 | [illegible] Daughter | [illegible] | Georgia | Ga. | Ga. |
| 153 224 | [illegible] John | W | M | [illegible] | | | [illegible] | [illegible] | [illegible] |
| | — Catherine | W | F | 55 | Wife | Keeping House | Germany | [illegible] | [illegible] |
| | — William M. | W | M | 31 | Son | Merchant | Georgia | S.C. | [illegible] |
| | — John F. | W | M | 28 | Son | At Home | Georgia | S.C. | [illegible] |
| | — Maggie [illegible] | W | F | 23 | Daughter | At Home | Georgia | S.C. | Ga. |
| | — [illegible] | W | F | 21 | Daughter | At Home | Georgia | S.C. | Ga. |
| | [illegible] Bob | B | M | 32 | | Cook | Georgia | Ga. | Ga. |
| 154 225 | King [illegible] | W | F | [illegible] | | [illegible] | S. Carolina | S.C. | S.C. |
| | — [illegible] | W | M | [illegible] | Son | At Home | Georgia | S.C. | S.C. |

Note D.—In making entries in columns 9, 10, 11, 12, 15 to 20, an affirmative mark only will be used, thus /, except in the case of divorced persons, column 11, when the letter "D" is to be used.
Note E.—Question No. 13 will only be asked in cases where an affirmative answer has been given either to question 12 or to question 14.
Note F.—Question No. 14 will only be asked in cases where a gainful occupation has been reported in column 13.
Note G.—In column 7 an abbreviation in the name of the month may be used, as Jan., Apr., Dec.

## Emma Walker in household of John Walker, "United States Census, 1880"

| | |
|---|---|
| name : | **Emma Walker** |
| event: | Census |
| event date: | 1880 |
| event place: | Perry, Houston, Georgia, United States |
| gender: | Female |
| age: | 33 |
| marital status : | Married |
| occupation : | Keeping House |
| race or color (original) : | |
| ethnicity (standardized) : | American |
| relationship to head : | Wife |
| birthplace : | Georgia, United States |
| birthdate : | 1847 |
| spouse's name : | John Walker |
| spouse's birthplace : | Georgia, United States |
| father's name : | |
| father's birthplace : | Georgia, United States |
| mother's name : | |
| mother's birthplace : | Georgia, United States |
| page : | 468 |
| page character : | A |
| entry number : | 6442 |
| nara film number : | T9-0153 |
| gs film number : | 1254153 |
| digital folder number: | 004240146 |
| image number: | 00139 |

| | Household | Gender | Age | Birthplace |
|---|---|---|---|---|
| self | John Walker | M | 38 | Georgia, United States |
| wife | Emma Walker | F | 33 | Georgia, United States |
| daughter | Evelin Walker | F | 18 | Georgia, United States |
| daughter | Gracey Walker | F | 13 | Georgia, United States |
| son | Johny Walker | M | 8 | Georgia, United States |
| daughter | Anna Walker | F | 4 | Georgia, United States |
| son | Milas Walker | M | 3 | Georgia, United States |
| daughter | Theodocia Walker | F | 0 | Georgia, United States |

**Citing this Record**

"United States Census, 1880," index and images, *FamilySearch* (https://familysearch.org/pal:/MM9.1.1/M8GH-Q3T : accessed 04 Dec 2012), Emma Walker in household of John Walker, Perry, Houston, Georgia, United States; citing sheet 468A, family 1, NARA microfilm publication T9-0153.

*...weeping may endure for a night...*
*Psalm 30:5*

The sunset of 1888 brought the sudden, untimely death of Big John Walker. This was an awfully dark period for the surviving Walker family members. Johnny took his father's death extremely hard. He and Milous had so much more to learn from him, and the interruption of that process was devastating. They were saddled with sharing new responsibilities, after the death of their father. Yet, deep inside, they knew he had prepared them well to overcome any obstacles they would face in life.

Milous was stunned to the point of total, unending concern and compassion for his mother and sisters. Emma was more than able to attend to the needs of each of her children, upon their father's death. Her strength had been much tested through the deaths of four of her ten children. Losing her husband would be a confirmation of that strength, for such a despairing time. Enduring the pain of her losses would be the expression of that strength, for hopeful times to come.

John and Milous continued their employ at the harness shop. Uncle Sol remained there and assumed paternal responsibility for them. They had actually learned a great deal about the business, from their father and uncle. The shop patrons could hardly miss Big John because the brothers bore such a strong physical resemblance to their father. They even had similar professional qualities like him. When times got rough, each would remind the other of Big John's words, his work ethic, and his wisdom. Milous and John were successful in bringing each other through episodes of grief.

John was nearing his 18th birthday, and his maturity was becoming obvious. He shouldered the responsibilities of being the oldest male in the household. As the older brother, he was very protective of his sisters.

Evaline also respected him, and she was ten years his senior. John's first, and foremost concern had become the well-being of his mother. Emma would want for nothing with John around.

Milous took careful notice of the changes in John. He admired his brother in the same way John had looked up to their father. During their weekly grooming visits to their father's friend, the neighborhood barber, Mr. Bill Russell, they would often have talks about their father as if he was right there with them. The road to recovery was long, but they would help each other on the journey.

The basic schooling that they were allowed to receive, was the foundation each of the children needed to promote their success in the changing times. The girls spent their time balancing school and chores, while the primary focus of the boys was earning a living for their family. The girls would teach the boys out of what they learned. Older family members would also become students of the children who were formally educated.

Emma was encouraged by the fact that her children were the first generation of her African heritage to get an education. The fear of the various degrees of punishment exacted on any enslaved male or female, was so prevalent during slavery that anything to do with learning, reading, or writing, was shunned by Emma and her ancestors. How proud Emma was of her children that they were able to benefit from being educated, and it was happening in her lifetime.

*...and with all thy getting, get understanding.*
*Proverbs 4:5-7*

**Black Barber in 1880s with client**

ancestry.com

## 1880 United States Federal Census

| | |
|---|---|
| Name: | **William Russel** |
| Home in 1880: | Upper Town, Houston, Georgia |
| Age: | 51 |
| Estimated Birth Year: | abt 1829 |
| Birthplace: | Virginia |
| Relation to Head of Household: | Self (Head) |
| Spouse's Name: | Hester Russel |
| Father's birthplace: | Virginia |
| Mother's birthplace: | Virginia |
| Neighbors: | |
| Occupation: | Barber |
| Marital Status: | Married |
| Race: | Mu |
| Gender: | Male |
| Cannot read/write: | |
| Blind: | |
| Deaf and dumb: | |
| Otherwise disabled: | |
| Idiotic or insane: | |
| Household Members: | Name |
| | William Russel |
| | Hester Russel |
| | Mary Russel |
| | Phillis Russel |
| | Willie Russel |
| | Neda Russel |

**Source Citation:** Year: *1880*; Census Place: *Upper Town, Houston, Georgia*; Roll: *153*; Family History Film: *1254153*; Page: *423B*; Enumeration District: *32*; Image: *0048*.

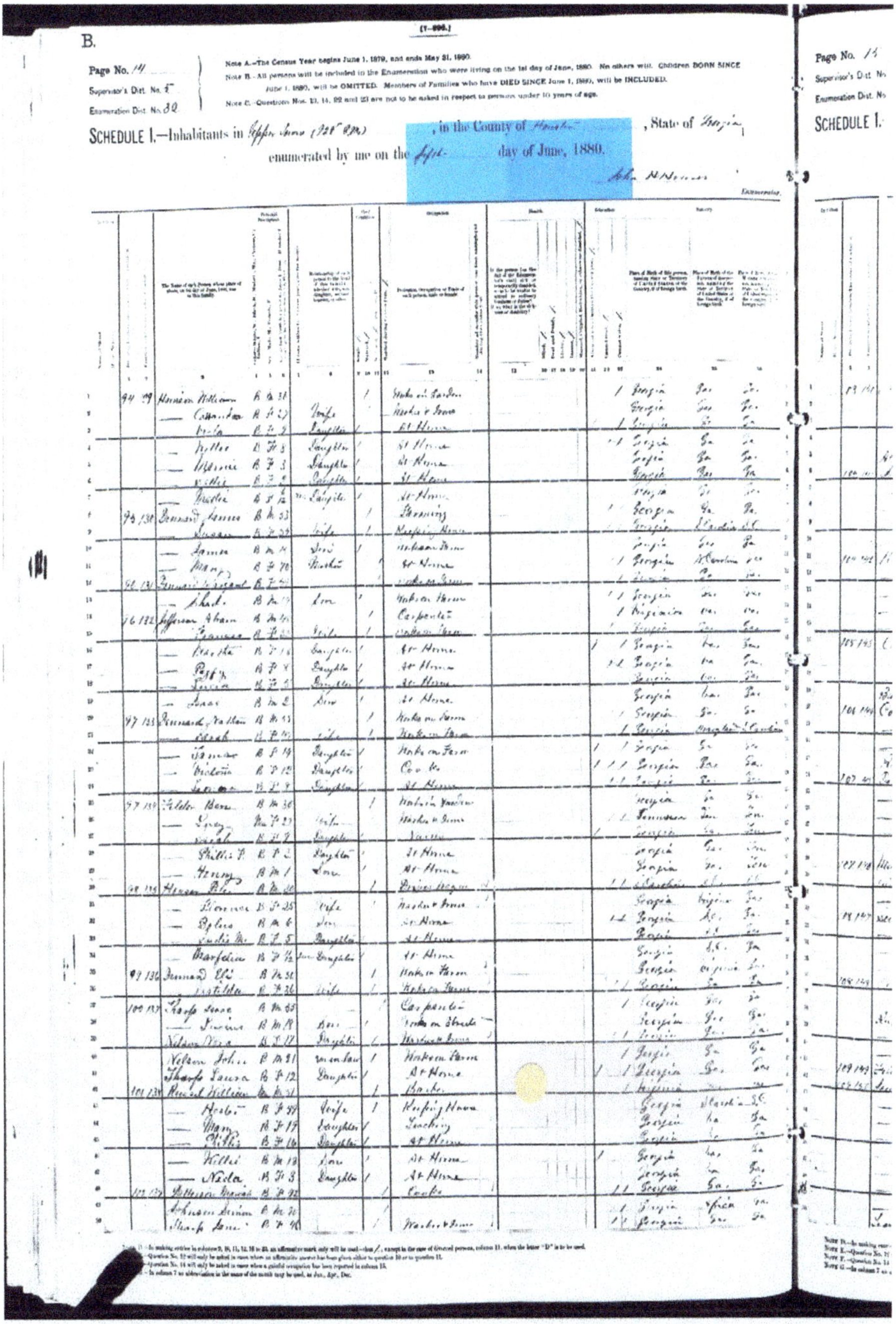

(7—096.)

B.

Page No. 14
Supervisor's Dist. No. 5
Enumeration Dist. No. 30

Note A.—The Census Year begins June 1, 1879, and ends May 31, 1880.
Note B.—All persons will be included in the Enumeration who were living on the 1st day of June, 1880. No others will. Children BORN SINCE June 1, 1880, will be OMITTED. Members of Families who have DIED SINCE June 1, 1880, will be INCLUDED.
Note C.—Questions Nos. 13, 14, 22 and 23 are not to be asked in respect to persons under 10 years of age.

SCHEDULE 1.—Inhabitants in Upper Town (728 Dis), in the County of Houston, State of Georgia, enumerated by me on the fifth day of June, 1880.

John H. Homes, Enumerator.

| Line | Dwelling | Family | Name | Color | Sex | Age | Relationship | Occupation | Place of Birth | Father's Birthplace | Mother's Birthplace |
|---|---|---|---|---|---|---|---|---|---|---|---|
| 1 | 94 | 129 | Hanson William | B | M | 31 | | Works in Garden | Georgia | Ga. | Ga. |
| 2 | | | — Cassandra | B | F | 27 | Wife | Works & House | Georgia | Ga. | Ga. |
| 3 | | | — Viola | B | F | 9 | Daughter | At Home | Georgia | Ga. | Ga. |
| 4 | | | — Willie | B | F | 8 | Daughter | At Home | Georgia | Ga. | Ga. |
| 5 | | | — Minnie | B | F | 3 | Daughter | At Home | Georgia | Ga. | Ga. |
| 6 | | | — Nellie | B | F | 2 | Daughter | At Home | Georgia | Ga. | Ga. |
| 7 | | | — Mattie | B | F | 6/12 | Daughter | At Home | Georgia | Ga. | Ga. |
| 8 | 95 | 130 | Bernard James | B | M | 53 | | Farming | Georgia | Ga. | Ga. |
| 9 | | | — Susan | B | F | 35 | Wife | Keeping House | Georgia | S. Carolina | S.C. |
| 10 | | | — James | B | M | 14 | Son | Works on Farm | Georgia | Ga. | Ga. |
| 11 | | | — Mary | B | F | 70 | Mother | At Home | Georgia | N. Carolina | Ga. |
| 12 | 96 | 131 | Bernard [illegible] | B | F | [illegible] | | Works on Farm | Georgia | Ga. | Ga. |
| 13 | | | — Shad. | B | M | 17 | Son | Works on Farm | Georgia | Ga. | Ga. |
| 14 | 96 | 132 | Jefferson Abram | B | M | 45 | | Carpenter | Virginia | Va. | Va. |
| 15 | | | — Frances | B | F | [illegible] | Wife | Works on Farm | Georgia | Ga. | Ga. |
| 16 | | | — Martha | B | F | 18 | Daughter | At Home | Georgia | Ga. | Ga. |
| 17 | | | — Patty | B | F | 8 | Daughter | At Home | Georgia | Va. | Ga. |
| 18 | | | — Lucia | B | F | 5 | Daughter | At Home | Georgia | Va. | Ga. |
| 19 | | | — Isaac | B | M | 2 | Son | At Home | Georgia | Va. | Ga. |
| 20 | 97 | 133 | Bernard Nathan | B | M | 53 | | Works on Farm | Georgia | Ga. | Ga. |
| 21 | | | — Sarah | B | F | [illegible] | Wife | Works on Farm | Georgia | [illegible] | S. Carolina |
| 22 | | | — Tamar | B | F | 14 | Daughter | Works on Farm | Georgia | Ga. | Ga. |
| 23 | | | — Victoria | B | F | 12 | Daughter | Cooks | Georgia | Ga. | Ga. |
| 24 | | | — [illegible] | B | F | 8 | Daughter | At Home | Georgia | Ga. | Ga. |
| 25 | 97 | 134 | Tileler Ben | B | M | 36 | | Works in Garden | Georgia | Ga. | Ga. |
| 26 | | | — Lucy | M | F | 23 | Wife | Works & House | Tennessee | Tenn. | Tenn. |
| 27 | | | — Sarah | B | F | 9 | Daughter | Nurse | Georgia | Ga. | Tenn. |
| 28 | | | — Phillis P. | B | F | 2 | Daughter | At Home | Georgia | Ga. | Tenn. |
| 29 | | | — Henry | B | M | 1 | Son | At Home | Georgia | Ga. | Tenn. |
| 30 | 98 | 135 | Hinson Pete | B | M | 30 | | Drives Wagon | S. Carolina | S.C. | S.C. |
| 31 | | | — Florence | B | F | 25 | Wife | Works & House | Georgia | Virginia | Ga. |
| 32 | | | — Sylvia | B | M | 6 | Son | At Home | Georgia | S.C. | Ga. |
| 33 | | | — Lula M. | B | F | 5 | Daughter | At Home | Georgia | S.C. | Ga. |
| 34 | | | — Marfelia | B | F | 1/12 | Daughter | At Home | Georgia | S.C. | Ga. |
| 35 | 99 | 136 | Bernard Eli | B | M | 31 | | Works on Farm | Georgia | Virginia | Ga. |
| 36 | | | — Matilda | B | F | 36 | Wife | Works on Farm | Georgia | Ga. | Ga. |
| 37 | 100 | 137 | Tharp Isaac | B | M | 55 | | Carpenter | Georgia | Ga. | Ga. |
| 38 | | | — Irvine | B | M | 18 | Son | Works on Streets | Georgia | Ga. | Ga. |
| 39 | | | Nelson Nora | B | F | 17 | Daughter | Works & House | Georgia | Ga. | Ga. |
| 40 | | | Nelson John | B | M | 21 | Son-in-law | Works on Farm | Georgia | Ga. | Ga. |
| 41 | | | Tharp Laura | B | F | 12 | Daughter | At Home | Georgia | Ga. | Ga. |
| 42 | 101 | 138 | Russel William | M | M | 31 | | Barber | Virginia | Va. | Va. |
| 43 | | | — Herb. | B | F | 37 | Wife | Keeping House | Georgia | S. Carolina | S.C. |
| 44 | | | — Mary | B | F | 17 | Daughter | Teaching | Georgia | Va. | Ga. |
| 45 | | | — Phillis | B | F | 16 | Daughter | At Home | Georgia | Va. | Ga. |
| 46 | | | — Willie | B | M | 13 | Son | At Home | Georgia | Va. | Ga. |
| 47 | | | — Neela | B | F | 3 | Daughter | At Home | Georgia | Va. | Ga. |
| 48 | 102 | 139 | Patterson Maria | B | F | 92 | | Cooks | Georgia | Ga. | Ga. |
| 49 | | | Johnson Simon | B | M | 70 | | | Georgia | Africa | Ga. |
| 50 | | | Tharp Jane | B | F | 40 | | Works & House | Georgia | Ga. | Ga. |

Note D.—In making entries in columns 9, 10, 11, 12, 16 to 23, an affirmative mark only will be used—thus /, except in the case of divorced persons, column 11, when the letter "D" is to be used.
Note E.—Question No. 12 will only be asked in cases where an affirmative answer has been given either to question 10 or to question 11.
Note F.—Question No. 14 will only be asked in cases where a gainful occupation has been reported in column 13.
Note G.—In column 7 no abbreviation in the name of the month may be used, as Jan., Apr., Dec.

ancestry.com

## 1870 United States Federal Census

| | |
|---|---|
| Name: | **William Russell** |
| Birth Year: | abt 1828 |
| Age in 1870: | 42 |
| Birthplace: | Virginia |
| Home in 1870: | Perry, Houston, Georgia |
| Race: | Mulatto (Black) |
| Gender: | Male |
| Value of real estate: | |
| Post Office: | Perry |

Household Members:

| Name | Age |
|---|---|
| William Russell | 42 |
| Hester Russell | 37 |
| Florence Russell | 16 |
| Augustus Russell | 15 |
| Mary F Russell | 9 |
| Phillis Russell | 6 |
| Willie T Russell | 4 |
| Infant Russell | 1/12 |

**Source Citation:** Year: *1870*; Census Place: *Perry, Houston, Georgia*; Roll: *M593_158*; Page: *143B*; Image: *291*; Family History Library Film: *545657*.

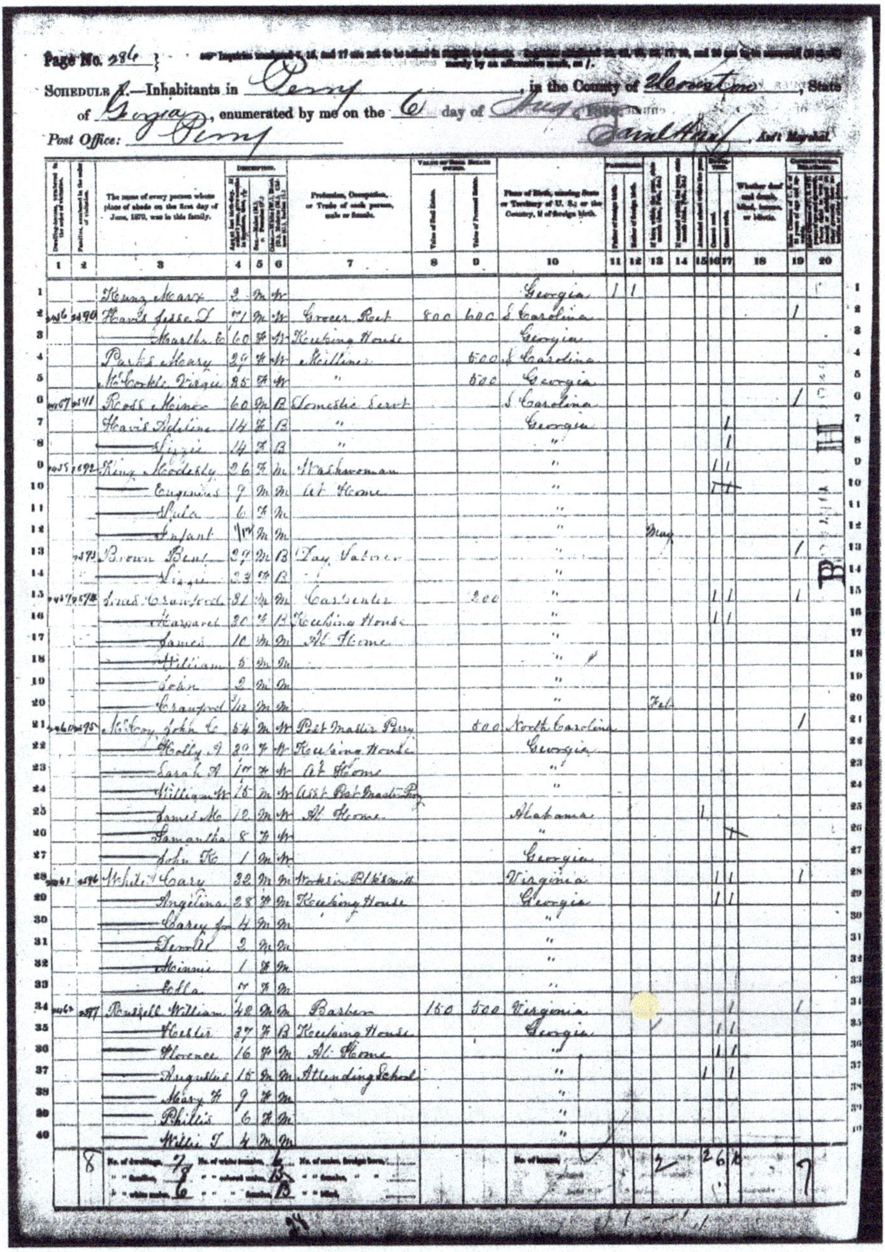

Page No. 286

SCHEDULE 1.—Inhabitants in Perry, in the County of Houston, State of Georgia, enumerated by me on the 6 day of Aug, 1870.

Post Office: Perry

Saml Hart, Ass't Marshal.

| | 1 | 2 | 3 | 4 | 5 | 6 | 7 | 8 | 9 | 10 | 11 | 12 | 13 | 14 | 15 | 16 | 17 | 18 | 19 | 20 |
|---|---|---|---|---|---|---|---|---|---|---|---|---|---|---|---|---|---|---|---|---|
| 1 | | | King Mary | 2 | M | W | | | | Georgia | 1 | 1 | | | | | | | | |
| 2 | 456 | 490 | Davis Jesse D | 71 | M | W | Grocer Reet | 800 | 600 | S Carolina | | | | | | | | | 1 | |
| 3 | | | —— Martha E | 60 | F | W | Keeping House | | | Georgia | | | | | | | | | | |
| 4 | | | Parks Mary | 29 | F | W | Milliner | | 500 | S Carolina | | | | | | | | | | |
| 5 | | | McCorkle Virgie | 25 | F | W | " | | 500 | Georgia | | | | | | | | | | |
| 6 | 457 | 491 | Ross Miner | 60 | M | B | Domestic Servt | | | S Carolina | | | | | | | | | 1 | |
| 7 | | | Davis Adeline | 14 | F | B | " | | | Georgia | | | | | | | 1 | | | |
| 8 | | | —— Lizzie | 14 | F | B | " | | | " | | | | | | | 1 | | | |
| 9 | 455 | 492 | King Modesty | 26 | F | M | Washwoman | | | " | | | | | | 1 | 1 | | | |
| 10 | | | —— Eugenius | 7 | M | M | At Home | | | " | | | | | | | | | | |
| 11 | | | —— Lula | 6 | F | M | | | | " | | | | | | | | | | |
| 12 | | | —— Infant | 1/12 | M | M | | | | " | | | May | | | | | | | |
| 13 | | 493 | Brown Benj | 27 | M | B | Day Laborer | | | " | | | | | | | | | 1 | |
| 14 | | | —— Lizzie | 23 | F | B | | | | " | | | | | | | | | | |
| 15 | 459 | 494 | Reed Crawford | 31 | M | M | Carpenter | | 200 | " | | | | | | 1 | 1 | | 1 | |
| 16 | | | —— Margaret | 30 | F | B | Keeping House | | | " | | | | | | 1 | 1 | | | |
| 17 | | | —— James | 10 | M | M | At Home | | | " | | | | | | | | | | |
| 18 | | | —— William | 5 | M | M | | | | " | | | | | | | | | | |
| 19 | | | —— John | 2 | M | M | | | | " | | | | | | | | | | |
| 20 | | | —— Crawford | 3/12 | M | M | | | | " | | | Feb | | | | | | | |
| 21 | 460 | 495 | McCoy John C | 54 | M | W | Post Master Perry | | 500 | North Carolina | | | | | | | | | 1 | |
| 22 | | | —— Holly A | 20 | F | W | Keeping House | | | Georgia | | | | | | | | | | |
| 23 | | | —— Sarah A | 17 | F | W | At Home | | | " | | | | | | | | | | |
| 24 | | | —— William W | 15 | M | W | Asst Post Master Perry | | | " | | | | | | | | | | |
| 25 | | | —— James M | 12 | M | W | At Home | | | Alabama | | | | | 1 | | | | | |
| 26 | | | —— Samantha | 8 | F | W | | | | " | | | | | | | | | | |
| 27 | | | —— John K | 1 | M | W | | | | Georgia | | | | | | | | | | |
| 28 | 461 | 496 | White Cary | 32 | M | M | Worker in Blksmith | | | Virginia | | | | | | 1 | 1 | | 1 | |
| 29 | | | —— Angelina | 28 | F | M | Keeping House | | | Georgia | | | | | | 1 | 1 | | | |
| 30 | | | —— Carey Jr | 4 | M | M | | | | " | | | | | | | | | | |
| 31 | | | —— Derrell | 2 | M | M | | | | " | | | | | | | | | | |
| 32 | | | —— Minnie | 1 | F | M | | | | " | | | | | | | | | | |
| 33 | | | —— Etta | 1/12 | F | M | | | | " | | | | | | | | | | |
| 34 | 462 | 497 | Russell William | 42 | M | M | Barber | 150 | 500 | Virginia | | | | | | | 1 | | 1 | |
| 35 | | | —— Hester | 37 | F | B | Keeping House | | | Georgia | | | | | | 1 | 1 | | | |
| 36 | | | —— Florence | 16 | F | M | At Home | | | " | | | | | | 1 | 1 | | | |
| 37 | | | —— Augustus | 15 | M | M | Attending School | | | " | | | | | 1 | | 1 | | | |
| 38 | | | —— Mary F | 9 | F | M | | | | " | | | | | | | | | | |
| 39 | | | —— Phillis | 6 | F | M | | | | " | | | | | | | | | | |
| 40 | | | —— Willie T | 4 | M | M | | | | " | | | | | | | | | | |

8 No. of dwellings, 7; No. of families, 8; No. of white males, 6; No. of white females, 6; No. of colored males, 13; No. of colored females, 13.

*...but joy comes in the morning.*
*Psalm 30:5*

The dawn of the 1890s arose with an excitement that indelibly marked the last decade of the 19th century with the moniker "The Gay Nineties". This was due to the many changes in fashion, industry, music & entertainment, communication, and transportation, just to mention a few. For all intents and purposes, John became the "man-of-the-house", taking on additional employment to maintain the family. The girls went to school and did their chores, and Milous followed in John's footsteps.

Emma continued her laundry business with the assistance of her daughter, Evaline, who forsook marriage for a life of loving devotion to her mother. Their clientele included many of their neighbors, both black and white. One particular neighbor, a recent widower by the name of Jefferson Swift, expressed an interest in Emma through his oft-repeated compliments of her flawless work. Emma had taken in his family's laundry during his wife's failing health.

Mr. Swift was nearly 20 years Emma's senior, and she respected him as such. Emma's mother, Grace, knew him as her contemporary, from years ago. Grace was actually more acquainted with the mother of Jefferson's deceased wife, Lucinda. When Grace was about to deliver Emma, Lucinda was five years old. Her mother was Grace's respected friend, so Lucinda and Grace decided to name the newborn baby girl in honor of Lucinda's mother, Emma.

It wasn't long before Mr. Swift would propose marriage to Emma. She accepted. It was a difficult decision for her, in light of the lifelong friendship Emma had with Lucinda. But, all she had to do was recall a conversation she held with Cindy, who asked that Emma continue to help Jeff with the household, and raising the younger children. She also hinted about Emma needing a man to take care of her and her children. Emma would smile as she reminisced about her match-making, thoughtful friend. Jefferson and Emma went to the Perry Court House to apply for their marriage license on Wednesday, March 5, 1890. Emma's younger brother, The Rev. Henry Felder, performed the ceremony that very day, and on Sunday, March 9, 1890, they attended church and were introduced as husband and wife.

**Map of Georgia**

MARRIAGE LICENSE.

**State of Georgia, Houston County.**

**By the ORDINARY of said County.**

To any JUDGE, JUSTICE OF THE PEACE or MINISTER OF THE GOSPEL,

**You are Hereby Authorized to Join**

Jeff Swift & Emma Felder

*In the Holy Estate of Matrimony, according to the Constitution and Laws of this State; and for so doing, this shall be your sufficient License.*

*And you are hereby required to return this License to me, with your Certificate hereon of the fact and date of the Marriage.*

*Given under my hand and seal of office, this* 5 *day of* Mch 1890

J. H. Houser [L.S.]
**Ordinary.**

*GEORGIA, Houston County.*

*I CERTIFY, that* Jeff Swift *and* Emma Felder *were joined in Matrimony by me,*

*this* 5 *day of* March *Eighteen Hundred and* ~~Eighty~~ 90

H. L. Felder M. G.

*Recorded:*

*Ordinary.*

L. W. BURKE & CO., PRINTERS, MACON, GA.

ancestry.com

## 1880 United States Federal Census

| | |
|---|---|
| Name: | **Henry Felder** |
| Home in 1880: | Perry, Houston, Georgia |
| Age: | 26 |
| Estimated Birth Year: | abt 1854 |
| Birthplace: | Georgia |
| Relation to Head of Household: | Self (Head) |
| Spouse's Name: | Grace Felder |
| Father's birthplace: | South Carolina |
| Mother's birthplace: | South Carolina |
| Neighbors: | |
| Occupation: | Col. D Minister |
| Marital Status: | Married |
| Race: | Black |
| Gender: | Male |
| Cannot read/write: | |
| Blind: | |
| Deaf and dumb: | |
| Otherwise disabled: | |
| Idiotic or insane: | |
| Household Members: | Name<br>Henry Felder<br>Grace Felder<br>Richard Dixon<br>John Dixon<br>Lotty Dixon |

**Source Citation:** Year: *1880*; Census Place: *Perry, Houston, Georgia*; Roll: *153*; Family History Film: *1254153*; Page: *468A*; Enumeration District: *33*; Image: *0136*.

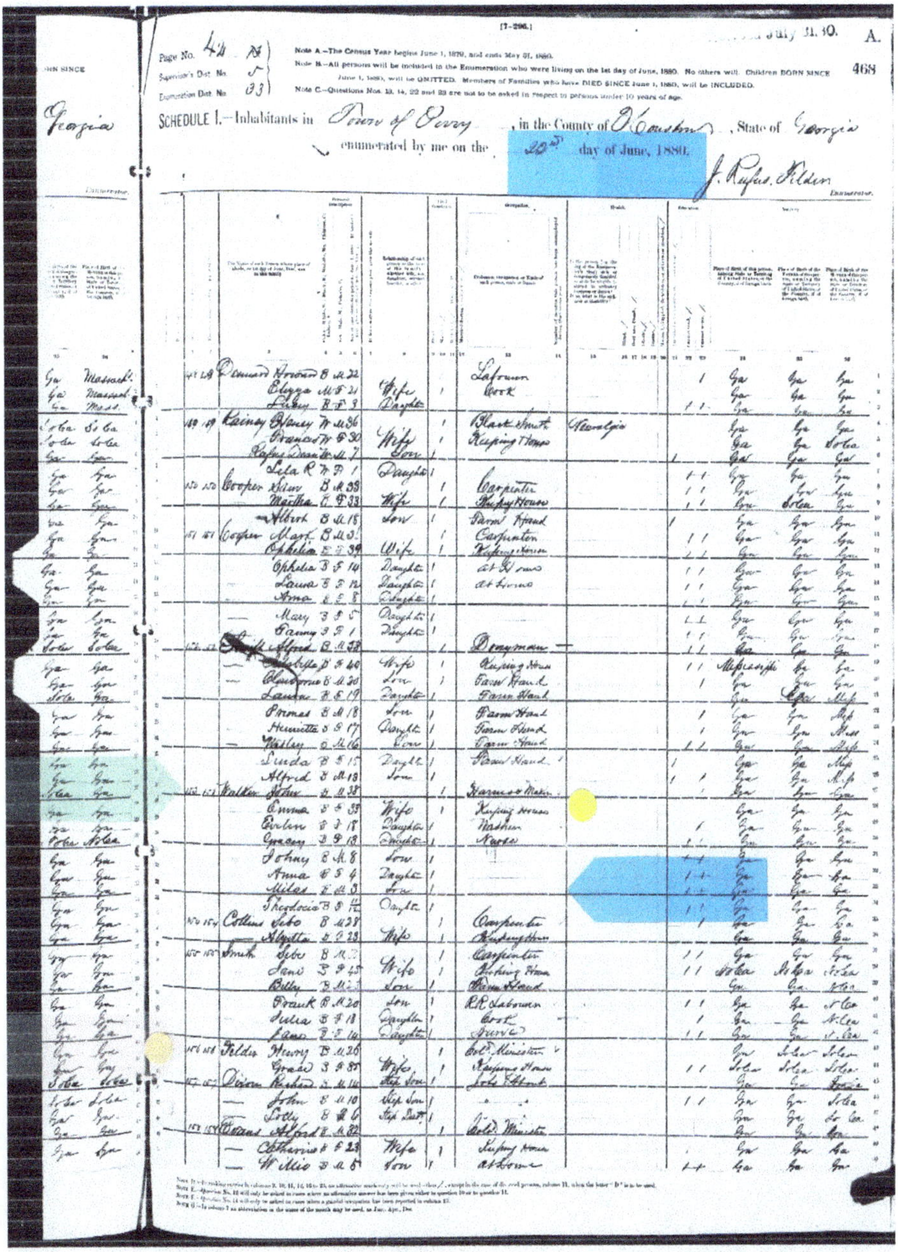

[7-296.]

July 31, 80. A.

468

Page No. 44 A | Supervisor's Dist. No. 5 | Enumeration Dist. No. 33

Note A.—The Census Year begins June 1, 1879, and ends May 31, 1880.

Note B.—All persons will be included in the Enumeration who were living on the 1st day of June, 1880. No others will. Children BORN SINCE June 1, 1880, will be OMITTED. Members of Families who have DIED SINCE June 1, 1880, will be INCLUDED.

Note C.—Questions Nos. 13, 14, 22 and 23 are not to be asked in respect to persons under 10 years of age.

SCHEDULE 1.—Inhabitants in Town of Perry, in the County of Houston, State of Georgia, enumerated by me on the 20th day of June, 1880. J. Rufus Felder, Enumerator.

| Dwelling | Family | Name | Color | Sex | Age | Relationship | Occupation | Sickness | Birthplace | Father's birthplace | Mother's birthplace |
|---|---|---|---|---|---|---|---|---|---|---|---|
| 148 | 148 | Dennard Howard | B | M | 22 | | Laborer | | Ga | Ga | Ga |
| | | Eliza | M | F | 21 | Wife | Cook | | Ga | Ga | Ga |
| | | Lucy | B | F | 3 | Daughter | | | Ga | Ga | Ga |
| 149 | 149 | Rainey Haney | W | M | 36 | | Black Smith | Neuralgia | Ga | Ga | Ga |
| | | Frances | W | F | 30 | Wife | Keeping House | | Ga | Ga | S Ca |
| | | Rufus Daniel | W | M | 7 | Son | | | Ga | Ga | Ga |
| | | Lila R | W | F | 1 | Daughter | | | Ga | Ga | Ga |
| 150 | 150 | Cooper Sam | B | M | 38 | | Carpenter | | Ga | Ga | Ga |
| | | Martha | B | F | 33 | Wife | Keeping House | | Ga | S Ca | Ga |
| | | Albert | B | M | 18 | Son | Farm Hand | | Ga | Ga | Ga |
| 151 | 151 | Cooper Mark | B | M | 3[illegible] | | Carpenter | | Ga | Ga | Ga |
| | | Ophelia | B | F | 39 | Wife | Keeping House | | Ga | Ga | Ga |
| | | Ophelia | B | F | 14 | Daughter | At Home | | Ga | Ga | Ga |
| | | Laura | B | F | 12 | Daughter | At Home | | Ga | Ga | Ga |
| | | Anna | B | F | 8 | Daughter | | | Ga | Ga | Ga |
| | | Mary | B | F | 5 | Daughter | | | Ga | Ga | Ga |
| | | Fanny | B | F | 1 | Daughter | | | Ga | Ga | Ga |
| 152 | 152 | [illegible] Alfred | B | M | 58 | | Drayman | | Ga | Ga | Ga |
| | | [illegible] | B | F | 40 | Wife | Keeping House | | Mississippi | Ga | Ga |
| | | Claiborne | B | M | 20 | Son | Farm Hand | | Ga | Ga | Ga |
| | | Laura | B | F | 19 | Daughter | Farm Hand | | Ga | Ga | Miss |
| | | Thomas | B | M | 18 | Son | Farm Hand | | Ga | Ga | Miss |
| | | Henrietta | B | F | 17 | Daughter | Farm Hand | | Ga | Ga | Miss |
| | | Wesley | B | M | 16 | Son | Farm Hand | | Ga | Ga | Miss |
| | | Linda | B | F | 15 | Daughter | Farm Hand | | Ga | Ga | Miss |
| | | Alfred | B | M | 13 | Son | | | Ga | Ga | Miss |
| 153 | 153 | Walker John | B | M | 38 | | Harness Maker | | Ga | Ga | Ga |
| | | Emma | B | F | 35 | Wife | Keeping House | | Ga | Ga | Ga |
| | | Evelin | B | F | 18 | Daughter | Washer | | Ga | Ga | Ga |
| | | Gracey | B | F | 13 | Daughter | Nurse | | Ga | Ga | Ga |
| | | Johny | B | M | 8 | Son | | | Ga | Ga | Ga |
| | | Anna | B | F | 4 | Daughter | | | Ga | Ga | Ga |
| | | Miles | B | M | 3 | Son | | | Ga | Ga | Ga |
| | | Theodocia | B | F | 11/12 | Daughter | | | Ga | Ga | Ga |
| 154 | 154 | Collins Sebo | B | M | 28 | | Carpenter | | Ga | Ga | Ga |
| | | Alzetta | B | F | 23 | Wife | Keeping House | | Ga | Ga | Ga |
| 155 | 155 | Smith Sebe | B | M | [illegible] | | Carpenter | | Ga | Ga | Ga |
| | | Jane | B | F | 45 | Wife | Keeping House | | S Ca | S Ca | S Ca |
| | | Billy | B | M | 2[illegible] | Son | Farm Hand | | Ga | Ga | S Ca |
| | | Frank | B | M | 20 | Son | RR Laborer | | Ga | Ga | N Ca |
| | | Julia | B | F | 18 | Daughter | Cook | | Ga | Ga | N Ca |
| | | Jane | B | F | 14 | Daughter | Nurse | | Ga | Ga | N Ca |
| 156 | 156 | Felder Henry | B | M | 26 | | Col'd Minister | | Ga | S Ca | S Ca |
| | | Grace | B | F | 35 | Wife | Keeping House | | S Ca | S Ca | S Ca |
| 157 | 157 | Dixon Richard | B | M | 14 | Step Son | Job Hunt | | Ga | Ga | [illegible] |
| | | John | B | M | 10 | Step Son | | | Ga | Ga | S Ca |
| | | Lolly | B | F | 6 | Step Daut. | | | Ga | Ga | S Ca |
| 158 | 158 | Evans Alford | B | M | 32 | | Col'd Minister | | Ga | Ga | Ga |
| | | Catharine | B | F | 23 | Wife | Keeping House | | Ga | Ga | Ga |
| | | Willie | B | M | 5 | Son | At Home | | Ga | Ga | Ga |

Note D.—In making entries in columns 9, 10, 11, 14, 16 to 23, an affirmative mark only will be used—thus /, except in the case of divorced persons, column 11, when the letter "D" is to be used.
Note E.—Question No. 12 will only be asked in cases where an affirmative answer has been given either to question 10 or to question 11.
Note F.—Question No. 14 will only be asked in cases where a gainful occupation has been reported in column 13.
Note G.—In column 7 an abbreviation of the name of the month may be used, as Jan., Apr., Dec.

ancestry.com

## 1880 United States Federal Census

| | |
|---|---|
| Name: | **Henry L. Felder** |
| Home in 1880: | Perry, Houston, Georgia |
| Age: | 24 |
| Estimated Birth Year: | abt 1856 |
| Birthplace: | Georgia |
| Relation to Head of Household: | Self (Head) |
| Spouse's Name: | Grace Felder |
| Father's birthplace: | Virginia |
| Mother's birthplace: | North Carolina |
| Neighbors: | |
| Occupation: | Minister Of The Gospel |
| Marital Status: | Married |
| Race: | Black |
| Gender: | Male |
| Cannot read/write: | |
| Blind: | |
| Deaf and dumb: | |
| Otherwise disabled: | |
| Idiotic or insane: | |
| Household Members: | Name<br>Henry L. Felder<br>Grace Felder<br>Richard Dickson<br>John Dickson<br>Lottie Dickson |

**Source Citation:** Year: *1880*; Census Place: *Perry, Houston, Georgia*; Roll: *153*; Family History Film: *1254153*; Page: *426D*; Enumeration District: *32*; Image: *0054*.

[7-296.]

D.

Page No. 30
Supervisor's Dist. No. 5
Enumeration Dist. No. 59

Note A.—The Census Year begins June 1, 1879, and ends May 31, 1880.
Note B.—All persons will be included in the Enumeration who were living on the 1st day of June, 1880. No others will. Children BORN SINCE June 1, 1880, will be OMITTED. Members of Families who have DIED SINCE June 1, 1880, will be INCLUDED.
Note C.—Questions Nos. 13, 14, 22 and 23 are not to be asked in respect to persons under 10 years of age.

SCHEDULE 1.—Inhabitants in Upper Town (725 G.M.), in the County of Houston, State of Georgia, enumerated by me on the Seventh day of June, 1880.

John N. Hearn, Enumerator.

| Line | Dwelling | Family | Name | Color | Sex | Age | Relationship | Occupation | Place of Birth | Father's Birthplace | Mother's Birthplace |
|---|---|---|---|---|---|---|---|---|---|---|---|
| 1 | 136 | 191 | Fielder Henry L. | B | M | 34 | | Minister of the Gospel | Georgia | Virginia | Virginia |
| 2 | | | Grace | B | F | 33 | Wife | Sewing | S. Carolina | S.C. | S.C. |
| 3 | | | Dickson Richard | B | M | 14 | [illegible] | Works on Farm | Georgia | Ga. | S.C. |
| 4 | | | — John | B | M | 11 | [illegible] | At Home | Georgia | Ga. | S.C. |
| 5 | | | — Lottie | B | F | 5 | S. Daughter | At Home | Georgia | Ga. | S.C. |
| 6 | 137 | 196 | McCants Jesse | B | M | [illegible] | | Works in Warehouse | S. Carolina | S.C. | S.C. |
| 7 | | | Margaret | B | F | 33 | Wife | Cooks | Georgia | S.C. | S.C. |
| 8 | | | — Annie | B | F | 17 | Daughter | Nurse | Georgia | S.C. | Ga. |
| 9 | | | [illegible] | B | M | [illegible] | Son | At Home | Georgia | S.C. | Ga. |
| 10 | | | Lonnie | B | M | 8 | Son | At Home | Georgia | S.C. | Ga. |
| 11 | | | — Mahalia | B | F | [illegible] | Daughter | At Home | Georgia | S.C. | Ga. |
| 12 | | | — Emma | B | F | [illegible] | Daughter | At Home | Georgia | S.C. | Ga. |
| 13 | 137 | 196 | Watson Cambrie | B | F | 45 | | Cooks | Georgia | Ga. | Ga. |
| 14 | | | Harper Betsy | B | F | 62 | | Works on Farm | Georgia | Ga. | Ga. |
| 15 | 138 | 197 | Cullen Anne | B | F | 38 | | Works on Farm | S. Carolina | S.C. | S.C. |
| 16 | | | Fannie | B | F | 15 | Daughter | Nurse | Georgia | S.C. | S.C. |
| 17 | | | — William | B | M | 10 | Son | At School | Georgia | S.C. | S.C. |
| 18 | | | Pilley Craig | B | F | 21 | | Works on Farm | Georgia | Ga. | Ga. |
| 19 | 139 | 198 | Nixon Alex | Mu | M | 61 | | Carpenter | S. Carolina | Va. | Virginia |
| 20 | | | — Amy | B | F | 57 | Wife | Keeping House | S. Carolina | S.C. | S.C. |
| 21 | | | Eliza | B | F | [illegible] | Daughter | Washer & Ironer | Georgia | S.C. | S.C. |
| 22 | 140 | 199 | Anant Benjamin F. | W | M | 44 | | Merchant | Georgia | Ga. | Ga. |
| 23 | | | — Mary A. | W | F | 38 | Wife | Keeping House | Georgia | Ala. | Ala. |
| 24 | | | Pilley Benjamin A. | W | M | 3 | Gr. Son | At Home | Georgia | Ga. | Ga. |
| 25 | | | — Mary A. | W | F | 1 | Gr. Daughter | At Home | Georgia | Ga. | Ga. |
| 26 | 141 | 200 | Holdridge Nathaniel | W | M | 65 | | Repairing Guns | Conn. | Conn. | Conn. |
| 27 | | | — Laura B. | W | F | 42 | Wife | Keeping House | Ala. | [illegible] | [illegible] |
| 28 | 141 | 201 | Pallman Sarah | B | F | [illegible] | | Cooks | Georgia | Ga. | Ga. |
| 29 | 142 | 202 | Dewitt Scot | B | M | 43 | | Carpenter | Georgia | Ga. | Ga. |
| 30 | | | — Lucy | B | F | 41 | Wife | Washer & Ironer | N. Carolina | N.C. | N.C. |
| 31 | | | — William | B | M | 21 | Son | Works on Farm | Georgia | Ga. | Ga. |
| 32 | | | — Frank | B | M | 20 | Son | Works in Stable | Georgia | Ga. | Ga. |
| 33 | | | — Julia | B | F | 19 | Daughter | Cooks | Georgia | Ga. | Ga. |
| 34 | | | — Jane | B | F | 14 | Daughter | Nurse | Georgia | Ga. | Ga. |
| 35 | | | John | B | M | 6/12 | Grandson | At Home | Georgia | Ga. | Ga. |
| 36 | 143 | 203 | Birch Rebecca T. | W | F | 53 | | Sewing | Georgia | Ga. | Ga. |
| 37 | | | Bateman Daniel L. | W | M | 27 | Son-in-law | Works in Printing Office | Georgia | Ga. | Ga. |
| 38 | | | Mary C. | W | F | 23 | Daughter | Sewing | Georgia | Ga. | Ga. |
| 39 | | | Claud N. | W | M | 4 | Gr. Son | At Home | Georgia | Ga. | Ga. |
| 40 | | | — Annie E. | W | F | 2 | Gr. Daughter | At Home | Georgia | Ga. | Ga. |
| 41 | 142 | 204 | Jones Sylvia | B | F | 37 | | Works on Farm | Georgia | Ga. | Ga. |
| 42 | | | — Mary E. | B | F | 14 | Daughter | Nurse | Georgia | Ga. | Ga. |
| 43 | | | — Ella | B | F | 9 | Daughter | At Home | Georgia | Ga. | Ga. |
| 44 | | | — Robert | B | M | 7 | Son | At Home | Georgia | Ga. | Ga. |
| 45 | | | — Trudy | B | F | 1 | Daughter | At Home | Georgia | Ga. | Ga. |
| 46 | 142 | 205 | Staley Clander | B | F | 60 | | Washer & Ironer | S. Carolina | S.C. | S.C. |
| 47 | 143 | 206 | Tuttle James M. | W | M | 29 | | Merchant | Kentucky | Ky. | Ky. |
| 48 | | | — Mary E. | W | F | 24 | Wife | Keeping House | S. Carolina | S.C. | S.C. |
| 49 | | | Choat Mariah | Mu | F | 35 | | Cooks | Georgia | Ga. | Ga. |
| 50 | | | Marshal Charles | W | M | 23 | | Clerk in Store | Georgia | Ga. | Ga. |

Note D.—In making entries in columns 9, 10, 11, 14, 15 to 23, an affirmative mark only will be used—thus /, except in the case of divorced persons, column 11, when the letter "D" is to be used.
Note E.—Question No. 12 will only be asked in cases where an affirmative answer has been given either to question 19 or to question 11.
Note F.—Question No. 14 will only be asked in cases where a gainful occupation has been reported in column 13.
Note G.—In column 7 an abbreviation in the name of the month may be used, as Jan., Apr., Dec.

## Jefferson Swift, "United States Census, 1880"

| | |
|---|---|
| name : | **Jefferson Swift** |
| event: | Census |
| event date: | 1880 |
| event place: | Upper Town, Houston, Georgia, United States |
| gender: | Male |
| age: | 50 |
| marital status : | Married |
| occupation : | Carpenter |
| race or color (original) : | |
| ethnicity (standardized) : | American |
| relationship to head : | Self |
| birthplace : | Georgia, United States |
| birthdate : | 1830 |
| spouse's name : | Lucinda Swift |
| spouse's birthplace : | Tennessee, United States |
| father's name : | |
| father's birthplace : | Alabama, United States |
| mother's name : | |
| mother's birthplace : | Alabama, United States |
| page : | 424 |
| page character : | C |
| entry number : | 2167 |
| nara film number : | T9-0153 |
| gs film number : | 1254153 |
| digital folder number: | 004240146 |
| image number: | 00051 |

| | Household | Gender | Age | Birthplace |
|---|---|---|---|---|
| self | Jefferson Swift | M | 50 | Georgia, United States |
| wife | Lucinda Swift | F | 40 | Tennessee, United States |
| daughter | Sylvester Swift | F | 23 | Tennessee, United States |
| son | Forrest Swift | M | 15 | Georgia, United States |

**Citing this Record**

"United States Census, 1880," index and images, *FamilySearch* (https://familysearch.org/pal:/MM9.1.1/M8G4-TTV : accessed 04 Dec 2012), Jefferson Swift, Upper Town, Houston, Georgia, United States; citing sheet 424C, family 0, NARA microfilm publication T9-0153.

ancestry

## 1880 United States Federal Census

| | |
|---|---|
| Name: | **Jefferson Swift** |
| Age: | 50 |
| Birth Year: | abt 1830 |
| Birthplace: | Georgia |
| Home in 1880: | Upper Town, Houston, Georgia |
| Race: | Black |
| Gender: | Male |
| Relation to Head of House: | Self (Head) |
| Marital Status: | Married |
| Spouse's Name: | Lucinda Swift |
| Father's Birthplace: | Alabama |
| Mother's Birthplace: | Alabama |
| Neighbors: | |
| Occupation: | |
| Cannot read/write: | |
| Blind: | |
| Deaf and dumb: | |
| Otherwise disabled: | |
| Idiotic or insane: | |
| Household Members: | Name / Age |

| Name | Age |
|---|---|
| Jefferson Swift | 50 |
| Lucinda Swift | 40 |
| Sylvester Swift | 23 |
| Forrest Swift | 15 |

**Source Citation:** Year: *1880*; Census Place: *Upper Town, Houston, Georgia*; Roll: *153*; Family History Film: *1254153*; Page: *424C*; Enumeration District: *032*; Image: *0049*.

*...So run that you may obtain.*
*I Corinthians 9:24*

The onset of the final ten years of the 19th Century were challenging for 19 year-old, John, and 14 year-old, Milous. Unbeknown to their mother, the adjustment to their stepfather would be filled with silent struggles. They discussed mutual plans to leave the nest in search of their independence.

Evaline would later die a young woman without issue, and Emma grieved the hardest over her death. She dearly loved her first child for giving up a future family life to help her with the business, and raising the younger children. Jefferson's solution to Emma's grief was to get away from the memories that were dredged up by Evaline's passing. So, the new Swift Family would move to Dublin, Laurens County, Georgia, a neighbor, 63 miles east of Houston County. Mr. Swift had two adult sons, William and Forrest, who lived and thrived there. However, the decision to move was divided. John and Milous had no desire to locate to Dublin.

They were informed, by a traveling patron of the harness shop, about employment with a very prosperous businessman in Macon, Georgia. This family was in need of hiring a coachman to drive their coaches, and to handle their horses. Other responsibilities would ensure their longevity and security with the new employer. With a mother's hesitancy, Emma encouraged them to pursue the offer, if they so desired. She truly loved her sons. As they got older, each of them reminded her more and more of her husband, John.

They also discussed the prospect with their Uncle Sol. They tried to convince him to make the journey with them, with his family in tow. Johnny and Milous wanted Uncle Sol to negotiate a deal to have the three of them work together. Solomon declined, gave them his blessing, and Milous and Johnny were soon bound for the city of Macon, the seat of Bibb County, Georgia.

*…and let us run with patience the race that is set before us…*
*Hebrews 12:1*

# *Chronicle II*

*Am I my brother's keeper?*
*Genesis 4:9*

**Downtown Macon, Georgia 1900**

The Walker Brothers were off to a good start in Macon, Bibb County, Georgia. Their mother and her new husband, Jeff Swift, arrived in Dublin, Laurens County, Georgia in the spring of 1891. Milous and big brother, John, left Perry, Georgia for Macon, Georgia, a few months later. Milous would turn 15 years old, that summer, and John would turn 20 in October.

Their destination was the residence of the William R. Rogers Family, a prominent merchant in the business district of Macon. The family lived at 375 College Street. The home was complete with a formal dining room, an expansive ballroom, and a functioning two-carriage coach house with upper-level living quarters. Milous and John shared the living space above the coach house, and readily attended to the traveling needs of the family, since they lived on-site. John was the chauffeur, while Milous functioned as the assistant caretaker, as well as a butler in the family home, along with the other in-house servants.

The Walker Brothers fared well in Macon, in just a few years. Due to the fact that Mr. Rogers was politically involved in the county, Milous and John were exposed to the prestigious families of that community. They were able to contract with some of those families, as their schedules, with the Rogers Family, allowed. Their skills, fostered by their father and uncle, made for a very sustainable livelihood for Milous and John.

The first half of the decade of the 1890s was a very profitable time for The Walker Brothers. The event that would change their "Brotherhood" was the marriage of John to a young woman by the name of Corine Smith, on Wednesday, April 18, 1894. Soon to be 18 years old, Milous was John's best man at the wedding, which was a small ceremony hosted by the Rogers Family at their home. Milous was never more proud of 22 ½ year-old John, as he took on the responsibility of starting a family of his own. The dynamic of their relationship would only flourish in the light of the progressive events that would continue to take place in each of their lives.

Milous continued to live at the Rogers Family's coach house, and took on the additional responsibility of driver, since he was older. John and his new bride, Corine, lived close by at 565 Monroe Street, which was a little under a mile from the Rogers Home. John regularly walked to work at the Rogers Household, and Milous would drive the coach to get him on days of inclement weather. They had such a well-organized working relationship, which kept them successful in their other business ventures. They were regularly recommended by their clients, and sought out by potential prospects who had the opportunity to observe their work.

John gained employment as a waiter for the Park Hotel, and also became employed as the driver for Dr. T. J. Dewberry. John was listed under each occupation in the 1899 Macon City Directory.

The Twentieth Century rolled into Macon, Georgia with reveling fanfare. Milous wanted to make a significant contribution to the excitement of the new century. So, on Monday afternoon, February 26, 1900, the marriage between Milous Wilburn Walker and Miss Loula Brown took place. Loula's mother, Alice Brown, cooked for one of the families with whom Milous had been acquainted through the Rogers Family. Mrs. Brown's first impression of Milous was so favorable that she arranged for him to meet her daughter, and the meeting proved to be a good match.

Alice Brown lived at 384 College Street, which was a distance of about 1/3 mile from the Rogers Home, where Milous worked. Milous maintained his residence at the Rogers Estate, but he also lived in the home of Alice Brown, with Loula, and Alice's younger children, 12 year-old Della, and 9 year-old James. However, the marriage was short-lived. Upon dissolving his marriage to Loula Brown, Milous left the Brown Household and returned to full-time residency at the Rogers' coach house apartment. He continued his excellent work there, but not without struggling with his recent marital situation.

# Georgia Marriages, 1808-1967 for John A. Walker

| | |
|---|---|
| Groom's Name: | John A. Walker |
| Groom's Birth Date: | |
| Groom's Birthplace: | |
| Groom's Age: | |
| Bride's Name: | Corine Smith |
| Bride's Birth Date: | |
| Bride's Birthplace: | |
| Bride's Age: | |
| Marriage Date: | 18 Apr 1894 |
| Marriage Place: | Bibb, Georgia |
| Groom's Father's Name: | |
| Groom's Mother's Name: | |
| Bride's Father's Name: | |
| Bride's Mother's Name: | |
| Groom's Race: | |
| Groom's Marital Status: | |
| Groom's Previous Wife's Name: | |
| Bride's Race: | |
| Bride's Marital Status: | |
| Bride's Previous Husband's Name: | |
| Indexing Project (Batch) Number: | M71212-2 |
| System Origin: | Georgia-EASy |
| Source Film Number: | 394118 |
| Reference Number: | |

**The First National Bank,** No. 1617—Organized 1865. Capital, $200,000. Surplus, $60,000.
**MACON, GEORGIA.**

G. S. & F. Ry.
Direct Pullman Buffet Sleeping Car Line Between Nashville and Jacksonville without change.
D. C. HALL, General Agent, 8 Kimball, Atlanta, Ga.



WILLIAMS ST.—Cont'd.
143 G C Aldrich,* molder
144 H B Campbell,* engr
149 Mrs M E Sanders
150 W J Hargrove,* painter
150 W J Hargrove,6 painter
153 J F Byrd,* carp
156 L E Moore,* carp
209 Frank Durden,* insptr

**WILLINGHAM STREET**
East Macon.

**WINGS HILL STREET**
South Macon.

**WOOD STREET**
South Macon, first south of Boundary, begins at Fourth, runs west to Second.
71 Vacant
73 Robert Lamar (c)
75 Wm J Jordan (c)
77 Cornelius Beal (c)
78 Benj Davis (c)
80 Betsy Holloway (c)
81 Preston Adams (c)
83 Mary James (c)
(W Boundary intersects)
100 Mary Asby (c)
101 Julia Baker (c)
101 Hattie Mitchell (c)
104 Philip Simmons (c)
108 John Young (c)
112 Robert Davis (c)
112 Wm Troy (c)
113 Geo Low (c),* shoemkr
115 Louisa Woolfolk (c)
116 Augustus Wright (c)
116 Wm Collins (c)
117 Ellen Benford (c)
117 Lula Odom (c)
125 Harvey Irving (c)
139 Annie Everedge (c)
141 Allen O'Neil (c)
143 Dora Harris (c)
145 G Lockhart (c)
147 Jas Luckey (c)
149(108) Wm P Martin (c)
151(215) S Searcy (c)
153 Monroe Roland (c)
155(86) Anderson Cheeves (c)
165 Silas Ivy (c)

**WOOLFOLK STREET**
East Macon.

**WRIGHT STREET**
South Macon.

**WYCHE STREET**
South Macon, begins at Third, runs northwest.

**DON'T LEND YOUR UMBRELLA.**

Did you ever lend your umbrella? If so, did you ever get it back? If you got it back, didn't you have to go after it or *hunt* for it?

Now, if you never loaned your DIRECTORY, we recommend you never to try it, for you will suffer a worse fate than with your parachute!

Borrowers, generally, are chronically such. Their conscience is "seared as with a hot iron." Beyond the shadowy vision of its ultimate reappearance, you will never see it again. The man who borrows a Directory never buys or subscribes for it (or for anything else). Ask him to do so, "he doesn't need it," "never has any use for it," "everybody knows him, he knows more about the people in this city than you can tell him." Yet the virgin freshness of its leaves has hardly been sullied by human touch before this individual wants to borrow your Directory. "He will bring it back right away."

**THIS IS PROPHETIC!**

Keep your Directory; it has cost you money; you can't buy another. It is out of print, for we publish only the number subscribed for.

There is Only One {Southern Dental Parlors} 614 Cherry st. Macon, Ga.
Our Reference—a Ten Years Record in Macon.
22 k. Gold Crowns $4.00
Bridge Work per tooth $4.00
Gold Fillings from $1 up.
Teeth Extracted without Pain.
All other work at Charges that will please you.
Set of Teeth on Rose Pearl, the prettiest, strongest and best plate made! $8 to $10.00
Set of Teeth on Rubber Plate $5 to $8.
Wm. G. Long, D. D. S., Propr. & Mgr.

KNOX HATS. **PHILLIPS,** HATTER and FURNISHER, 566 CHERRY ST. FINE TIES.

Ship and Travel via Georgia Railroad and Atlantic Coast Line.
Pullman Sleeping Cars Between Macon and New York.



**VOLUME X.**

# MALONEY'S

18  99

**MACON, GA.**

# CITY DIRECTORY.

The asterisk thus (*) opp name denotes married.

ALWAYS carry your Prescriptions to THE BRUNNER DRUG COMPANY. Phone 430. Opp. Union Depot.

ABBOTT, DON Q.* SUPT PUBLIC SCHOOLS, 654 Mulberry, r 588 Madison.
" Hunley, student, r 588 Madison
" W C, student Ga-Ala Bus Col, bds 154 4th
Abel, Chas E.* wks Abel Pkg Co, r 314 Shamrock
" Cornelius, W, mess W U Tel Co, r 314 Shamrock
" Edna M, Miss, wks Winn-J Co, r 1059 Hazel
" Elizabeth (wid Henry), r 424 Adams
" Frederick T, r Columbus road
" Lewey D, (Abel Packing Co), r 421 Adams
" Mary B Miss, wks Winn-J Co, r 1059 Hazel
" Milo F,* mech So Ry Shop, r Columbus road
" Packing Co, (L D Abel, Geo R & E Napier), whol & ret meats, 620 Cherry & stalls 7 & 10 city mkt
" Sarah C (wid John H), r 1059 Hazel
" Wm M,* sanitary inspr, r 339 Ross

—THE— Franklin Printing and Publishing Co. Printers, Publishers and Blank Book Manufacturers. 65-71 IVY STREET, ATLANTA, GA.

**F. W. Goette,** ARTISTIC TAILORING
123 COTTON AVENUE.



THIS HOUSE is conveniently located, being directly on the M. & Electric Car Line, and in one block of every street c line in the City. Next door to Opera House. Tab First-Class.
**Stubblefield House,** 663 Mulberry Street.

Walker, Jas (c), lab Central shops
" Jerry (c), wks Ga Cot Oil Co
" John (c), wks Acme B Co, r 156 Bay
" John (c),* waiter Park Hotel, r 565 Monroe
" John (c), driver Dr T J Dewberry, r same
" John (c),* lab So Ry shops, r Columbus rd
" John H (c), lab, r rear 620 Spring
" John H (c),* clk R M S, r 230 Jones
" Jos (c), lab, r 156 Bay
" Josephine (c), laund, r rear 419 Elbert
" Joshua (c), porter H J Lamar & S, r Craft nr 1st av
" Julia (c), cook, r 422 Elbert
" Lizzie (c), wks J A Braswell, r same
" Lula (c), cook, r Lynn ave V'ville
" Mamie (c), nurse, r 124 Ross
" Mary (c), wks Cres Stm Ldry, r rear 409 Spring
" Ned (c), lab, r 314 Poplar
" Peter (c),* lab English J & Co, r 159 Bay

**THE BROWN HOUSE** T. C. Parker, Prop. Rates, $2.50 to $4.

" Richd F (c),* brick layer, r 132 Jones
" Robt (c), lab, r 604 5th
" Squire (c),* wks R H Plant, r Forsyth rd
" Susie (c), nurse, r 329 Forsyth
" Thos (c), wks Brown Hse
" Tyler (c),* lab, r rear 354 Elm
" Vina (c), r 811 Pine
" Wm T (c), barber R Ruff, r Williams S M
Wall, Wm (c), wks Bibb Mfg Co, r Ft Hill E M
Wallace, Addie (c), laund, r 216 6th
" Anna (c), laund, r 156 Madison
" C Augustus (c),* plasterer, r 220 Jones
" David (c),* lab, r 625 New
" Frank (c), wks Jelks & Taylor, r 165 Tupelo
" Geo (c), lab, r 921 Ocmulgee
" Geo (c),* plasterer, r 218 Jones
" Henry (c),* lab, r 217 Jefferson
" Henry (c), lab, r 221 Orange
" Jas (c), butcher, r rear 952 Oglethorpe
" John H (c), wks W A Smith, r 220 Jones

**A. T. HOLT,** Real Estate and Insurance Agent.
PHONE 22.
Special Attention to Rent Collections. 652 Cherry Street.

ancestry.com

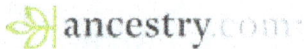

## 1900 United States Federal Census

| | |
|---|---|
| Name: | **Milas Walker** |
| Home in 1900: | Macon, Bibb, Georgia [Macon, Bibb, Georgia] |
| Age: | 24 |
| Birth Date: | Jul 1876 |
| Birthplace: | Georgia |
| Race: | Black |
| Gender: | Male |
| Relationship to head-of-house: | Servant |
| Father's Birthplace: | Georgia |
| Mother's Birthplace: | Georgia |
| Marital Status: | Single |
| Occupation: | |

Household Members:

| Name | Age |
|---|---|
| William R Rogers | 63 |
| Julia C Rogers | 59 |
| Julia C Rogers | 36 |
| Mattie H Rogers | 31 |
| William R Rogers | 26 |
| Julia R Goodwyn | 9 |
| Grey Goodwyn | 3 |
| Mary Bennet | 50 |
| Sarah Brogswell | 45 |
| Milas Walker | 24 |
| Julia Blackshea | 59 |

**Source Citation:** Year: *1900*; Census Place: *Macon, Bibb, Georgia*; Roll: *T623_181*; Page: *1B*; Enumeration District: *27*.

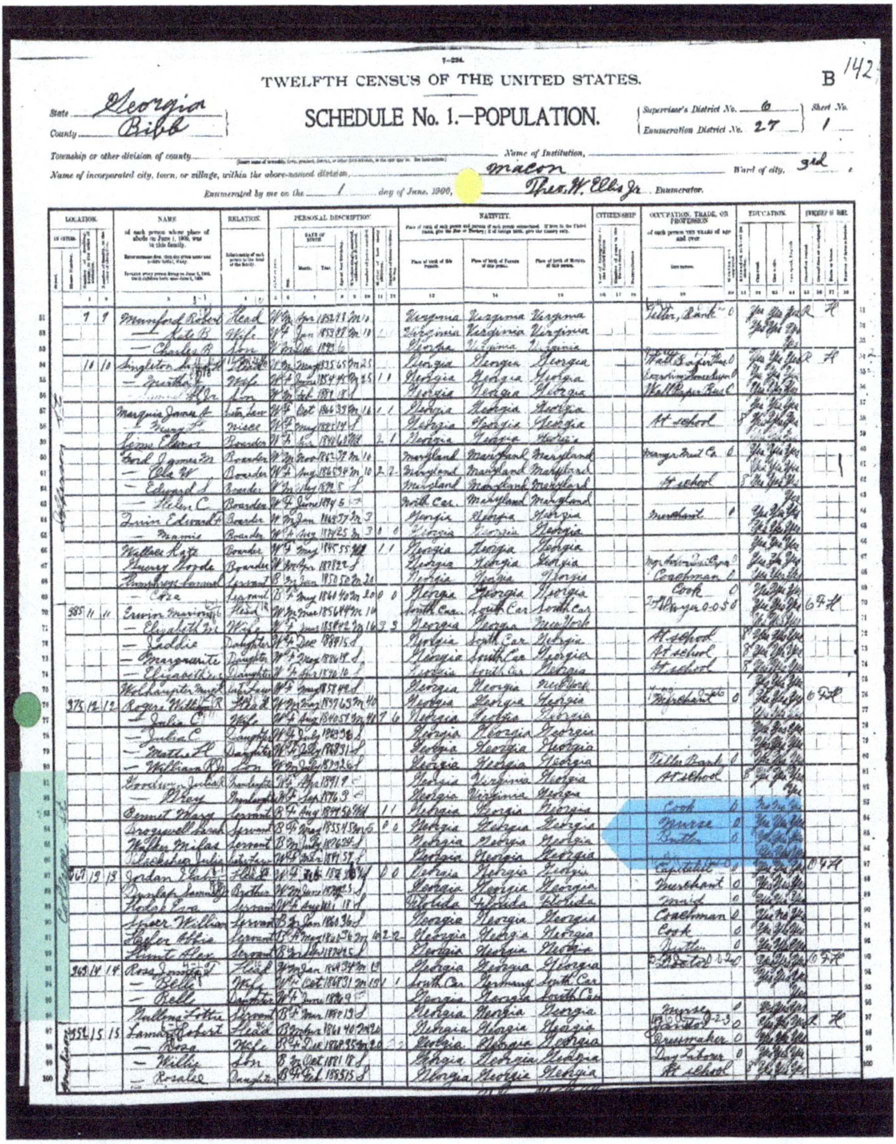

T-294.

TWELFTH CENSUS OF THE UNITED STATES. B 142

SCHEDULE No. 1.—POPULATION.

State: Georgia
County: Bibb
Supervisor's District No. 6
Enumeration District No. 27
Sheet No. 1
Name of incorporated city, town, or village: Macon
Ward of city: 3rd
Enumerated by me on the 1 day of June, 1900, Theo. W. Ellis Jr, Enumerator.

| Dwelling | Family | Name | Relation | Color/Sex | Birth | Age | Marital | Birthplace | Father's birthplace | Mother's birthplace | Occupation |
|---|---|---|---|---|---|---|---|---|---|---|---|
| 9 | 9 | Mumford Robert | Head | W M | Apr 1852 | 48 | M | Virginia | Virginia | Virginia | Teller, Bank |
| | | — Kate B | Wife | W F | Jan 1853 | 47 | M | Virginia | Virginia | Virginia | |
| | | — Charles B | Son | W M | Dec 189[illegible] | [illegible] | | Georgia | Virginia | Virginia | |
| 10 | 10 | Singleton [illegible] | Head | W M | May 1835 | 65 | M | Georgia | Georgia | Georgia | Wall Paper [illegible] |
| | | — Martha | Wife | W F | June 1854 | 45 | M | Georgia | Georgia | Georgia | [illegible] |
| | | [illegible] H Jr | Son | W M | Feb 1881 | 18 | S | Georgia | Georgia | Georgia | Wall Paper [illegible] |
| | | Marquis Jane A | Sister-Law | W F | Oct 1866 | 33 | M | Georgia | Georgia | Georgia | |
| | | — Mary L | Niece | W F | May 1885 | 14 | S | Georgia | Georgia | Georgia | At school |
| | | Lane Elnor | Boarder | W F | [illegible] 1840 | 60 | Wd | Georgia | Georgia | Georgia | |
| | | Ford James M | Boarder | W M | Nov 1862 | 37 | M | Maryland | Maryland | Maryland | Manager Meat Co. |
| | | — Ola W | Boarder | W F | Aug 1865 | 34 | M | Maryland | Maryland | Maryland | |
| | | — Edward L | Boarder | W M | May 1892 | 8 | S | Maryland | Maryland | Maryland | At school |
| | | — Helen C | Boarder | W F | June 1894 | 5 | | North Car. | Maryland | Maryland | |
| | | Quin Edward F | Boarder | W M | Jan 1863 | 37 | M | Georgia | Georgia | Georgia | Merchant |
| | | — Mamie | Boarder | W F | Aug 1874 | 25 | M | Georgia | Georgia | Georgia | |
| | | Wallace Kate | Boarder | W F | May 1845 | 55 | Wd | Georgia | Georgia | Georgia | |
| | | Henry Lloyde | Boarder | W M | Apr 1878 | 22 | S | Georgia | Georgia | Georgia | [illegible] |
| | | Humphreys Samuel | Servant | B M | Jan 1850 | 50 | M | Georgia | Georgia | Georgia | Coachman |
| | | — Cora | Servant | B F | May 1860 | 40 | M | Georgia | Georgia | Georgia | Cook |
| 11 | 11 | Erwin Marion | Head | W M | Mar 1856 | 44 | M | South Car. | South Car | South Car | [illegible] |
| | | — Elizabeth M | Wife | W F | June 1858 | 42 | M | Georgia | Georgia | New York | |
| | | — Sadie | Daughter | W F | Dec 1884 | 15 | S | Georgia | South Car | Georgia | At school |
| | | — Marguerite | Daughter | W F | May 1886 | 14 | S | Georgia | South Car | Georgia | At school |
| | | — Elizabeth | Daughter | W F | Apr 1890 | 10 | S | Georgia | South Car | Georgia | At school |
| | | Wolhaupter Mary | Sister-Law | W F | May 1858 | 42 | S | Georgia | Georgia | New York | |
| 12 | 12 | Rogers William R | Head | W M | May 1837 | 63 | M | Georgia | Georgia | Georgia | Merchant |
| | | — Julia C | Wife | W F | Aug 1840 | 57 | M | Georgia | Georgia | Georgia | |
| | | — Julia C | Daughter | W F | July 1862 | 38 | S | Georgia | Georgia | Georgia | |
| | | — Mattie H | Daughter | W F | July 1868 | 31 | S | Georgia | Georgia | Georgia | |
| | | — William R Jr | Son | W M | July 1873 | 26 | S | Georgia | Georgia | Georgia | Teller Bank |
| | | Goodwyn Julia | Granddaughter | W F | Apr 1891 | 9 | | Georgia | Virginia | Georgia | At school |
| | | — [illegible] | Granddaughter | W F | Sep 1896 | 3 | | Georgia | Virginia | Georgia | |
| | | Bennet Mary | Servant | B F | Aug 1844 | 56 | Wd | Georgia | Georgia | Georgia | Cook |
| | | Brogswell Sarah | Servant | B F | May 1855 | 45 | M | Georgia | Georgia | Georgia | Nurse |
| | | Walker Milas | Servant | B M | July 1876 | 24 | S | Georgia | Georgia | Georgia | Butler |
| | | [illegible] Julia | Sister-Law | W F | Mar 1841 | 59 | S | Georgia | Georgia | Georgia | |
| 13 | 13 | Jordan [illegible] | Head | W F | [illegible] | [illegible] | Wd | Georgia | Georgia | Georgia | Capitalist |
| | | Dunlap Samuel | Brother | W M | June 187[illegible] | [illegible] | S | Georgia | Georgia | Georgia | Merchant |
| | | [illegible] Eva | Servant | W F | Aug 18[illegible] | 18 | S | Florida | Florida | Florida | Maid |
| | | Spicer William | Servant | B M | Jan 1860 | 36 | S | Georgia | Georgia | Georgia | Coachman |
| | | Hafer Abbie | Servant | B F | May 18[illegible] | [illegible] | M | Georgia | Georgia | Georgia | Cook |
| | | Hunt Alex | Servant | B M | [illegible] 187[illegible] | 25 | S | Georgia | Georgia | Georgia | Butler |
| 14 | 14 | Ross [illegible] | Head | W M | Jan 18[illegible] | 34 | M | Georgia | Georgia | Georgia | Doctor |
| | | — Belle | Wife | W F | Oct 1868 | 31 | M | South Car | Germany | South Car | |
| | | — Belle | Daughter | W F | June 18[illegible] | [illegible] | | Georgia | Georgia | South Car | |
| | | [illegible] Lottie | Servant | B F | Mar 1880 | 19 | S | Georgia | Georgia | Georgia | Nurse |
| 15 | 15 | Lamar Robert | Head | B M | [illegible] 1861 | 40 | M | Georgia | Georgia | Georgia | Janitor |
| | | — Rosa | Wife | B F | Dec 1868 | 35 | M | Georgia | Georgia | Georgia | Dressmaker |
| | | — Willie | Son | B M | Oct 1881 | 18 | S | Georgia | Georgia | Georgia | Day Laborer |
| | | — Rosalee | Daughter | B F | Feb 1885 | 15 | S | Georgia | Georgia | Georgia | At school |

Milous Walker, Sr.*The Musician

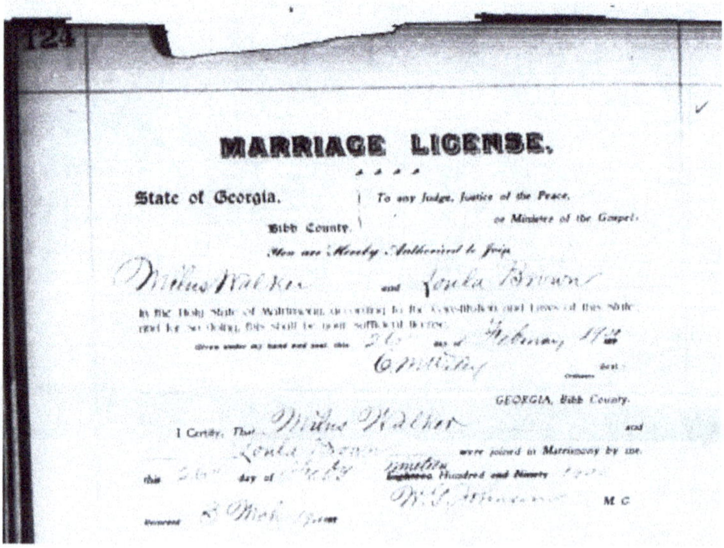

124

MARRIAGE LICENSE.

State of Georgia, Bibb County. | To any Judge, Justice of the Peace, or Minister of the Gospel.

You are Hereby Authorized to Join

Milus Walker and Loula Brown

in the Holy State of Matrimony, according to the Constitution and Laws of this State, and for so doing, this shall be your sufficient license.

Given under my hand and seal, this 26 day of February 1902

C. M. Wiley Ordinary. Seal.

GEORGIA, Bibb County.

I Certify, That Milus Walker and Loula Brown were joined in Matrimony by me, this 26 day of Feby Nineteen Hundred and Ninety two

M. G.

Recorded

# Georgia Marriages, 1808-1967 for Milus Walker

| | |
|---|---|
| Groom's Name: | Milus Walker |
| Groom's Birth Date: | |
| Groom's Birthplace: | |
| Groom's Age: | |
| Bride's Name: | Loula Brown |
| Bride's Birth Date: | |
| Bride's Birthplace: | |
| Bride's Age: | |
| Marriage Date: | 26 Feb 1900 |
| Marriage Place: | , Bibb, Georgia |
| Groom's Father's Name: | |
| Groom's Mother's Name: | |
| Bride's Father's Name: | |
| Bride's Mother's Name: | |
| Groom's Race: | |
| Groom's Marital Status: | |
| Groom's Previous Wife's Name: | |
| Bride's Race: | |
| Bride's Marital Status: | |
| Bride's Previous Husband's Name: | |
| Indexing Project (Batch) Number: | M71212-3 |
| System Origin: | Georgia-EASy |
| Source Film Number: | 394119 |
| Reference Number: | |

ancestry.com

1900 United States Federal Census

| | |
|---|---|
| Name: | **Milus Walker** |
| Home in 1900: | Macon, Bibb, Georgia [Macon, Bibb, Georgia] |
| Age: | 23 |
| Birth Date: | May 1877 |
| Birthplace: | Georgia |
| Race: | Black |
| Gender: | Male |
| Relationship to head-of-house: | Son-in-Law |
| Father's Birthplace: | Georgia |
| Mother's Birthplace: | Georgia |
| Spouse's Name: | Lula Walker |
| Marriage year: | 1900 |
| Marital Status: | Married |
| Years married: | 0 |
| Occupation: | |

Household Members:

| Name | Age |
|---|---|
| Alice Brown | 35 |
| Lula Walker | 20 |
| Milus Walker | 23 |
| Della Brown | 12 |
| James Brown | 7 |

**Source Citation:** Year: *1900*; Census Place: *Macon, Bibb, Georgia*; Roll: *T623_181*; Page: *11A*; Enumeration District: *27*.

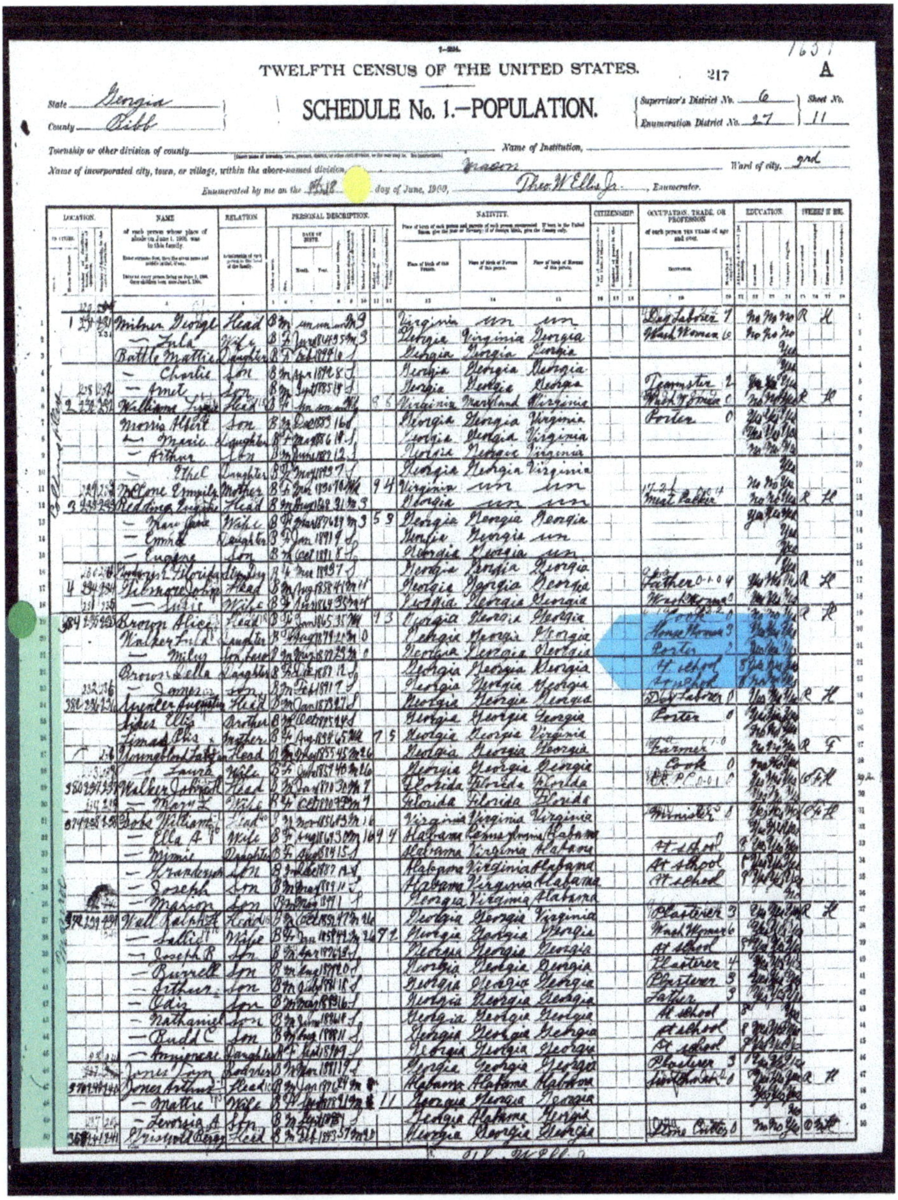
TWELFTH CENSUS OF THE UNITED STATES. 217 A

SCHEDULE No. 1.—POPULATION.

State Georgia
County Bibb
Supervisor's District No. 6
Enumeration District No. 27
Sheet No. 11

Township or other division of county ______ Name of Institution, ______
Name of incorporated city, town, or village, within the above-named division, Macon. Ward of city, 3rd
Enumerated by me on the 18 day of June, 1900, Theo. W. Ellis Jr., Enumerator.

| Line | Name | Relation | Birthplace of person | Birthplace of father | Birthplace of mother | Occupation |
|---|---|---|---|---|---|---|
| 1 | Milner George | Head | Virginia | un | un | Day Laborer |
| 2 | — Lula | Wife | Georgia | Virginia | Georgia | Wash Woman |
| 3 | Battle Mattie | Daughter | Georgia | Georgia | Georgia | |
| 4 | — Charlie | Son | Georgia | Georgia | Georgia | |
| 5 | — Arnet | Son | Georgia | Georgia | Georgia | Teamster |
| 6 | Williams Lizzie | Head | Virginia | Maryland | Virginia | Wash Woman |
| 7 | Morris Albert | Son | Georgia | Georgia | Virginia | Porter |
| 8 | — Marie | Daughter | Georgia | Georgia | Virginia | |
| 9 | — Arthur | Son | Georgia | Georgia | Virginia | |
| 10 | — Ethel | Daughter | Georgia | Georgia | Virginia | |
| 11 | McCone Emmily | Mother | Virginia | un | un | |
| 12 | Redding Eugene | Head | Georgia | un | un | Meat Packer |
| 13 | — Jane | Wife | Georgia | Georgia | Georgia | |
| 14 | — Emma | Daughter | Georgia | Georgia | un | |
| 15 | — Eugene | Son | Georgia | Georgia | un | |
| 16 | [illegible] Florida | Step Daughter | Georgia | Georgia | Georgia | |
| 17 | Gilmore John | Head | Georgia | Georgia | Georgia | Farmer |
| 18 | — Susie | Wife | Georgia | Georgia | Georgia | Wash Woman |
| 19 | Brown Alice | Head | Georgia | Georgia | Georgia | Cook |
| 20 | Walker Frida | Daughter | Georgia | Georgia | Georgia | House Woman |
| 21 | — Miley | Son-in-law | Georgia | Georgia | Georgia | Porter |
| 22 | Brown Della | Daughter | Georgia | Georgia | Georgia | At school |
| 23 | — James | Son | Georgia | Georgia | Georgia | At school |
| 24 | Spencer Augustin | Head | Georgia | Georgia | Georgia | Day Laborer |
| 25 | Sikes Ellis | Brother | Georgia | Georgia | Georgia | Porter |
| 26 | Simas Elis | Mother | Georgia | Georgia | Virginia | |
| 27 | Youngblood Fate | Head | Georgia | Georgia | Georgia | Farmer |
| 28 | — Laura | Wife | Georgia | Georgia | Georgia | Cook |
| 29 | Walker John | Head | Florida | Florida | Florida | R. R. P[illegible] |
| 30 | — Mary L | Wife | Florida | Florida | Florida | |
| 31 | Bobe William | Head | Virginia | Virginia | Virginia | Minister |
| 32 | — Ella A | Wife | Alabama | [illegible] | Alabama | At school |
| 33 | — Mimie | Daughter | Alabama | Virginia | Alabama | At school |
| 34 | — Granderson | Son | Alabama | Virginia | Alabama | At school |
| 35 | — Joseph | Son | Alabama | Virginia | Alabama | |
| 36 | — Marion | Son | Georgia | Virginia | Alabama | |
| 37 | Wall Ralph H | Head | Georgia | Georgia | Virginia | Plasterer |
| 38 | — Sallie | Wife | Georgia | Georgia | Georgia | Wash Woman |
| 39 | — Joseph R | Son | Georgia | Georgia | Georgia | At school |
| 40 | — Burrell | Son | Georgia | Georgia | Georgia | Plasterer |
| 41 | — Arthur | Son | Georgia | Georgia | Georgia | Plasterer |
| 42 | — Odis | Son | Georgia | Georgia | Georgia | Father |
| 43 | — Nathaniel | Son | Georgia | Georgia | Georgia | At school |
| 44 | — Budd C | Son | Georgia | Georgia | Georgia | At school |
| 45 | — Anniemae | Daughter | Georgia | Georgia | Georgia | At school |
| 46 | Jones Tom | Boarder | Georgia | Georgia | Georgia | Plasterer |
| 47 | Jones Arthur | Head | Alabama | Alabama | Alabama | [illegible] |
| 48 | — Mattie | Wife | Georgia | Georgia | Georgia | |
| 49 | — Georgia A | Son | Georgia | Alabama | Georgia | |
| 50 | Griswold Perry | Head | Georgia | Georgia | Georgia | Stone Cutter |

## A. The Alice Brown Residence to
## B. The Wm. R. Rogers Residence

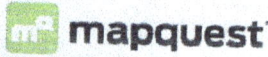

**mapquest**

Trip to:

**375 College St**
Macon, GA 31201-1651
0.31 miles / 1 minute
Notes

(A) **384 Monroe St**, Macon, GA 31201-6555

| | | |
|---|---|---|
| 1. Start out going north on **Monroe St** toward **2nd Ave.** Map | **0.06 Mi** | *0.06 Mi Total* |
| 2. Take the 1st **right** onto **2nd Ave.** Map<br>*If you reach Green Smith Ln you've gone a little too far* | **0.2 Mi** | *0.3 Mi Total* |
| 3. Turn **right** onto **College St.** Map | **0.04 Mi** | *0.3 Mi Total* |
| 4. **375 COLLEGE ST** is on the **right.** Map<br>*If you reach Georgia Ave you've gone a little too far* | | |

(B) **375 College St**, Macon, GA 31201-1651

Total Travel Estimate: **0.31 miles - about 1 minute**

©2012 MapQuest, Inc. Use of directions and maps is subject to the MapQuest Terms of Use. We make no guarantee of the accuracy of their content, road conditions or route usability. You assume all risk of use. View Terms of Use

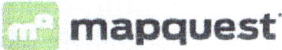

**mapquest**

Trip to:

**384 Monroe St**
Macon, GA 31201-6555
0.22 miles /

**565 Monroe St**, Macon, GA 31201-1419

1. Start out going **north** on **Monroe St** toward **Hardeman Ave.** Map — **0.2 Mi** *0.2 Mi Total*

2. **384 MONROE ST** is on the **right**. Map
*Your destination is just past Jefferson St*
*If you reach 2nd Ave you've gone a little too far*

**384 Monroe St**, Macon, GA 31201-6555

Total Travel Estimate: **0.22 miles - about**

©2012 MapQuest, Inc. Use of directions and maps is subject to the MapQuest Terms of Use. We make no guarantee of the accuracy of their content, road conditions or route usability. You assume all risk of use. View Terms of Use

**A. John Walker's Residence to**
**B. The Alice Brown Residence**

ancestry.com

## 1900 United States Federal Census

| | |
|---|---|
| Name: | **John Walker** |
| Home in 1900: | Macon, Bibb, Georgia [Macon, Bibb, Georgia] |
| Age: | 25 |
| Birth Date: | Oct 1874 |
| Birthplace: | Georgia |
| Race: | Black |
| Gender: | Male |
| Relationship to head-of-house: | Head |
| Spouse's Name: | Corinne Walker |
| Marriage year: | 1895 |
| Marital Status: | Married |
| Years married: | 5 |
| Occupation: | |

Household Members:

| Name | Age |
|---|---|
| John Walker | 25 |
| Corinne Walker | 23 |

**Source Citation:** Year: *1900*; Census Place: *Macon, Bibb, Georgia*; Roll: *T623_181*; Page: *8B*; Enumeration District: *34*.

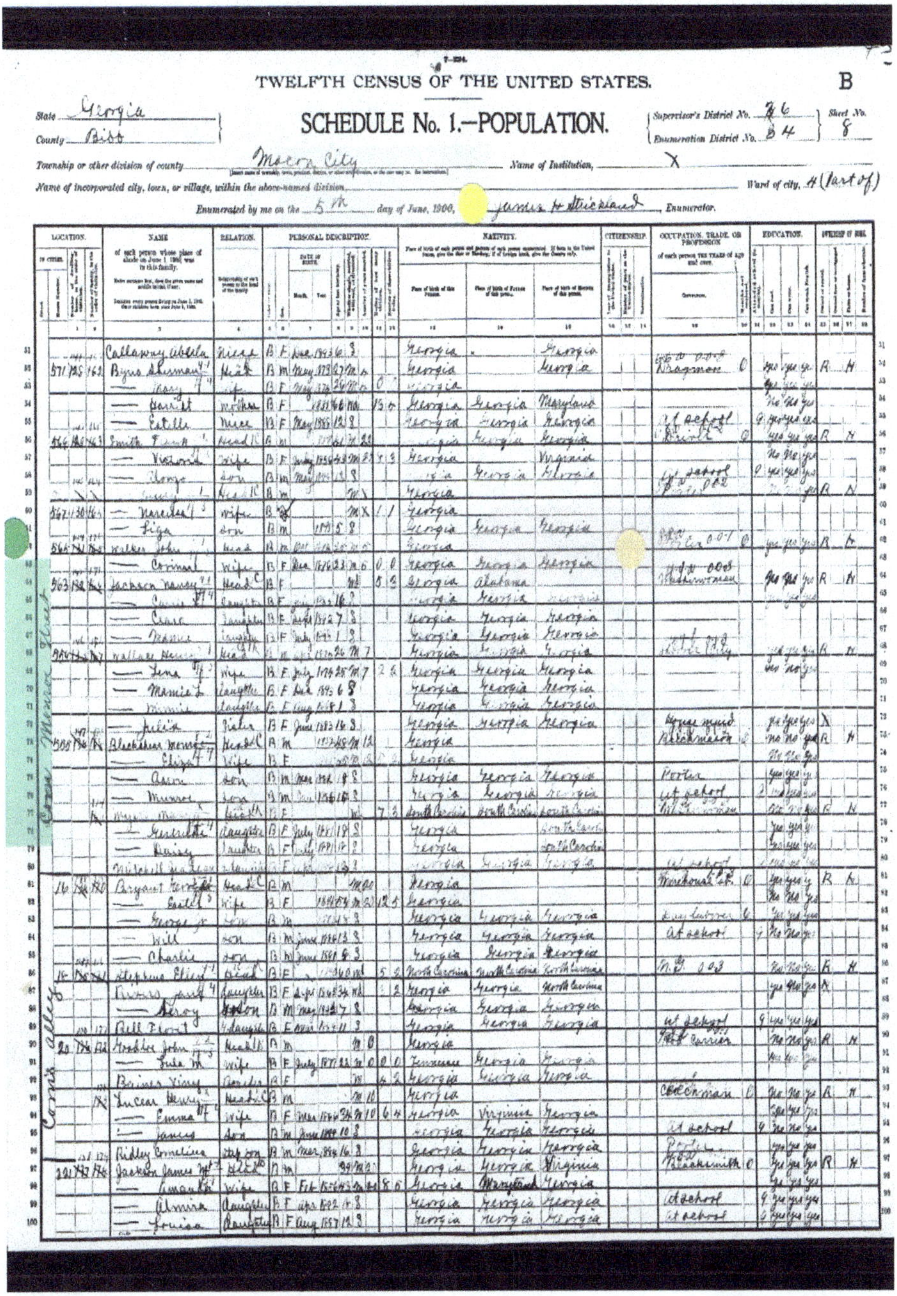

7-224.

TWELFTH CENSUS OF THE UNITED STATES. B

SCHEDULE No. 1.—POPULATION.

State: Georgia
County: Bibb
Township or other division of county: Macon City
Name of Institution: X
Name of incorporated city, town, or village, within the above-named division:
Supervisor's District No. 6
Enumeration District No. 84
Sheet No. 8
Ward of city, 4 (Part of)
Enumerated by me on the 5th day of June, 1900, James H Strickland, Enumerator.

Cross Monroe Street

Corn's alley

| Line | House / Dwelling / Family no. | Name | Relation | Color | Sex | Month | Year | Age | Marital | Yrs. married | Children born | Living | Birthplace | Father's birthplace | Mother's birthplace | Occupation | Months not employed | Months in school | Read | Write | Speak English | Owned / Rented, Farm / House |
|---|---|---|---|---|---|---|---|---|---|---|---|---|---|---|---|---|---|---|---|---|---|---|
| 51 | | Callaway Abella | Niece | B | F | Dec | 1893 | 6 | S | | | | Georgia | | Georgia | | | | | | | |
| 52 | 571 125 162 | Byus Sherman | Head | B | M | May | 1873 | 27 | M | | | | Georgia | | Georgia | Drayman | 0 | | yes | yes | yes | R H |
| 53 | | — Mary | Wife | B | F | May | 1874 | 26 | M | | 0 | | Georgia | | | | | | yes | yes | yes | |
| 54 | | — Harriet | Mother | B | F | | 1833 | 66 | Wd | | 13 | 6 | Georgia | Georgia | Maryland | | | | No | No | yes | |
| 55 | | — Estelle | Niece | B | F | May | 1885 | 12 | S | | | | Georgia | Georgia | Georgia | At school | | 9 | yes | yes | yes | |
| 56 | 566 126 163 | Smith Frank | Head | B | M | | [illegible] | [illegible] | M | 22 | | | Georgia | Georgia | Georgia | [illegible] | 0 | | yes | yes | yes | R H |
| 57 | | — Victoria | Wife | B | F | July | 1856 | 43 | M | 22 | 4 | 3 | Georgia | | Virginia | | | | No | No | yes | |
| 58 | | — Alonzo | Son | B | M | May | [illegible] | [illegible] | S | | | | Georgia | Georgia | Georgia | At school | | 9 | yes | yes | yes | |
| 59 | | [illegible] | Head | B | M | | | | M | | | | Georgia | | | Porter | | | | | yes | R H |
| 60 | 567 130 164 | — Narcissa | Wife | B | | | | | M | | 1 | 1 | Georgia | | | | | | | | | |
| 61 | | — Liga | Son | B | M | | 1895 | 5 | S | | | | Georgia | Georgia | Georgia | | | | | | | |
| 62 | 564 | Walker John | Head | B | M | Oct | [illegible] | [illegible] | M | 5 | | | Georgia | | | [illegible] | 0 | | yes | yes | yes | R H |
| 63 | | — Corinna | Wife | B | F | Dec | 1876 | 23 | M | 5 | 0 | 0 | Georgia | Georgia | Georgia | | | | | | | |
| 64 | 563 132 | Jackson Nancy | Head | B | F | | | | Wd | | 5 | 3 | Georgia | Alabama | | Washerwoman | | | yes | yes | yes | R H |
| 65 | | — Carrie | Daughter | B | F | July | 1883 | 16 | S | | | | Georgia | Georgia | Georgia | | | | yes | yes | yes | |
| 66 | | — Clara | Daughter | B | F | Sept | 1892 | 7 | S | | | | Georgia | Georgia | Georgia | | | | | | | |
| 67 | | — Mamie | Daughter | B | F | July | 1898 | 1 | S | | | | Georgia | Georgia | Georgia | | | | | | | |
| 68 | | Wallace Henry | Head | B | M | Apr | 1874 | 26 | M | 7 | | | Georgia | Georgia | Georgia | [illegible] | | | yes | yes | yes | R H |
| 69 | | — Lena | Wife | B | F | July | 1874 | 25 | M | 7 | 2 | 2 | Georgia | Georgia | Georgia | | | | yes | no | yes | |
| 70 | | — Mamie L | Daughter | B | F | Dec | 1893 | 6 | S | | | | Georgia | Georgia | Georgia | | | | | | | |
| 71 | | — Minnie | Daughter | B | F | Aug | 1898 | 1 | S | | | | Georgia | Georgia | Georgia | | | | | | | |
| 72 | | — Julia | Sister | B | F | June | 1883 | 16 | S | | | | Georgia | Georgia | Georgia | House maid | | | yes | yes | yes | |
| 73 | 565 136 | Blackshear Monroe | Head | B | M | | 1852 | 48 | M | 12 | | | Georgia | | | Brickmason | | | no | no | yes | R H |
| 74 | | — Eliza | Wife | B | F | | [illegible] | [illegible] | M | 12 | | | Georgia | | | | | | No | No | yes | |
| 75 | | — Aaron | Son | B | M | Mar | 1882 | 18 | S | | | | Georgia | Georgia | Georgia | Porter | | | yes | yes | yes | |
| 76 | | — Monroe | Son | B | M | Jan | 1884 | 16 | S | | | | Georgia | Georgia | Georgia | At school | | 2 | yes | yes | yes | |
| 77 | | Myers [illegible] | Head | B | F | | | | Wd | | 7 | 3 | South Carolina | South Carolina | South Carolina | Washerwoman | | | [illegible] | no | yes | R H |
| 78 | | — Henrietta | Daughter | B | F | July | 1881 | 18 | S | | | | Georgia | | South Carolina | | | | yes | yes | yes | |
| 79 | | — Daisy | Daughter | B | F | July | 1881 | 18 | S | | | | Georgia | | South Carolina | | | | yes | yes | yes | |
| 80 | | Mitchell [illegible] | Granddaughter | B | F | | [illegible] | [illegible] | S | | | | Georgia | Georgia | Georgia | At school | | | | | | |
| 81 | 16 120 | Bryant George | Head | B | M | | | | M | 20 | | | Georgia | | | Warehouse lab. | 0 | | yes | yes | yes | R H |
| 82 | | — Castell | Wife | B | F | | 1846 | 54 | M | 20 | 12 | 5 | Georgia | | | | | | No | No | yes | |
| 83 | | — George Jr | Son | B | M | | [illegible] | 18 | S | | | | Georgia | Georgia | Georgia | Day laborer | 6 | | yes | yes | yes | |
| 84 | | — Will | Son | B | M | June | 1886 | 13 | S | | | | Georgia | Georgia | Georgia | At school | | 9 | No | No | yes | |
| 85 | | — Charlie | Son | B | M | June | 1891 | 8 | S | | | | Georgia | Georgia | Georgia | | | | | | | |
| 86 | 18 | Stephens Eliza | Head | B | F | | 1840 | 60 | Wd | | 5 | 2 | North Carolina | North Carolina | North Carolina | [illegible] | | | No | No | yes | R H |
| 87 | | Rivers Jane | Daughter | B | F | Sept | 1865 | 34 | Wd | | | 2 | Georgia | Georgia | North Carolina | | | | yes | No | yes | R |
| 88 | | — Leroy | Grandson | B | M | May | 1892 | 7 | S | | | | Georgia | Georgia | Georgia | | | | | | | |
| 89 | | Bell Flora | Granddaughter | B | F | Mar | 1889 | 11 | S | | | | Georgia | Georgia | Georgia | At school | | 9 | yes | yes | yes | |
| 90 | 20 | Grubbs John | Head | B | M | | | | M | 0 | | | Georgia | | | [illegible] Carrier | | | No | No | yes | R H |
| 91 | | — Lula M | Wife | B | F | July | 1877 | 22 | M | 0 | 0 | 0 | Tennessee | Georgia | Georgia | | | | yes | yes | yes | |
| 92 | | Baines Viney | Boarder | B | F | | | | Wd | | 4 | 2 | Georgia | Georgia | Georgia | | | | | | | |
| 93 | | Lucear Henry | Head | B | M | | | | M | 10 | | | Georgia | | | Coachman | 0 | | No | No | yes | R H |
| 94 | | — Emma | Wife | B | F | Mar | 1866 | 34 | M | 10 | 6 | 4 | Georgia | Virginia | Georgia | | | | yes | yes | yes | |
| 95 | | — James | Son | B | M | June | 1889 | 10 | S | | | | Georgia | Georgia | Georgia | At school | | 9 | No | No | yes | |
| 96 | | Ridley Cornelius | Step son | B | M | Mar | 1884 | 16 | S | | | | Georgia | Georgia | Georgia | Porter | | | yes | yes | yes | |
| 97 | 221 | Jackson James | Head | B | M | | | 34 | M | [illegible] | | | Georgia | Georgia | Virginia | Blacksmith | 0 | | yes | yes | yes | R H |
| 98 | | — Amanda | Wife | B | F | Feb | 1856 | 43 | M | [illegible] | 8 | 6 | Georgia | Maryland | Georgia | | | | yes | yes | yes | |
| 99 | | — Almira | Daughter | B | F | Apr | 1892 | 8 | S | | | | Georgia | Georgia | Georgia | At school | | 9 | yes | yes | yes | |
| 100 | | — Louisa | Daughter | B | F | Aug | 1887 | 12 | S | | | | Georgia | Georgia | Georgia | At school | | 6 | yes | yes | yes | |

**Rev. Norman G. McCall**

*Without counsel purposes are disappointed:*
*but in the multitude of counselors they are established.*
*Proverbs 15:22*

Milous took counsel from his big brother, during that time. John suggested that he should take a break just to clear his mind a little. He had been exchanging letters with their mother in Dublin, Georgia, so he urged Milous to visit Emma and Jeff to see how they were doing. John would manage Milous' duties while he was gone.

Milous went to Dublin, Georgia and had a pleasant visit with his mother and her husband, Jeff Swift. Jeff's granddaughter, Jennie Nelson, was a nine year-old who lived with them. Jeff's daughter, Sylvester, was Jennie's mother. Also in the Swift Household was Jeff's 21 year-old grandson, Jefferson Swift II. Milous knew the younger Jefferson Swift, as they grew up together, and were a few years apart in age.

Milous ended the weekend visit with his mother by going to church with her at the Dublin First Baptist Church. The presiding pastor was Rev. Norman G. McCall. During the service, Milous sat between his mother and his little niece, Jennie. She nudged Milous, and pointed out her schoolteacher, who was sitting across the aisle and a few rows closer to the front. Milous turned to his mother, on his left, and asked about Jennie's teacher, after he had gotten a profile glimpse of her, as she looked toward the pulpit. Emma immediately shushed him until after the service. Milous was rather inattentive to what was coming from the pulpit, as he anticipated the end of the service so he could get more information about Jennie's teacher.

The time for a congregational song was at hand. A young woman stood up across the aisle, and it was Jennie's teacher. As she moved in the direction of the piano, Milous watched her every step. When she got to the piano and played the first chord, it was literally and figuratively music to his ears. His eyes also enjoyed the vision he beheld. Her name was Louisa Rebecca McCall. She was a niece of the pastor. Having an inclination and love for music, himself, Milous was taken in by Miss McCall's ability at the piano, and her voice, as she led the congregational songs. His attention to the worship service was regenerated.

After the service, Pastor McCall greeted everyone at the door, as they exited the church. Emma waited to make a special introduction of her son to the pastor. As Milous and Rev. McCall talked for a few minutes, the pastor asked Jennie to politely go over and get her teacher's attention for him. He beckoned her to him, and introduced her to Milous as his niece, Lula McCall. How ironic could it be that the young woman who impressed him so much would have the same name as Milous' recently estranged wife? He found out later that Lula was a nickname by which her family referred to her. Her given name was Louisa, after the mother of her maternal grandfather, Hamlet McCall. The irony posed no problem for Milous, because several months later, on Friday, August 9, 1901, he was back at the Dublin First Baptist Church exchanging wedding vows with Miss Louisa Rebecca McCall, officiated by her uncle, the Rev. Norman G. McCall.

When Milous and Louisa got married, she had been living with her maternal grandmother, Patsey McCall. Louisa's teen-aged brother, Henry James, and her first cousin, schoolteacher, Miss Nettie Freeman, also lived with Grandmother Patsey. Milous moved into the home with his wife, and lived in Dublin for the first few years of their marriage. Nettie later moved out when she married, and Henry James moved to Houston, Texas where his other sister, Mattie, had gone to live with their mother's niece, Julia

Thomas Hester, the wife of Alexander Z. Hester. Julia, their first cousin, was about 20 years his senior, so Henry James was raised by the Hesters as their son, since 1901, when he was 16 years old.

When Milous left Macon, he never returned. John and his wife, Corine, made the trip to Dublin for the wedding, and John stood as Milous' best man. The time shared between Emma and her sons was quite enjoyable for each of them. If her daughters, Annie and Theodosia, had attended, it would have been a treat for Emma to have spent time with her four surviving children out of the ten children she birthed. Emma would later console and empathize with Lula and Milous after the loss of their first two babies. Grandmother Patsey was also there as a support, since she was a midwife, and had delivered many of the babies born in the town of Dublin, Georgia.

Brother John and his wife, Corine, were unsuccessful with trying to have children. Several miscarriages put a strain on their marriage, and it ended in 1904. John later met a woman named Viola McComb. They were married in Macon, on Tuesday, November 14, 1905.

Dublin, Georgia proved to be a decent place for Milous to live, after all. He was reunited with his mother, he found a beautiful wife to share his life, and he was gainfully employed in a thriving city.

Jumping the Broom

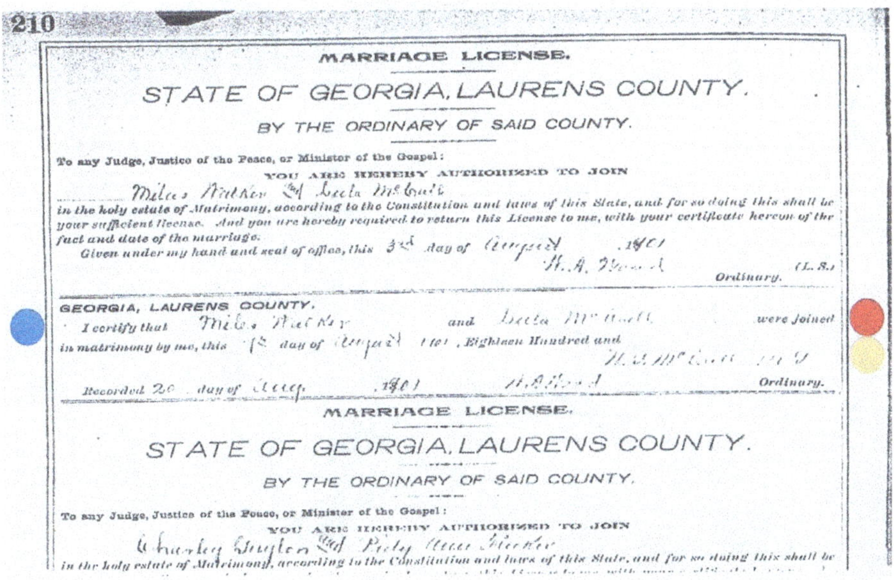

210

MARRIAGE LICENSE.

STATE OF GEORGIA, LAURENS COUNTY.

BY THE ORDINARY OF SAID COUNTY.

To any Judge, Justice of the Peace, or Minister of the Gospel:

YOU ARE HEREBY AUTHORIZED TO JOIN

Miles Walker and Leila McCall in the holy estate of Matrimony, according to the Constitution and laws of this State, and for so doing this shall be your sufficient license. And you are hereby required to return this License to me, with your certificate hereon of the fact and date of the marriage.

Given under my hand and seal of office, this 3rd day of August 1901

H. A. Wood (L. S.)
Ordinary.

GEORGIA, LAURENS COUNTY.

I certify that Miles Walker and Leila McCall were joined in matrimony by me, this 4th day of August 1901, Eighteen Hundred and

W. S. McCall M. G.

Recorded 20 day of Aug. 1901 H. A. Wood Ordinary.

MARRIAGE LICENSE.

STATE OF GEORGIA, LAURENS COUNTY.

BY THE ORDINARY OF SAID COUNTY.

To any Judge, Justice of the Peace, or Minister of the Gospel:

YOU ARE HEREBY AUTHORIZED TO JOIN

Charley Guyton and Poly Ann Hooker in the holy estate of Matrimony, according to the Constitution and laws of this State, and for so doing this shall be

MC CALL, N.G. (REV.) 46

## PROMINENT NEGRO DIED SUDDENLY WEDNESDAY

Rev. N. G. McCall, pastor of the Dublin First Baptist church, colored, president of the colored State Baptist Sunday School Convention, a member of the executive board of Central City College, and a very prominent negro, fell dead in his field near the city Wednesday morning.

Rev McCall had been afflicted with dropsy of the heart for several months.

He was a good negro and was well liked by both white and colored.

He had been pastor of the church here nineteen years and was 47 years old at the time of his death.

Rev. McCall was a member of every colored secret order in Dublin, with the exception of the Knights of Pythias—being a Mason, Odd Fellow and Laboring Friend.

He was a man of large build and almost herculean strength and was one of the most prominent negroes in the state.

The funeral Thursday afternoon was perhaps the largest ever held here, as negroes from all over the county were in attendance, and the procession to the cemetery was nearly a mile in length.

The funeral sermon was preached by Rev. Dr. W. R. Fobbs, of Macon.

DUBLIN TIMES June 18, 1904

***A MIGHTY PREACHER MAN*** - The Rev. Norman G. McCall served as pastor of the First African Baptist Church of Dublin for nineteen years. Rev. McCall was a giant of a man and known all over for his Herculean strength. Rev. McCall worked on the riverboats and it was said that he could swim across the river with two sacks of fertilizer under his arms. Rev. McCall was active in the organization of the schools in the black community in the 1880s. His family lived in the southwestern portion of Dublin between Marcus and Marion Streets. Rev. McCall served on the Executive Board of Central City College and as President of the State Sunday School Board of Education. He was a member of the Masons, the Odd Fellows, and the Laboring Friends. On June 15, 1904, after suffering for several months with dropsy, Rev. McCall fell dead in his field. His funeral procession was one of the longest in Dublin's history, nearly one mile long. *Dublin Times, June 18, 1904, p. 1.*

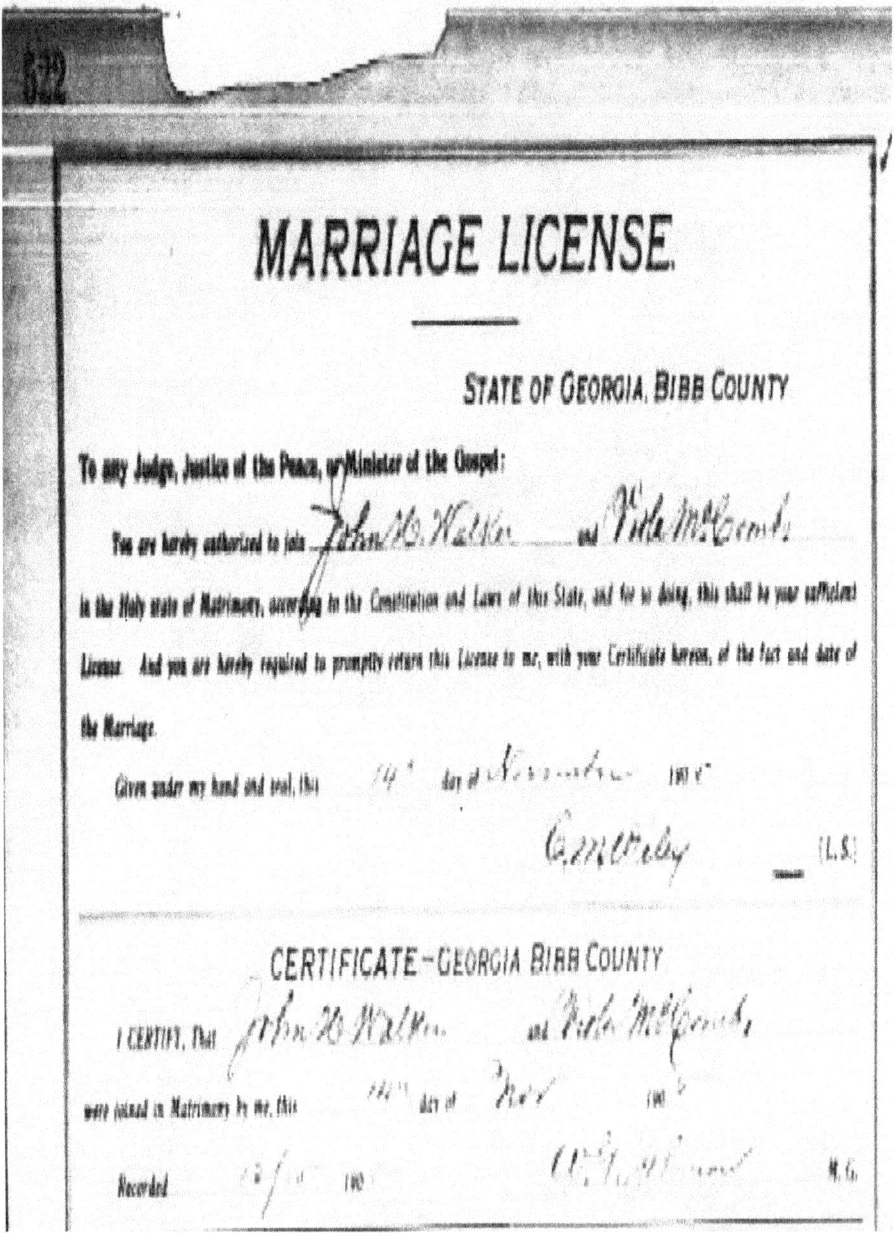

MARRIAGE LICENSE.

STATE OF GEORGIA, BIBB COUNTY

To any Judge, Justice of the Peace, or Minister of the Gospel:

You are hereby authorized to join John W. Walker and Viola McComb in the Holy state of Matrimony, according to the Constitution and Laws of this State, and for so doing, this shall be your sufficient License. And you are hereby required to promptly return this License to me, with your Certificate hereon, of the fact and date of the Marriage.

Given under my hand and seal, this 14th day of November 190[illegible]

C. M. Wiley [L.S.]

CERTIFICATE—GEORGIA BIBB COUNTY

I CERTIFY, That John W. Walker and Viola McComb were joined in Matrimony by me, this 14th day of Nov 190[illegible]

Recorded 12/15 190[illegible] [illegible] M.G.

# Georgia Marriages, 1808-1967 for John H. Walker

| | |
|---|---|
| Groom's Name: | John H. Walker |
| Groom's Birth Date: | |
| Groom's Birthplace: | |
| Groom's Age: | |
| Bride's Name: | Viola Mc Combs |
| Bride's Birth Date: | |
| Bride's Birthplace: | |
| Bride's Age: | |
| Marriage Date: | 14 Nov 1905 |
| Marriage Place: | , Bibb, Georgia |
| Groom's Father's Name: | |
| Groom's Mother's Name: | |
| Bride's Father's Name: | |
| Bride's Mother's Name: | |
| Groom's Race: | |
| Groom's Marital Status: | |
| Groom's Previous Wife's Name: | |
| Bride's Race: | |
| Bride's Marital Status: | |
| Bride's Previous Husband's Name: | |
| Indexing Project (Batch) Number: | M71212-3 |
| System Origin: | Georgia-EASy |
| Source Film Number: | 394119 |
| Reference Number: | |

**Dublin First African Baptist Church**
**405 Telfair Street**
**Dublin, Laurens Co., GA 31021**

Milous became an active member of the Dublin First Baptist Church, and was a comfort to the entire McCall Family after the death of Lula's uncle, Rev. Norman G. McCall, on Wednesday, June 15, 1904. Milous took an active part in the church's Music Department along with his wife, who actually taught him how to read music.

During the next year, the family endured two more deaths, when Emma's husband, Jefferson Swift, died in the spring, and Lula's grandmother, Patsey Yopp McCall, died in late August of 1905. Lula was grief-stricken, since Patsey raised her, and her younger siblings, Mattie and Henry James, after their mother died. Patsey's daughter, Tena McCall, was Lula's mother. Lula's father was a white man named John Stanley. Tena and John were not married. However, the white Stanleys and the white McCalls intermarried, as both were prominent families in the county.

Mattie and Henry James shared the same father, who was a man with the surname, Thomas. They were raised in Houston, Texas by Mr. and Mrs. Julia C. and Alexander Z. Hester. Julia's mother was Patsey's daughter, Antoinette, who died in childbirth, bringing her only child into the world. Patsey was the midwife who delivered Julia, and subsequently had to raise her granddaughter as her own child. Julia's father was a young, white lawyer named James A. Thomas, who lived and practiced law in the Dublin community. After Julia's birth on Monday, December 18, 1865, he took his practice to a neighboring county, where he and his family resided for several years. Julia's parents were not married.

Mattie and Henry James were Julia's younger first cousins – their mothers, Antoinette and Tena, were sisters. Since the surname of Mattie and Henry James' alleged father was the same as Julia's natural father, the three of them may have been cousins on both sides of their families.

When Patsey died, her will was recorded on Monday, September 4, 1905, and had been written, and x-marked by her 13 years earlier, on Wednesday, March 30, 1892. She bequeathed her real estate of five acres and the houses that were built on the land, to her children, and her granddaughters, Julia Thomas Hester, and Lula McCall Walker. Her husband, Hamlet McCall, was not mentioned in the will, and it is likely that he died between 1890 and 1892.

The irony in Patsey's history was such that just 41 years earlier, in 1853, she, her husband and children were, themselves, the property of Judge Jeremiah Yopp, who bequeathed his Negroes to his children, along with his other items of property. How interesting it is that the documented history of any one person could drastically change from a situation of perpetual despair to the fullness of hope, in two generations. Lula's Grandma Patsey, had such a history, which was certainly a type of Wilderness Experience, similar to that of Moses, as he lead the Israelites out of Egypt and into The Promised Land.

*A good man (woman) leaves an inheritance*
*to his (her) children's children...*
*Proverbs 13:22*

Soon, after Patsey's estate was settled, Milous and Lula located to Atlanta, Fulton County, Georgia. Once they secured a comfortable living space, Milous' recently widowed mother, Emma Swift, came to live with them. She stopped in Macon to spend a few days with her oldest son, John, and his new wife, Viola, before settling in Atlanta with Lula and Milous.

Now, Lula had left Dublin, Laurens County, Georgia, but her family history was always with her. Her grandparents, Hamlet and Patsey Yopp McCall, were born into slavery under two prominent families in Georgia. Hamlet belonged to Elizabeth Mary Ann Smith McCall and Thomas McCall, the brother of Hugh McCall, who wrote the first history of Georgia. In 1830, Mrs. Elizabeth McCall wrote a four-page will, listing all of her property which she passed down to her five daughters. Her youngest daughters were twins, and to the twin, Margaret Sanders McCall Yopp, she bequeathed her Negroes, which included an eight year-old boy named Hamlet. The parents and siblings of Hamlet were also given to Margaret. His parents were Will and Louisa. Lula was named after her great-grandmother.

Margaret was married to Judge Jeremiah Yopp, and Hamlet grew into manhood on the Yopp Plantation. Patsey was born under the Yopps. By 1853, Patsey and Hamlet were a family with several children. Judge Yopp died that year, and he was pre-deceased by his wife, the year before. His taxable inventory listed the value of all of his property, including his Negroes. Hamlet, 31 years old, was valued at $1200.00, while 30 year-old Patsey was valued at $750.00. The values of their children ranged from $500.00 to $200.00. Lula's mother, Tena, was born to Hamlet and Patsey in 1858. She became the mother of three children, lived in one of her mother's houses, rent-free, as stated in the 1892 draft of Patsey's will, and before the census was taken in June of 1900, Tena McCall died.

When Lula was born in 1880, Tena McCall was not married. Lula's father was a man by the name of John Stanley. It is alleged that he was white. In a family story about the childhood relationship between Lula and her younger sister, Mattie Ellen, it was told that whenever a conversation between the sisters turned into an argument, Mattie would tease Lula with the statement, "Well, at least my father isn't white", to which Lula would respond, "Well, at least my father's gonna build me a house". Years later, the sisters would laugh about their youthful taunts, whenever they shared that story.

The white Stanleys were another very prominent family in Dublin, Georgia. They intermarried with the white McCalls. It is likely that as a young woman, Tena McCall may have been under the employ of the Stanley Family, during the late 1870s, and Lula was conceived with one John Stanley, during that arrangement. On the 1880 census, Tena lived in the household of the Calvin Johnson Family, who lived next door to her parents, Patsey and Hamlet McCall. Tena was listed as Calvin's 22 year-old cousin, and her baby, Louisa (misspelled Lucia), was just three months old. The girl of 14 years old, named Julia Thompson (misspelling of Thomas), who also lived in the Johnson Household was Tena's niece. She later became Julia C. Hester, who would raise her Aunt Tena's younger two children, Mattie Ellen and Henry James McCall. A five year-old Julia lived with her grandparents, Patsey and Hamlet McCall on the census of 1870. She was listed as a McCall. Julia would list on the United States Decennial Censuses for the next seven decades until her passing on Tuesday, December 20, 1940.

On the 1870 census, where Hamlet and Patsey were listed for the first time, as people and not property, 12 year-old Tena was in the household with her parents, siblings, and Peggy McCall, who was Patsey's mother, or possibly her grandmother, considering the 33-year age difference between Patsey and Peggy. On the 1880 census, Peggy was listed with Hamlet and Patsey as Peggy Yopp. Her age was listed as 100. Ten years earlier, she was listed as 80 years old. On the 1853 Tax Inventory Assessment of Judge Yopp, her value was listed as $250.00. Peggy was thus valued because she was well into her sixties or seventies, and of lesser value than a female of childbearing age, or a female with any tolerance for rigorous labor. Among the enslaved females, it was not uncommon for a grandmother to be under 40 years old, as girls as young as 12 years old were often given to older men to bear their children and to manage a household, as a married couple.

Certainly Lula was not likely to leave or forget any part of her heritage or history in Dublin, Georgia. As rich, and as interesting as it was, she would be able to tell those stories in years to come, to her children, her grandchildren, and her great-grandchildren.

Remember the days of old,
Consider the years of many generations: ...
Deuteronomy 32:7

**Mrs. Julia C. Thomas Hester**

**Mr. Alexander Z. Hester**

ancestry library edition

## 1900 United States Federal Census

| | |
|---|---|
| Name: | **Mattie Mccall** |
| Age: | 16 |
| Birth Date: | Jan 1884 |
| Birthplace: | Georgia |
| Home in 1900: | Justice Precinct 1, Harris, Texas [Harris] |
| Race: | Black |
| Gender: | Female |
| Relation to Head of House: | Cousin |
| Marital Status: | Single |
| Father's Birthplace: | Georgia |
| Mother's Birthplace: | Georgia |
| Occupation: | |

Household Members:

| Name | Age |
|---|---|
| Alex Z Hester | 35 |
| Julia A Hester | 35 |
| Mattie Mccall | 16 |

**Source Citation:** Year: *1900*; Census Place: *Justice Precinct 1, Harris, Texas*; Roll: *1642*; Page: *2B*; Enumeration District: *0092*; FHL microfilm: *1241642*.

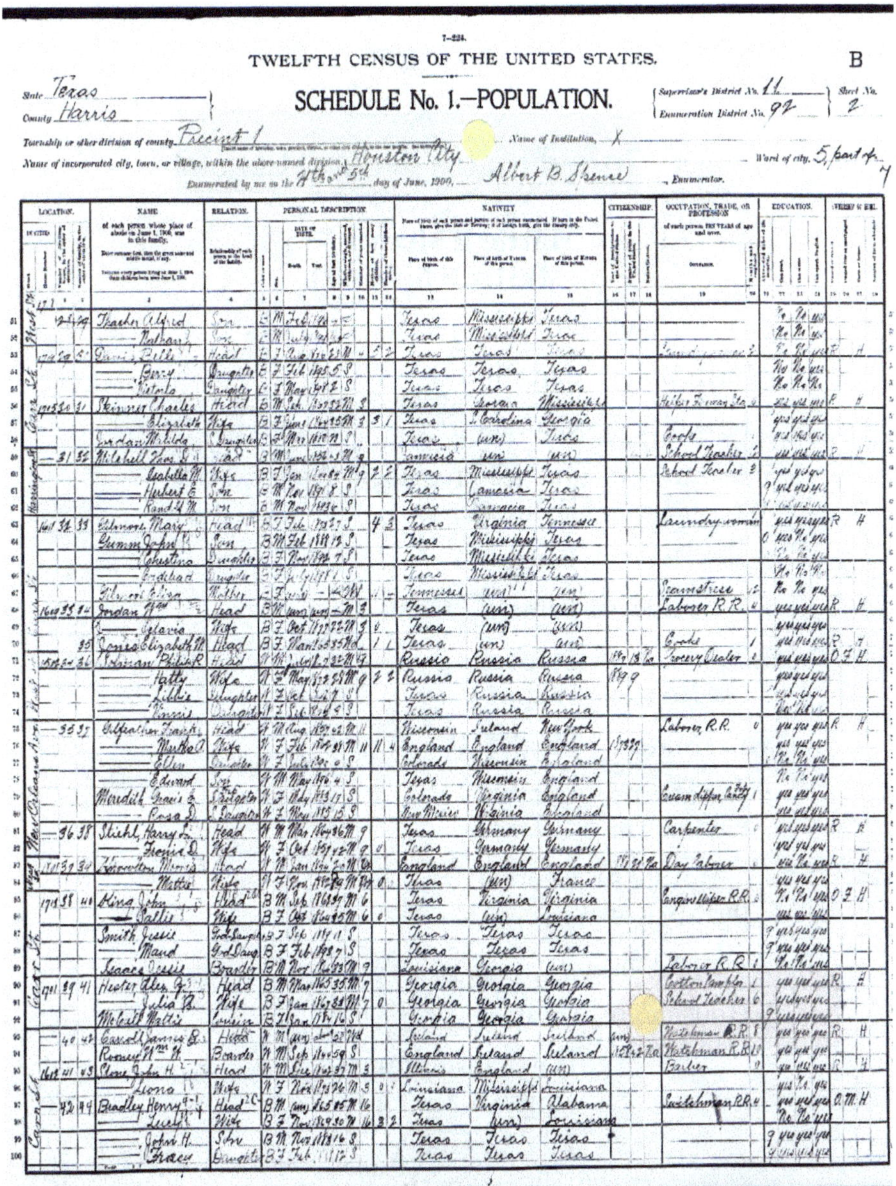

7-224.

TWELFTH CENSUS OF THE UNITED STATES. B

State Texas
County Harris

SCHEDULE No. 1.—POPULATION.

Supervisor's District No. 11
Enumeration District No. 92
Sheet No. 2

Township or other division of county Precinct 1 — Name of Institution, X

Name of incorporated city, town, or village, within the above-named division, Houston City — Ward of city, 5 part of 7

Enumerated by me on the 4th and 5th day of June, 1900, Albert B. Spence, Enumerator.

| Line | Name | Relation | Color | Sex | Month | Year | Age | Conj. | Birthplace | Father's birthplace | Mother's birthplace | Occupation |
|---|---|---|---|---|---|---|---|---|---|---|---|---|
| 51 | Thacker, Alfred | Son | B | M | Feb | 18[illegible] | [illegible] | | Texas | Mississippi | Texas | |
| 52 | Nathan | Son | B | M | July | [illegible] | [illegible] | | Texas | Mississippi | Texas | |
| 53 | Davis, Bellie | Head | B | F | Aug | 18[illegible] | [illegible] | W | Texas | Texas | Texas | Laundress |
| 54 | Berry | Daughter | B | F | Feb | 1895 | 5 | S | Texas | Texas | Texas | |
| 55 | Victoria | Daughter | B | F | May | 1898 | 2 | S | Texas | Texas | Texas | |
| 56 | Skinner, Charles | Head | B | M | Feb | 18[illegible] | 52 | M | Texas | Georgia | Mississippi | Helper Foreman Sta. |
| 57 | Elizabeth | Wife | B | F | June | 1864 | 35 | M | Texas | S. Carolina | Georgia | |
| 58 | Jordan, Matilda | S. Daughter | B | F | Mar | 18[illegible] | [illegible] | S | Texas | (un) | Texas | Cook |
| 59 | Mitchell, Thos. G. | Head | B | M | [illegible] | 18[illegible] | [illegible] | M | Jamaica | (un) | (un) | School Teacher |
| 60 | Isabella M. | Wife | B | F | Jan | 18[illegible] | [illegible] | M | Texas | Mississippi | Texas | School Teacher |
| 61 | Herbert E. | Son | B | M | Nov | 1891 | 8 | S | Texas | Jamaica | Texas | |
| 62 | Randolph M. | Son | B | M | Nov | 1893 | 6 | S | Texas | Jamaica | Texas | |
| 63 | Gilmore, Mary | Head | B | F | Feb | 18[illegible] | [illegible] | S | Texas | Virginia | Tennessee | Laundry woman |
| 64 | Gumm, John | Son | B | M | Feb | 1888 | 12 | S | Texas | Mississippi | Texas | |
| 65 | Christina | Daughter | B | F | Nov | 1892 | 7 | S | Texas | Mississippi | Texas | |
| 66 | [illegible] | Daughter | B | F | July | 1898 | 1 | S | Texas | Mississippi | Texas | |
| 67 | Gilmore, Eliza | Mother | B | F | [illegible] | [illegible] | [illegible] | W | Tennessee | (un) | (un) | Seamstress |
| 68 | Jordan, Wm. | Head | B | M | (un) | (un) | — | M | Texas | (un) | (un) | Laborer R.R. |
| 69 | Octavia | Wife | B | F | Oct | 1877 | 22 | M | Texas | (un) | (un) | |
| 70 | Jones, Elizabeth M. | Head | B | F | Mar | 1865 | 35 | Wd | Texas | (un) | (un) | Cook |
| 71 | [illegible], Philip R. | Head | W | M | July | [illegible] | 32 | M | Russia | Russia | Russia | Grocery Dealer |
| 72 | Hatty | Wife | W | F | May | [illegible] | [illegible] | M | Russia | Russia | Russia | |
| 73 | Libbie | Daughter | W | F | Oct | [illegible] | 7 | S | Texas | Russia | Russia | |
| 74 | [illegible] | Daughter | W | F | Sep | [illegible] | 4 | S | Texas | Russia | Russia | |
| 75 | Gilfeather, Frank | Head | W | M | Aug | 18[illegible] | [illegible] | M | Wisconsin | Ireland | New York | Laborer R.R. |
| 76 | Martha A. | Wife | W | F | Feb | 18[illegible] | 38 | M | England | England | England | |
| 77 | Ellen | Daughter | W | F | July | 18[illegible] | [illegible] | S | Colorado | Wisconsin | England | |
| 78 | Edward | Son | W | M | May | 1896 | 4 | S | Texas | Wisconsin | England | |
| 79 | Meredith, Travis E. | S. Daughter | W | F | May | 1883 | 17 | S | Colorado | Virginia | England | Cream dipper, candy factory |
| 80 | Rosa D. | S. Daughter | W | F | May | 1885 | 15 | S | New Mexico | Virginia | England | |
| 81 | Stiehl, Harry L. | Head | W | M | Mar | 1864 | 36 | M | Texas | Germany | Germany | Carpenter |
| 82 | Fronie D. | Wife | W | F | Oct | 1857 | 42 | M | Texas | Germany | Germany | |
| 83 | [illegible], Morris | Head | W | M | Jan | [illegible] | [illegible] | M | England | England | England | Day Laborer |
| 84 | Mattie | Wife | W | F | Nov | [illegible] | [illegible] | M | Texas | (un) | France | |
| 85 | King, John | Head | B | M | Sep | 1863 | 37 | M | Texas | Virginia | Virginia | Engine Wiper R.R. |
| 86 | Callie | Wife | B | F | Oct | 1864 | 35 | M | Texas | (un) | Louisiana | |
| 87 | Smith, Jessie | Grd. Daughter | B | F | Sep | 1889 | 11 | S | Texas | Texas | Texas | |
| 88 | Maud | Grd. Daug. | B | F | Feb | 1893 | 7 | S | Texas | Texas | Texas | |
| 89 | Isaacs, Jessie | Boarder | B | M | Nov | 18[illegible] | [illegible] | M | Louisiana | Georgia | (un) | Laborer R.R. |
| 90 | Hester, Alex. G. | Head | B | M | Mar | 1865 | 35 | M | Georgia | Georgia | Georgia | Cotton Sampler |
| 91 | Julia B. | Wife | B | F | Jan | 18[illegible] | [illegible] | M | Georgia | Georgia | Georgia | School Teacher |
| 92 | McCall, Mattie | Cousin | B | F | Jan | 1884 | 16 | S | Georgia | Georgia | Georgia | |
| 93 | Carroll, James E. | Head | W | M | (un) | [illegible] | [illegible] | Wd | Ireland | Ireland | Ireland | Watchman R.R. |
| 94 | Rooney, Wm. H. | Boarder | W | M | Sep | 18[illegible] | [illegible] | S | England | Ireland | Ireland | Watchman R.R. |
| 95 | Stone, John H. | Head | W | M | Dec | 18[illegible] | 37 | M | Illinois | England | (un) | Barber |
| 96 | Leona | Wife | W | F | Nov | 18[illegible] | [illegible] | M | Louisiana | Mississippi | Louisiana | |
| 97 | Bradley, Henry | Head | B | M | (un) | 18[illegible] | [illegible] | M | Texas | Virginia | Alabama | Switchman R.R. |
| 98 | Lucy | Wife | B | F | Nov | 18[illegible] | 30 | M | Texas | (un) | Louisiana | |
| 99 | John H. | Son | B | M | Nov | 18[illegible] | [illegible] | S | Texas | Texas | Texas | |
| 100 | Tracy | Daughter | B | F | Feb | [illegible] | [illegible] | S | Texas | Texas | Texas | |

ancestry library edition

## 1900 United States Federal Census

| | |
|---|---|
| Name: | **Mattie E Mccall [Mattie E Mc Call]** |
| Age: | 20 |
| Birth Date: | Jan 1880 |
| Birthplace: | Georgia |
| Home in 1900: | Justice Precinct 6, Waller, Texas [Waller] |
| Race: | Black |
| Gender: | Female |
| Relation to Head of House: | Student [Pupil] |
| Marital Status: | Single |
| Father's Birthplace: | Georgia |
| Mother's Birthplace: | Georgia |
| Occupation: | |

Household Members:

| Name | Age |
|---|---|
| Harriet Kimbro | 54 |
| Mattie E Mccall | 20 |
| Ella Alexander | 17 |
| Lillie E Smith | 17 |
| Mabel Hallaway | 17 |

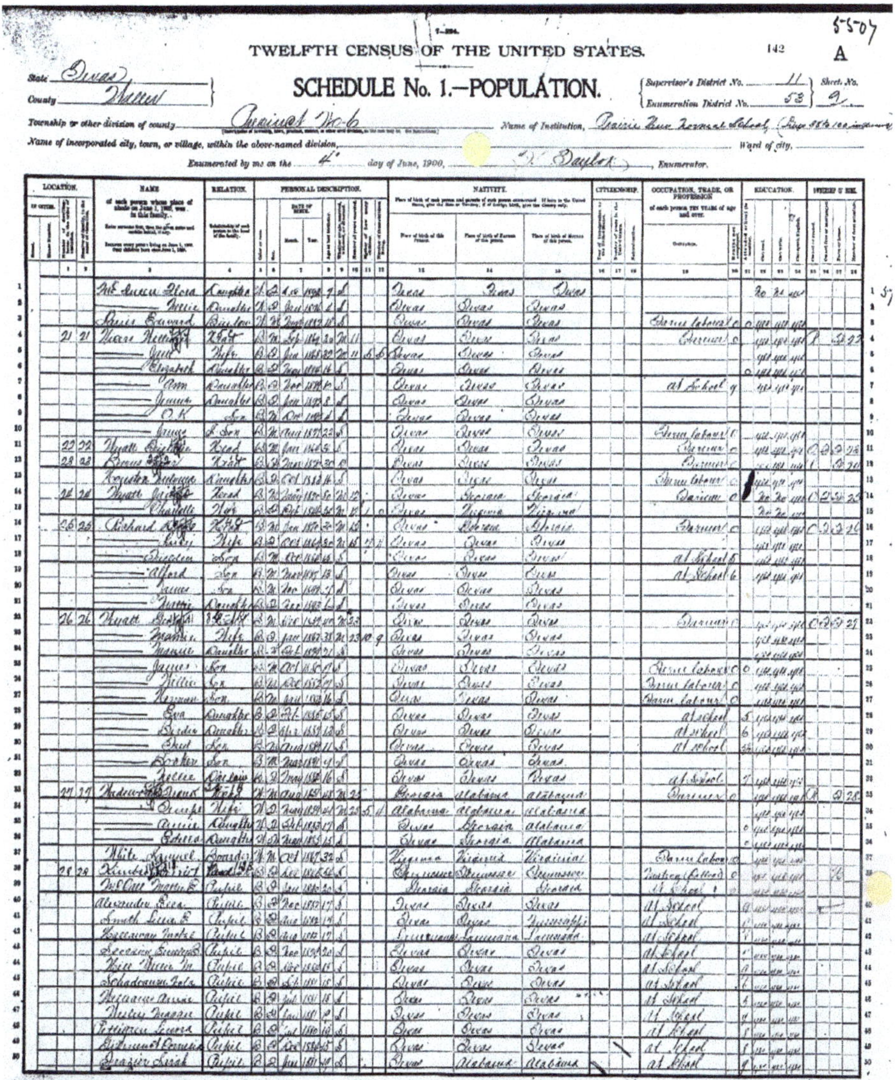
5-5-07

142 A

TWELFTH CENSUS OF THE UNITED STATES.

SCHEDULE No. 1.—POPULATION.

State: Texas
County: Waller
Township or other division of county: Precinct No. 6
Name of incorporated city, town, or village, within the above-named division:
Supervisor's District No. 11
Enumeration District No. 53
Sheet No. 9
Name of Institution, Prairie View Normal School
Ward of city,
Enumerated by me on the 4 day of June, 1900, [illegible], Enumerator.

| Line | Dwelling | Family | Name | Relation | Color | Sex | Month | Year | Age | Marital | Yrs married | Children born | Living | Birthplace | Father's birthplace | Mother's birthplace | Occupation | Months not employed | School months | Read | Write | English | Owned/rented | Free/mortg. | Farm/house | Farm sched. |
|---|---|---|---|---|---|---|---|---|---|---|---|---|---|---|---|---|---|---|---|---|---|---|---|---|---|---|
| 1 | | | McQueen Flora | Daughter | [illegible] | F | [illegible] | 1892 | 9 | S | | | | Texas | Texas | Texas | | | | no | no | yes | | | | |
| 2 | | | — Minnie | Daughter | [illegible] | F | Jan | 1896 | 4 | S | | | | Texas | Texas | Texas | | | | | | | | | | |
| 3 | | | Davis Edward | Boarder | [illegible] | M | [illegible] | 1882 | 18 | S | | | | Texas | Texas | Texas | Farm labourer | 0 | 0 | yes | yes | yes | | | | |
| 4 | 21 | 21 | Ware [illegible] | Head | B | M | Sep | 1869 | 30 | M | 11 | | | Texas | Texas | Texas | Farmer | 0 | | yes | yes | yes | R | | F | 22 |
| 5 | | | — Jane | Wife | B | F | Jan | 1865 | 32 | M | 11 | 6 | 6 | Texas | Texas | Texas | | | | yes | yes | yes | | | | |
| 6 | | | — Elizabeth | Daughter | B | F | [illegible] | 1886 | 14 | S | | | | Texas | Texas | Texas | | | 0 | yes | yes | yes | | | | |
| 7 | | | — Ann | Daughter | B | F | Nov | 1888 | 11 | S | | | | Texas | Texas | Texas | at School | 9 | | yes | yes | yes | | | | |
| 8 | | | — Jennie | Daughter | B | F | Jan | 1892 | 8 | S | | | | Texas | Texas | Texas | | | | | | | | | | |
| 9 | | | — O. K. | Son | B | M | Dec | 1895 | 4 | S | | | | Texas | Texas | Texas | | | | | | | | | | |
| 10 | | | — [illegible] | S. Son | B | M | Aug | 1877 | 22 | S | | | | Texas | Texas | Texas | Farm labourer | 0 | | yes | yes | yes | | | | |
| 11 | 22 | 22 | Wyatt [illegible] | Head | B | M | Jan | 1865 | 35 | S | | | | Texas | Texas | Texas | Farmer | 0 | | yes | yes | yes | O | F | F | 23 |
| 12 | 23 | 23 | [illegible] | Head | B | M | [illegible] | 1870 | 30 | [illegible] | | | | Texas | Texas | Texas | Farmer | 0 | | yes | yes | yes | R | | F | 24 |
| 13 | | | Houston [illegible] | Daughter | B | F | Oct | 1883 | 16 | S | | | | Texas | Texas | Texas | Farm labourer | 0 | | yes | yes | yes | | | | |
| 14 | 24 | 24 | Wyatt [illegible] | Head | B | M | [illegible] | 1850 | 50 | M | 12 | | | Texas | Georgia | Georgia | Farmer | 0 | | no | no | yes | O | F | F | 25 |
| 15 | | | — Charlotte | Wife | B | F | Sep | 1860 | 39 | M | 12 | 1 | 0 | Texas | Virginia | Virginia | | | | no | no | yes | | | | |
| 16 | 25 | 25 | Richard [illegible] | Head | B | M | Jan | 1870 | 30 | M | 15 | | | Texas | Alabama | Alabama | Farmer | 0 | | yes | yes | yes | O | F | F | 26 |
| 17 | | | — [illegible] | Wife | B | F | Oct | 1864 | 35 | M | 15 | [illegible] | [illegible] | Texas | Texas | Texas | | | | yes | yes | yes | | | | |
| 18 | | | — [illegible] | Son | B | M | Oct | 1884 | 15 | S | | | | Texas | Texas | Texas | at School | 6 | | yes | yes | yes | | | | |
| 19 | | | — Alford | Son | B | M | Mar | 1887 | 13 | S | | | | Texas | Texas | Texas | at School | 6 | | yes | yes | yes | | | | |
| 20 | | | — James | Son | B | M | Nov | 1892 | 7 | S | | | | Texas | Texas | Texas | | | | | | | | | | |
| 21 | | | — [illegible] | Daughter | B | F | Nov | 1893 | 6 | S | | | | Texas | Texas | Texas | | | | | | | | | | |
| 22 | 26 | 26 | Wyatt [illegible] | Head | B | M | Dec | 1859 | 40 | M | 23 | | | Texas | Texas | Texas | Farmer | 0 | | yes | yes | yes | O | F | F | 27 |
| 23 | | | — Mamie | Wife | B | F | Jan | 1867 | 33 | M | 23 | 10 | 9 | Texas | Texas | Texas | | | | yes | yes | yes | | | | |
| 24 | | | — Mamie | Daughter | B | F | Feb | 1879 | 21 | S | | | | Texas | Texas | Texas | | | | yes | yes | yes | | | | |
| 25 | | | — James | Son | B | M | Oct | 1880 | 19 | S | | | | Texas | Texas | Texas | Farm labourer | 0 | 0 | yes | yes | yes | | | | |
| 26 | | | — Willie | Son | B | M | Dec | 1882 | 17 | S | | | | Texas | Texas | Texas | Farm labourer | 0 | | yes | yes | yes | | | | |
| 27 | | | — Herman | Son | B | M | Apr | 1884 | 16 | S | | | | Texas | Texas | Texas | Farm labourer | 0 | | yes | yes | yes | | | | |
| 28 | | | — Eva | Daughter | B | F | Feb | 1886 | 15 | S | | | | Texas | Texas | Texas | at school | | 5 | yes | yes | yes | | | | |
| 29 | | | — Birdie | Daughter | B | F | Apr | 1887 | 13 | S | | | | Texas | Texas | Texas | at school | | 6 | yes | yes | yes | | | | |
| 30 | | | — Fred | Son | B | M | Aug | 1888 | 11 | S | | | | Texas | Texas | Texas | at school | | 5 | yes | yes | yes | | | | |
| 31 | | | — Booker | Son | B | M | Mar | 1891 | 9 | S | | | | Texas | Texas | Texas | | | | | | | | | | |
| 32 | | | — Hollie | Cousin | B | F | May | 1884 | 16 | S | | | | Texas | Texas | Texas | at School | | 7 | yes | yes | yes | | | | |
| 33 | 27 | 27 | Underwood Frank | Head | W | M | Aug | 1851 | 48 | M | 25 | | | Georgia | Alabama | Alabama | Farmer | 0 | | yes | yes | yes | R | | F | 28 |
| 34 | | | — [illegible] | Wife | W | F | Aug | 1854 | 44 | M | 25 | 5 | 4 | Alabama | Alabama | Alabama | | | | yes | yes | yes | | | | |
| 35 | | | — Annie | Daughter | W | F | Feb | 1883 | 17 | S | | | | Texas | Georgia | Alabama | | | 0 | yes | yes | yes | | | | |
| 36 | | | — Edna | Daughter | W | F | Mar | 1885 | 15 | S | | | | Texas | Georgia | Alabama | | | 0 | yes | yes | yes | | | | |
| 37 | | | White Samuel | Boarder | W | M | Oct | 1867 | 32 | S | | | | Virginia | Virginia | Virginia | Farm labor | 0 | | yes | yes | yes | | | | |
| 38 | 28 | 29 | Kimbell [illegible] | Head | B | F | Dec | 1866 | [illegible] | S | | | | Tennessee | Tennessee | Tennessee | Teaching (School) | 0 | | yes | yes | yes | | | H | |
| 39 | | | McCall Mattie E. | Pupil | B | F | Jan | 1880 | 20 | S | | | | Georgia | Georgia | Georgia | At School | | [illegible] | yes | yes | yes | | | | |
| 40 | | | Alexander [illegible] | Pupil | B | F | Nov | 1882 | 17 | S | | | | Texas | Texas | Texas | At School | | 9 | yes | yes | yes | | | | |
| 41 | | | Smith Lucie E. | Pupil | B | F | Aug | 1882 | 17 | S | | | | Texas | Texas | Mississippi | At School | | [illegible] | yes | yes | yes | | | | |
| 42 | | | [illegible] | Pupil | B | F | Aug | 1882 | 17 | S | | | | Louisiana | Louisiana | Louisiana | At School | | [illegible] | yes | yes | yes | | | | |
| 43 | | | [illegible] | Pupil | B | F | Nov | 1879 | 20 | S | | | | Texas | Texas | Texas | At School | | [illegible] | yes | yes | yes | | | | |
| 44 | | | [illegible] | Pupil | B | F | Dec | 1884 | 15 | S | | | | Texas | Texas | Texas | At School | | 9 | yes | yes | yes | | | | |
| 45 | | | [illegible] | Pupil | B | F | Sep | 1884 | 15 | S | | | | Texas | Texas | Texas | At School | | [illegible] | yes | yes | yes | | | | |
| 46 | | | [illegible] Annie | Pupil | B | F | Jul | 1881 | 18 | S | | | | Texas | Texas | Texas | At School | | 5 | yes | yes | yes | | | | |
| 47 | | | Wesley Maggie | Pupil | B | F | Jan | 1881 | [illegible] | S | | | | Texas | Texas | Texas | At School | | 9 | yes | yes | yes | | | | |
| 48 | | | Pettigrew Lenora | Pupil | B | F | Jul | 1880 | 19 | S | | | | Texas | Texas | Texas | At School | | [illegible] | yes | yes | yes | | | | |
| 49 | | | [illegible] | Pupil | B | F | Dec | 1884 | 15 | S | | | | Texas | Texas | Texas | At School | | [illegible] | yes | yes | yes | | | | |
| 50 | | | Frazier Sarah | Pupil | B | F | Jun | 1881 | 19 | S | | | | Texas | Alabama | Alabama | At School | | 9 | yes | yes | yes | | | | |

ancestry.com

## 1900 United States Federal Census

| | |
|---|---|
| Name: | **Louisa Mccall [Loura Mccall] [Louisa Freeman]** |
| Home in 1900: | Dublin, Laurens, Georgia [Dublin, Laurens, Georgia] |
| Age: | 20 |
| Birth Date: | Jan 1880 |
| Birthplace: | Georgia |
| Race: | Black |
| Gender: | Female |
| Relationship to head-of-house: | Granddaughter |
| Father's Birthplace: | Georgia |
| Mother's Birthplace: | Georgia |
| Marital Status: | Single |
| Occupation: | |

Household Members:

| Name | Age |
|---|---|
| Patsy Mccall | 78 |
| Nettie R Mccall | 24 |
| Louisa Mccall | 20 |
| Henry S Mccall | 14 |

**Source Citation:** Year: *1900*; Census Place: *Dublin, Laurens, Georgia*; Roll: *T623_208*; Page: *10A*; Enumeration District: *58*.

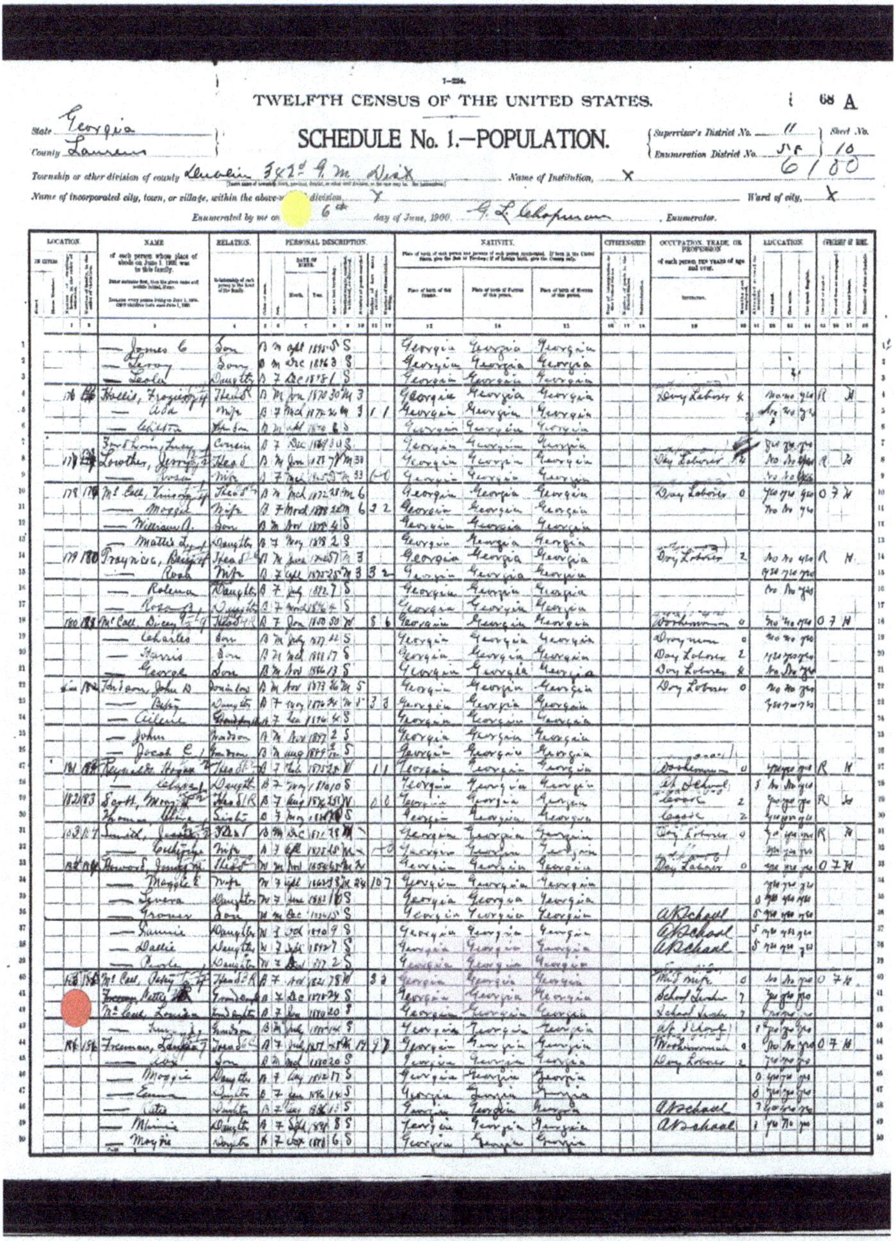

1—224.

TWELFTH CENSUS OF THE UNITED STATES. 68 A

SCHEDULE No. 1.—POPULATION.

State Georgia
County Laurens
Supervisor's District No. 11
Enumeration District No. 58 / 61
Sheet No. 10 / 80
Township or other division of county Dublin 342nd G. M. Dist
Name of Institution, X
Name of incorporated city, town, or village, within the above-named division, X
Ward of city, X
Enumerated by me on the 6th day of June, 1900. G. L. Chapman, Enumerator.

| Line | Dwelling | Family | Name | Relation | Color | Sex | Month | Year | Age | Marital | Yrs married | Children born | Living | Birthplace | Father | Mother | Occupation | Months not employed | School months | Read / Write / English | Home |
|---|---|---|---|---|---|---|---|---|---|---|---|---|---|---|---|---|---|---|---|---|---|
| 1 | | | — James C | Son | B | M | Apl | 1895 | 5 | S | | | | Georgia | Georgia | Georgia | | | | | |
| 2 | | | — Leroy | Son | B | M | Dec | 1896 | 3 | S | | | | Georgia | Georgia | Georgia | | | | | |
| 3 | | | — Leola | Daughter | B | F | Dec | 1898 | 1 | S | | | | Georgia | Georgia | Georgia | | | | | |
| 4 | 176 | [illegible] | Hollis, Frazier | Head | B | M | Jan | 1870 | 30 | M | 3 | | | Georgia | Georgia | Georgia | Day Laborer | 4 | | No No Yes | R H |
| 5 | | | — Ada | Wife | B | F | Mch | 1878 | 22 | M | 3 | 1 | 1 | Georgia | Georgia | Georgia | | | | Yes No Yes | |
| 6 | | | — Wilton | Step Son | B | M | Apl | 1896 | 6 | S | | | | Georgia | Georgia | Georgia | | | | | |
| 7 | | | Tomlin, Lucy | Cousin | B | F | Dec | 1869 | 30 | S | | | | Georgia | Georgia | Georgia | | | | Yes Yes Yes | |
| 8 | 177 | [illegible] | Lowther, Jerry | Head | B | M | Jan | 1827 | 71 | M | 33 | | | Georgia | Georgia | Georgia | Day Laborer | 4 | | No No Yes | R H |
| 9 | | | — Rosa | Wife | B | F | Mch | 1850 | [illegible] | M | 33 | 1 | 0 | Georgia | Georgia | Georgia | | | | No No Yes | |
| 10 | 178 | 179 | McCall, Timothy | Head | B | M | Mch | 1872 | 28 | M | 6 | | | Georgia | Georgia | Georgia | Day Laborer | 0 | | Yes Yes Yes | O F H |
| 11 | | | — Maggie | Wife | B | F | Mch | 1878 | 22 | M | 6 | 2 | 2 | Georgia | Georgia | Georgia | | | | No No Yes | |
| 12 | | | — William A. | Son | B | M | Nov | 1895 | 4 | S | | | | Georgia | Georgia | Georgia | | | | | |
| 13 | | | — Mattie L. | Daughter | B | F | May | 1898 | 2 | S | | | | Georgia | Georgia | Georgia | | | | | |
| 14 | 179 | 180 | Traynire, Benj | Head | B | M | June | 1865 | 37 | M | 3 | | | Georgia | Georgia | Georgia | Day Laborer | 2 | | No No Yes | R H |
| 15 | | | — Rosa | Wife | B | F | Apl | 1875 | 25 | M | 3 | 3 | 2 | Georgia | Georgia | Georgia | | | | Yes Yes Yes | |
| 16 | | | — Rolena | Daughter | B | F | July | 1892 | 7 | S | | | | Georgia | Georgia | Georgia | | | | No No Yes | |
| 17 | | | — Rosa B. | Daughter | B | F | Mch | 1896 | 4 | S | | | | Georgia | Georgia | Georgia | | | | | |
| 18 | 180 | 181 | McCall, Dicey | Head | B | F | Jan | 1850 | 50 | Wd | | 8 | 6 | Georgia | Georgia | Georgia | Washerwoman | 0 | | No No Yes | O F H |
| 19 | | | — Charles | Son | B | M | July | 1877 | 22 | S | | | | Georgia | Georgia | Georgia | Drayman | 0 | | No No Yes | |
| 20 | | | — Harris | Son | B | M | Mch | 1883 | 17 | S | | | | Georgia | Georgia | Georgia | Day Laborer | 2 | | Yes Yes Yes | |
| 21 | | | — George | Son | B | M | Nov | 1886 | 13 | S | | | | Georgia | Georgia | Georgia | Day Laborer | 4 | | No No Yes | |
| 22 | [illegible] | 182 | Johnson, John D | Son-in-law | B | M | Nov | 1873 | 26 | M | 5 | | | Georgia | Georgia | Georgia | Day Laborer | 0 | | No No Yes | |
| 23 | | | — Betsy | Daughter | B | F | May | 1876 | 24 | M | 5 | 3 | 3 | Georgia | Georgia | Georgia | | | | Yes Yes Yes | |
| 24 | | | — Aileine | Granddaughter | B | F | Jan | 1896 | 4 | S | | | | Georgia | Georgia | Georgia | | | | | |
| 25 | | | — John | Grandson | B | M | Nov | 1897 | 2 | S | | | | Georgia | Georgia | Georgia | | | | | |
| 26 | | | — Jacob C | Grandson | B | M | Aug | 1899 | 9/12 | S | | | | Georgia | Georgia | Georgia | | | | | |
| 27 | 181 | 184 | Reynolds, Hogan | Head | B | F | Feb | 1875 | 25 | Wd | | 1 | 1 | Georgia | Georgia | Georgia | Washerwoman | 0 | | Yes Yes Yes | R H |
| 28 | | | — Clara | Daughter | B | F | May | 1890 | 10 | S | | | | Georgia | Georgia | Georgia | At School | | 5 | No No Yes | |
| 29 | 182 | 183 | Scott, Mary | Head | B | F | Aug | 1874 | 25 | Wd | | 0 | 0 | Georgia | Georgia | Georgia | Cook | 2 | | Yes Yes Yes | R H |
| 30 | | | Thomas, Eliza | Sister | B | F | May | 1880 | [illegible] | S | | | | Georgia | Georgia | Georgia | Cook | 2 | | Yes Yes Yes | |
| 31 | 183 | 184 | Smith, Jessie | Head | B | M | Dec | 1871 | 28 | M | | | | Georgia | Georgia | Georgia | Day Laborer | 4 | | Yes Yes Yes | R H |
| 32 | | | — Cathjohn | Wife | B | F | Apl | 1875 | 25 | M | | | 0 | Georgia | Georgia | Georgia | | | | No Yes Yes | |
| 33 | 184 | 185 | Howard, Jerry M | Head | W | M | Nov | 1856 | 43 | M | 24 | | | Georgia | Georgia | Georgia | Day Laborer | 0 | | Yes Yes Yes | O F H |
| 34 | | | — Maggie E | Wife | W | F | Apl | 1862 | 38 | M | 24 | 10 | 7 | Georgia | Georgia | Georgia | | | | Yes Yes Yes | |
| 35 | | | — Severa | Daughter | W | F | June | 1883 | 16 | S | | | | Georgia | Georgia | Georgia | | | 0 | Yes Yes Yes | |
| 36 | | | — Grover | Son | W | M | Dec | 1884 | 15 | S | | | | Georgia | Georgia | Georgia | At School | | 5 | Yes Yes Yes | |
| 37 | | | — Fannie | Daughter | W | F | Oct | 1890 | 9 | S | | | | Georgia | Georgia | Georgia | At School | | 5 | Yes Yes Yes | |
| 38 | | | — Dallie | Daughter | W | F | Sept | 1892 | 7 | S | | | | Georgia | Georgia | Georgia | At School | | 5 | Yes Yes Yes | |
| 39 | | | — Pearle | Daughter | W | F | Oct | 1897 | 2 | S | | | | Georgia | Georgia | Georgia | | | | | |
| 40 | 185 | 186 | McCall, Betsy | Head | B | F | Nov | 1821 | 78 | Wd | | 3 | 2 | Georgia | Georgia | Georgia | [illegible] | 0 | | No No Yes | O F H |
| 41 | | | Freeman, Nettie | Granddaughter | B | F | Dec | 1875 | 24 | S | | | | Georgia | Georgia | Georgia | School Teacher | 7 | | Yes Yes Yes | |
| 42 | | | McCall, Louisa | Granddaughter | B | F | Jan | 1880 | 20 | S | | | | Georgia | Georgia | Georgia | School Teacher | 7 | | Yes Yes Yes | |
| 43 | | | — [illegible] | Grandson | B | M | July | 1889 | [illegible] | S | | | | Georgia | Georgia | Georgia | At School | | 7 | Yes Yes Yes | |
| 44 | 186 | 187 | Freeman, Louisa | Head | B | F | July | 1857 | 42 | Wd | | 9 | 7 | Georgia | Georgia | Georgia | Washerwoman | 0 | | No No Yes | O F H |
| 45 | | | — Roy | Son | B | M | Mch | 1880 | 20 | S | | | | Georgia | Georgia | Georgia | Day Laborer | 2 | | Yes Yes Yes | |
| 46 | | | — Maggie | Daughter | B | F | Aug | 1882 | 17 | S | | | | Georgia | Georgia | Georgia | | | 0 | Yes Yes Yes | |
| 47 | | | — Emma | Daughter | B | F | Jan | 1886 | 14 | S | | | | Georgia | Georgia | Georgia | | | 0 | Yes Yes Yes | |
| 48 | | | — Katie | Daughter | B | F | Aug | 1886 | 13 | S | | | | Georgia | Georgia | Georgia | At School | | 7 | Yes Yes Yes | |
| 49 | | | — Minnie | Daughter | B | F | Sept | 1891 | 8 | S | | | | Georgia | Georgia | Georgia | At School | | 1 | Yes No Yes | |
| 50 | | | — Mayhe | Daughter | B | F | Oct | 1893 | 6 | S | | | | Georgia | Georgia | Georgia | | | | | |

ancestry.com

## 1900 United States Federal Census

| | |
|---|---|
| Name: | **Emma Swift** |
| Age: | 56 |
| Birth Date: | Jun 1843 |
| Birthplace: | Georgia |
| Home in 1900: | Dublin, Laurens, Georgia |
| Race: | Black |
| Gender: | Female |
| Relation to Head of House: | Wife |
| Marital Status: | Married |
| Spouse's Name: | Jefferson Swift |
| Year: | 1890 |
| Years Married: | 10 |
| Father's Birthplace: | Georgia |
| Mother's Birthplace: | Georgia |
| Mother: number of living children: | 4 |
| Mother: How many children: | 10 |
| Occupation: | |

Household Members:

| Name | Age |
|---|---|
| Jefferson Swift | 72 |
| Emma Swift | 56 |
| Jennie Nelson | 9 |
| Jefferson Swift | 21 |
| Thomas Mitchel | 28 |

**Source Citation:** Year: *1900*; Census Place: *Dublin, Laurens, Georgia*; Roll: *208*; Page: *25A*; Enumeration District: *0059*; FHL microfilm: *1240208*.

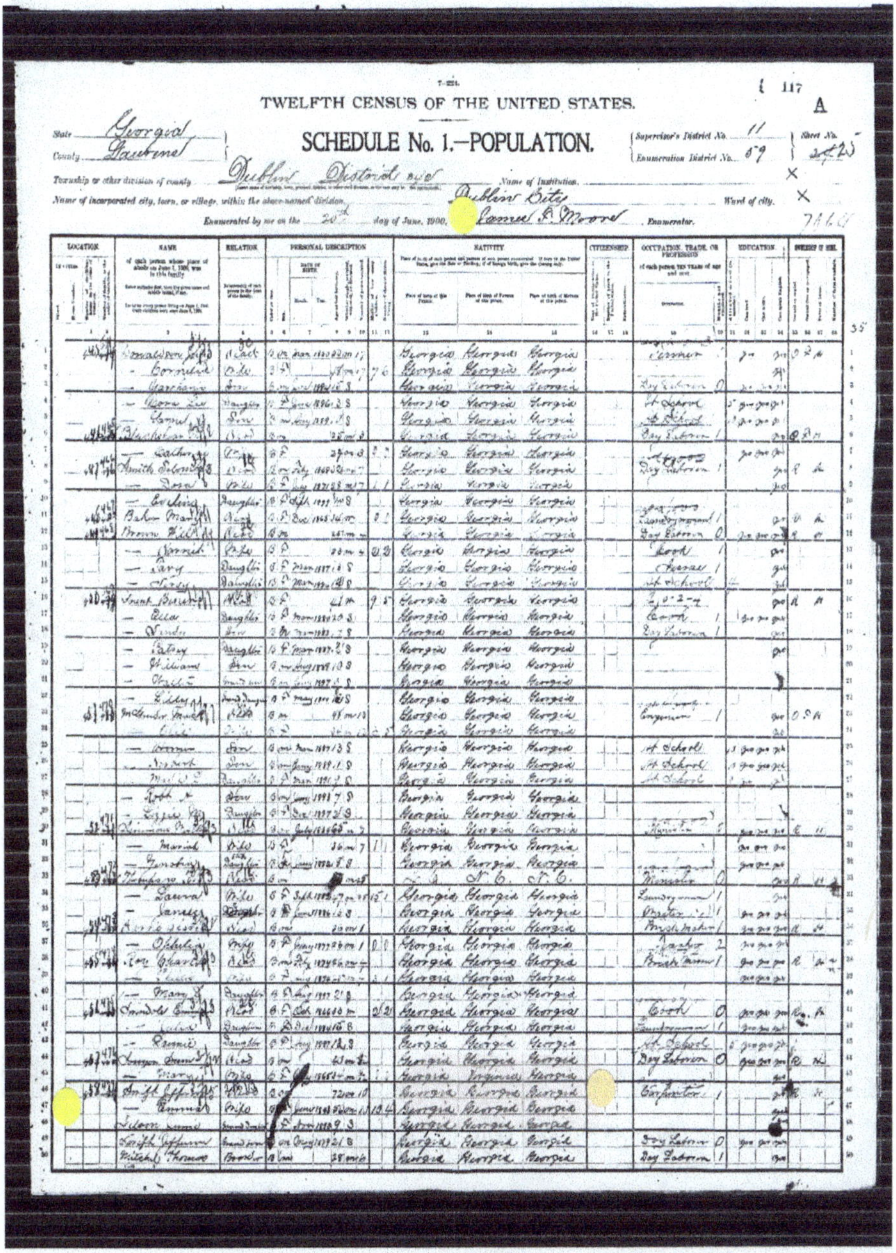

7-224.

117

A

TWELFTH CENSUS OF THE UNITED STATES.

SCHEDULE No. 1.—POPULATION.

State: Georgia
County: Laurens
Township or other division of county: Dublin District
Name of incorporated city, town, or village, within the above-named division: Dublin City
Supervisor's District No. 11
Enumeration District No. 59
Sheet No. [illegible]
Enumerated by me on the 20 day of June, 1900, James F. Moore, Enumerator.

| Line | Name | Relation | Place of birth of this person | Place of birth of Father | Place of birth of Mother | Occupation |
|---|---|---|---|---|---|---|
| 1 | Donaldson Joseph | Head | Georgia | Georgia | Georgia | Farmer |
| 2 | — Cornelia | Wife | Georgia | Georgia | Georgia | |
| 3 | — [illegible] | Son | Georgia | Georgia | Georgia | Day Laborer |
| 4 | — Mora Lee | Daughter | Georgia | Georgia | Georgia | At School |
| 5 | — Samuel | Son | Georgia | Georgia | Georgia | At School |
| 6 | Blackshear [illegible] | Head | Georgia | Georgia | Georgia | Day Laborer |
| 7 | — Catherine | Wife | Georgia | Georgia | Georgia | |
| 8 | Smith Solomon | Head | Georgia | Georgia | Georgia | Day Laborer |
| 9 | — Dora | Wife | Georgia | Georgia | Georgia | |
| 10 | — Eveline | Daughter | Georgia | Georgia | Georgia | |
| 11 | Baker Mary | Head | Georgia | Georgia | Georgia | Laundrywoman |
| 12 | Brown Will | Head | Georgia | Georgia | Georgia | Day Laborer |
| 13 | — Jannie | Wife | Georgia | Georgia | Georgia | Cook |
| 14 | — Lucy | Daughter | Georgia | Georgia | Georgia | Nurse |
| 15 | — [illegible] | Daughter | Georgia | Georgia | Georgia | At School |
| 16 | [illegible] | Head | Georgia | Georgia | Georgia | [illegible] |
| 17 | — Ella | Daughter | Georgia | Georgia | Georgia | Cook |
| 18 | — [illegible] | Son | Georgia | Georgia | Georgia | Day Laborer |
| 19 | — Patsy | Daughter | Georgia | Georgia | Georgia | |
| 20 | — William | Son | Georgia | Georgia | Georgia | |
| 21 | — [illegible] | Grandson | Georgia | Georgia | Georgia | |
| 22 | — Libby | Granddaughter | Georgia | Georgia | Georgia | |
| 23 | McClendon Frank | Head | Georgia | Georgia | Georgia | Engineer |
| 24 | — [illegible] | Wife | Georgia | Georgia | Georgia | |
| 25 | — Warren | Son | Georgia | Georgia | Georgia | At School |
| 26 | — [illegible] | Son | Georgia | Georgia | Georgia | At School |
| 27 | — [illegible] | Daughter | Georgia | Georgia | Georgia | At School |
| 28 | — Robt. A. | Son | Georgia | Georgia | Georgia | |
| 29 | — Lizzie | Daughter | Georgia | Georgia | Georgia | |
| 30 | [illegible] | Head | Georgia | Georgia | Georgia | [illegible] |
| 31 | — Mariah | Wife | Georgia | Georgia | Georgia | |
| 32 | — [illegible] | Daughter | Georgia | Georgia | Georgia | |
| 33 | Thompson [illegible] | Head | N.C. | N.C. | N.C. | Minister |
| 34 | — Laura | Wife | Georgia | Georgia | Georgia | Laundrywoman |
| 35 | — [illegible] | Daughter | Georgia | Georgia | Georgia | [illegible] |
| 36 | [illegible] | Head | Georgia | Georgia | Georgia | Brick Maker |
| 37 | — Ophelia | Wife | Georgia | Georgia | Georgia | Teacher |
| 38 | [illegible] Charles | Head | Georgia | Georgia | Georgia | Brick Mason |
| 39 | — [illegible] | Wife | Georgia | Georgia | Georgia | |
| 40 | — Mary J. | Daughter | Georgia | Georgia | Georgia | |
| 41 | [illegible] | Head | Georgia | Georgia | Georgia | Cook |
| 42 | — Julia | Daughter | Georgia | Georgia | Georgia | Laundrywoman |
| 43 | — Rennie | Daughter | Georgia | Georgia | Georgia | At School |
| 44 | [illegible] | Head | Georgia | Georgia | Georgia | Day Laborer |
| 45 | — Mary | Wife | Georgia | Virginia | Georgia | |
| 46 | Smith Jefferson | Head | Georgia | Georgia | Georgia | Carpenter |
| 47 | — Emma | Wife | Georgia | Georgia | Georgia | |
| 48 | [illegible] | Granddaughter | Georgia | Georgia | Georgia | |
| 49 | Smith Jefferson | Grandson | Georgia | Georgia | Georgia | Day Laborer |
| 50 | Mitchell Thomas | Boarder | Georgia | Georgia | Georgia | Day Laborer |

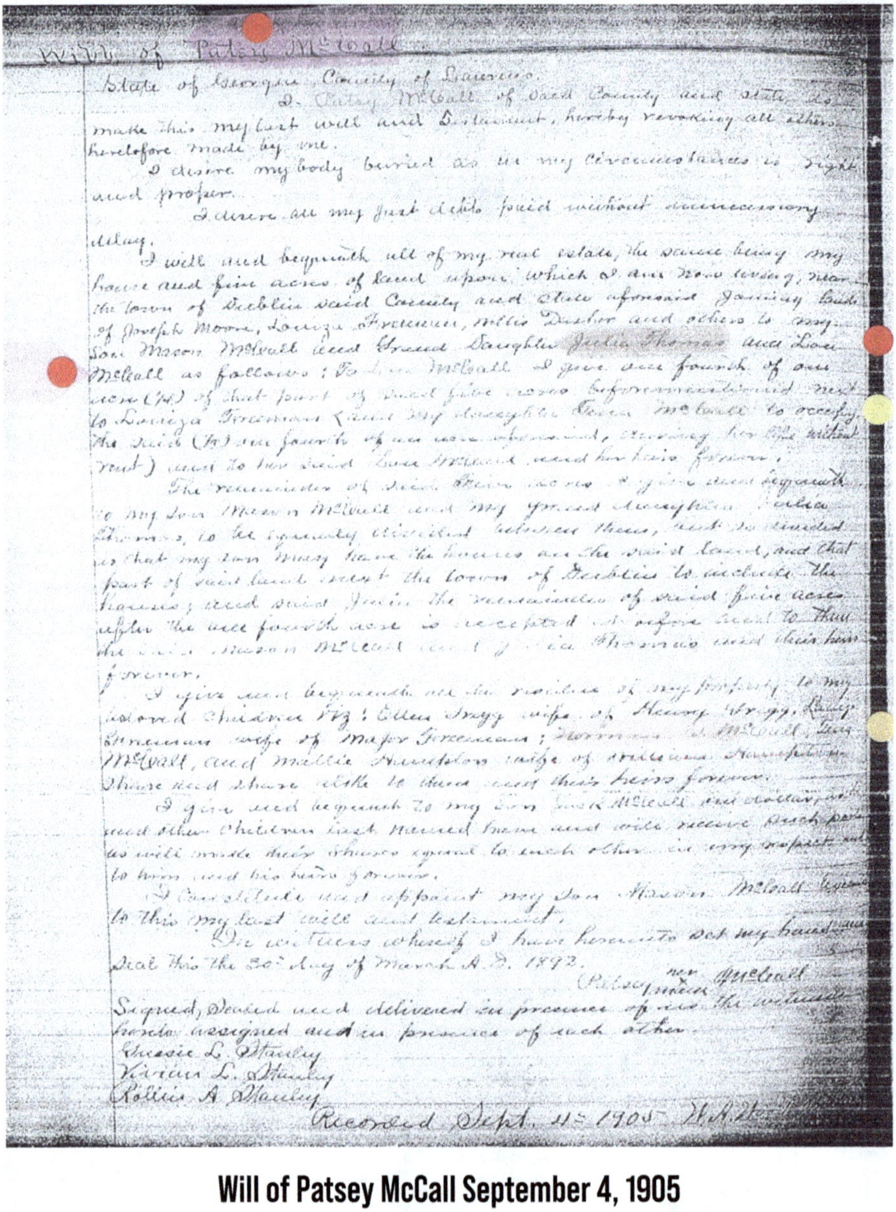

Will of Patsey McCall

State of Georgia, County of Laurens.

I, Patsey McCall of said County and State, do make this my last will and Testament, hereby revoking all others heretofore made by me.

I desire my body buried as in my circumstances is right and proper.

I desire all my just debts paid without unnecessary delay.

I will and bequeath all of my real estate, the same being my house and five acres of land upon which I am now living, near the town of Dublin said County and State aforesaid joining lands of Joseph Moore, Louiza Freeman, Willis Dasher and others to my Son Mason McCall and Grand Daughter Julia Thomas and Lou McCall as follows: To Lou McCall I give one fourth of one acre (¼) of that part of said five acres beforementioned next to Louiza Freeman (and my daughter Lou McCall to occupy the said (¼) one fourth of an acre aforesaid, during her life without rent) and to her said Lou McCall and her heirs forever.

The remainder of said five acres I give and bequeath to my Son Mason McCall and my grand daughter Julia Thomas, to be equally divided between them, and to divided so that my son may have the houses on the said land, and that part of said land next the town of Dublin to include the houses; and said Julia the remainder of said five acres after the one fourth acre is excepted as before said to them the said Mason McCall and Julia Thomas and their heirs forever.

I give and bequeath all the residue of my property to my beloved Children Viz: Ellen Trigg wife of Henry Trigg, Louiza Freeman wife of Major Freeman; [illegible] McCall, Lou McCall, and Mollie Hampton wife of William Hampton share and share alike to them and their heirs forever.

I give and bequeath to my son Jack McCall one dollar, [illegible] and other Children last named have and will receive such [illegible] as will make their shares equal to each other in any respect [illegible] to him and his heirs forever.

I Constitute and appoint my Son Mason McCall Executor to this my last will and testament.

In witness whereof I have hereunto set my hand and Seal this the 30th day of March A.D. 1892.

Patsey her x mark McCall

Signed, Sealed and delivered in presence of us the witnesses hereto assigned and in presence of each other.

Chessie L. Stanley

Vivian L. Stanley

Rollin A. Stanley

Recorded Sept. 4th 1905 [illegible]

Will of Patsey McCall September 4, 1905

## Will of Patsy McCall

State of Georgia, County of Laurens.
I, Patsy McCall of said county and state, do make this my last will and testament, hereby revoking all others heretofore made by me.
I desire my body buried as in my circumstances is right and proper.
I desire all my just debts paid without unnecessary delay.
I will and bequeath all of my real estate, the same being my house and five acres of land upon which I am now living, near the town of Dublin said county and state aforesaid, joining lands of Joseph Moore, Louiza Freeman, Willis Dasher, and others. To my son, Mason McCall and grand daughter, Julia Thomas and Lou McCall as follows: To Lou McCall, I give one fourth of one acre (1/4) of that part of said five acres beforementioned. Next, to Louiza Freeman ( and my daughter Tena McCall to occupy the said (1/4) one fourth of an acre aforesaid, during her life without rent) and to her said Lou McCall and her heirs forever.
The remainder of said five acres I give and bequeath to my son Mason McCall and my grand daughter, Julia Thomas, to be equally divided between them, but so divided in that my son may have the houses on the said land, and that part of said land next the town of Dublin to include the houses; and said Julia the remainder of said five acres after the one fourth acre is accepted as before and to them the said Mason McCall and Julia Thomas and their heirs forever.
I give and bequeath all the residue of my property to my beloved children viz: Ellen Gregg, wife of Henry Gregg, Louiza Freeman, wife of Major Freeman; Norman G. McCall; **Tena McCall,** and Mattie Hampton, wife of William Hampton, share and share alike to them and their heirs forever.
I give and bequeath to my son, Jack McCall, one dollar, as is, and other children last named have and will receive such parts as will make their shares equal to each other in my respect and to him and his heirs forever.
I constitute and appoint my son, Mason McCall, executor to this my last will and testament.
In witness whereof I have hereunto set my hand and seal this the $30^{th}$ day of March A.D. 1892.
her

Patsey X McCall
mark

Signed, Sealed and delivered in presence of us the witnesses hereto assigned and in presence of each other.
Gussie L. Stanley
Vivian L. Stanley
Rollin A. Stanley
Recorded Sept. $4^{th}$ 1905 W. A. Wood Ordinary

ancestry.com

## 1870 United States Federal Census

| | |
|---|---|
| Name: | **Louisa Mccall** |
| Age in 1870: | 85 |
| Birth Year: | abt 1785 |
| Birthplace: | Georgia |
| Home in 1870: | Militia District 342, Laurens, Georgia |
| Race: | Mulatto |
| Gender: | Female |
| Post Office: | Dublin |
| Value of real estate: | |

Household Members:

| Name | Age |
|---|---|
| Samuel Mitchel | 38 |
| Rhoda Mitchel | 35 |
| Hamlet Mitchel | 13 |
| Ever Mitchel | 12 |
| Elick Mitchel | 9 |
| Louisa Mccall | 85 |

**Source Citation:** Year: *1870*; Census Place: *Militia District 342, Laurens, Georgia*; Roll: *M593_161*; Page: *319B*; Image: *26*; Family History Library Film: *545660*.

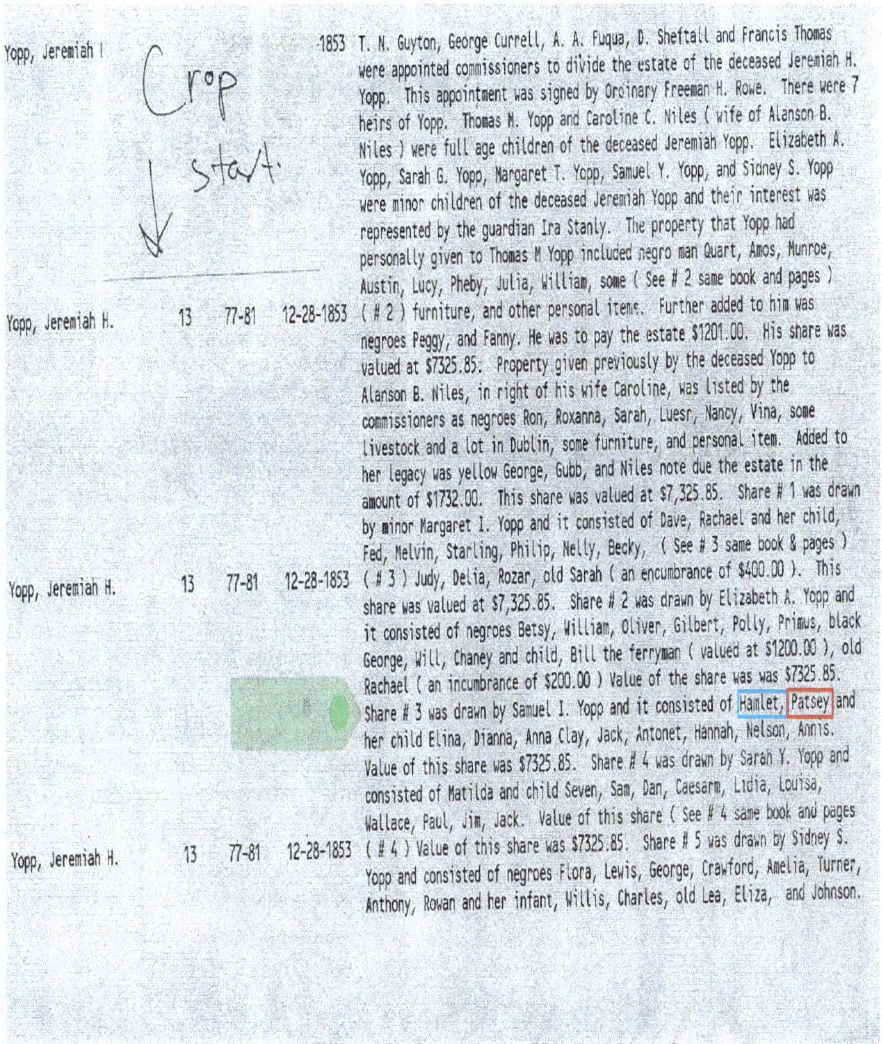


| | | | | |
|---|---|---|---|---|
| Yopp, Jeremiah H | | | 1853 | T. N. Guyton, George Currell, A. A. Fuqua, D. Sheftall and Francis Thomas were appointed commissioners to divide the estate of the deceased Jeremiah H. Yopp. This appointment was signed by Ordinary Freeman H. Rowe. There were 7 heirs of Yopp. Thomas M. Yopp and Caroline C. Niles ( wife of Alanson B. Niles ) were full age children of the deceased Jeremiah Yopp. Elizabeth A. Yopp, Sarah G. Yopp, Margaret T. Yopp, Samuel Y. Yopp, and Sidney S. Yopp were minor children of the deceased Jeremiah Yopp and their interest was represented by the guardian Ira Stanly. The property that Yopp had personally given to Thomas M Yopp included negro man Quart, Amos, Munroe, Austin, Lucy, Pheby, Julia, William, some ( See # 2 same book and pages ) |
| Yopp, Jeremiah H. | 13 | 77-81 | 12-28-1853 | ( # 2 ) furniture, and other personal items. Further added to him was negroes Peggy, and Fanny. He was to pay the estate $1201.00. His share was valued at $7325.85. Property given previously by the deceased Yopp to Alanson B. Niles, in right of his wife Caroline, was listed by the commissioners as negroes Ron, Roxanna, Sarah, Luesr, Nancy, Vina, some livestock and a lot in Dublin, some furniture, and personal item. Added to her legacy was yellow George, Gubb, and Niles note due the estate in the amount of $1732.00. This share was valued at $7,325.85. Share # 1 was drawn by minor Margaret I. Yopp and it consisted of Dave, Rachael and her child, Fed, Melvin, Starling, Philip, Nelly, Becky, ( See # 3 same book & pages ) |
| Yopp, Jeremiah H. | 13 | 77-81 | 12-28-1853 | ( # 3 ) Judy, Delia, Rozar, old Sarah ( an encumbrance of $400.00 ). This share was valued at $7,325.85. Share # 2 was drawn by Elizabeth A. Yopp and it consisted of negroes Betsy, William, Oliver, Gilbert, Polly, Primus, black George, Will, Chaney and child, Bill the ferryman ( valued at $1200.00 ), old Rachael ( an incumbrance of $200.00 ) Value of the share was $7325.85. Share # 3 was drawn by Samuel I. Yopp and it consisted of Hamlet, Patsey and her child Elina, Dianna, Anna Clay, Jack, Antonet, Hannah, Nelson, Annis. Value of this share was $7325.85. Share # 4 was drawn by Sarah Y. Yopp and consisted of Matilda and child Seven, Sam, Dan, Caesarm, Lidia, Louisa, Wallace, Paul, Jim, Jack. Value of this share ( See # 4 same book and pages |
| Yopp, Jeremiah H. | 13 | 77-81 | 12-28-1853 | ( # 4 ) Value of this share was $7325.85. Share # 5 was drawn by Sidney S. Yopp and consisted of negroes Flora, Lewis, George, Crawford, Amelia, Turner, Anthony, Rowan and her infant, Willis, Charles, old Lea, Eliza, and Johnson. |

**1853 Will of J.H. Yopp**

## 1853 Tax List of J.H. Yopp

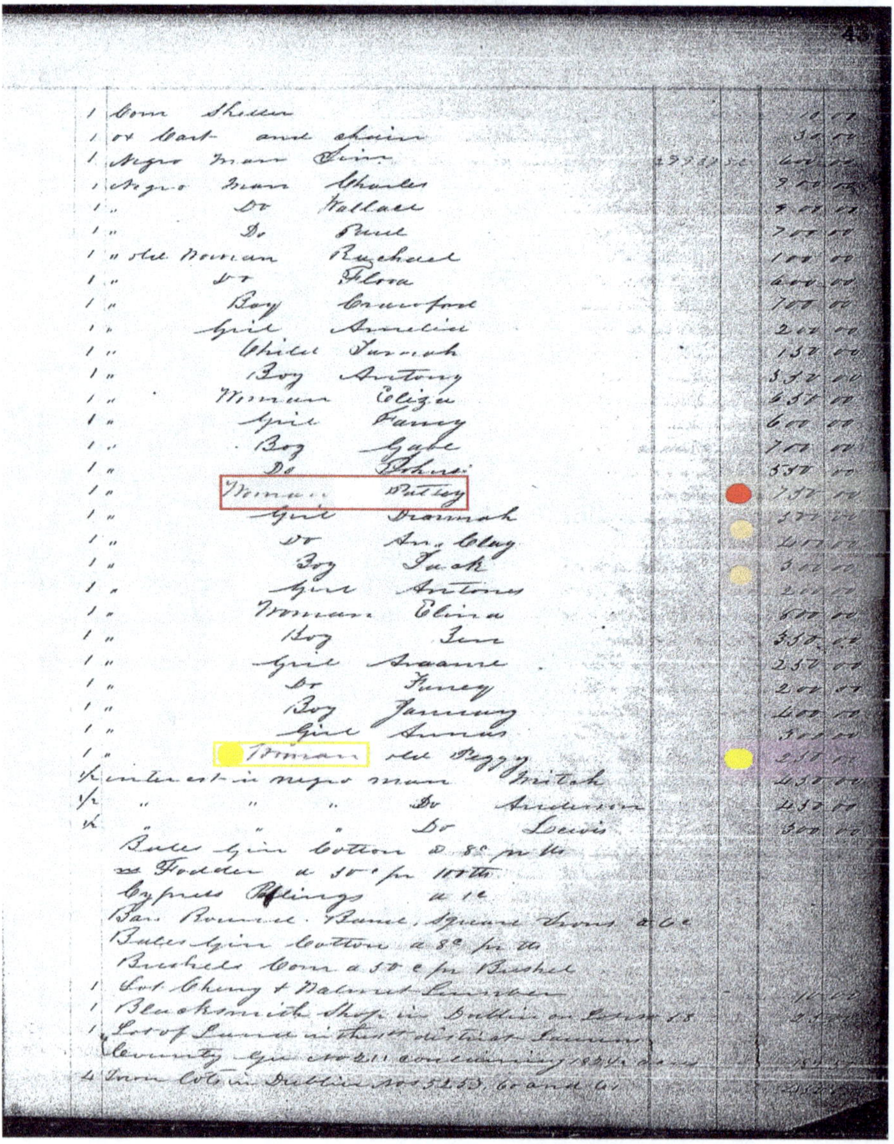

| | | | | |
|---|---|---|---|---|
| 1 | Corn Sheller | | | 10 00 |
| 1 | Ox Cart and chains | | | 30 00 |
| 1 | Negro man Jim | 29937 50 | | 600 00 |
| 1 | Negro man Charles | | | 900 00 |
| 1 | " Do Wallace | | | 900 00 |
| 1 | " Do Paul | | | 700 00 |
| 1 | " old Woman Rachael | | | 100 00 |
| 1 | " Do Flora | | | 600 00 |
| 1 | " Boy Crawford | | | 700 00 |
| 1 | " Girl Amelia | | | 200 00 |
| 1 | " Child Hannah | | | 150 00 |
| 1 | " Boy Antony | | | 350 00 |
| 1 | " Woman Eliza | | | 650 00 |
| 1 | " Girl Fanny | | | 600 00 |
| 1 | " Boy Gabe | | | 700 00 |
| 1 | " Do [illegible] | | | 550 00 |
| 1 | " Woman Patsy | | | 750 00 |
| 1 | " Girl Hannah | | | 500 00 |
| 1 | " Do Ann Clay | | | 400 00 |
| 1 | " Boy Jack | | | 300 00 |
| 1 | " Girl Antonia | | | 200 00 |
| 1 | " Woman Elina | | | 600 00 |
| 1 | " Boy Jim | | | 350 00 |
| 1 | " Girl Susanne | | | 250 00 |
| 1 | " Do Finney | | | 200 00 |
| 1 | " Boy Jimmy | | | 400 00 |
| 1 | " Girl Annas | | | 300 00 |
| 1 | " Woman old Peggy | | | 250 00 |
| 1/2 | interest in negro man Mitch | | | 450 00 |
| 1/2 | " " " Do Anderson | | | 450 00 |
| 1/2 | " " " Do Lewis | | | 300 00 |
| | Bales Gin Cotton @ 8c per lb | | | |
| | Fodder @ 50c per 100 lb | | | |
| | Cypress Shingles @ 1c | | | |
| | Bar Round Band Square Iron @ 6c | | | |
| | Bales Gin Cotton @ 8c per lb | | | |
| | Bushels Corn @ 50c per Bushel | | | |
| 1 | Lot Cherry & Walnut Lumber | | | 10 00 |
| 1 | Blacksmith Shop in Dublin on Lot No 13 | | | [illegible] |
| 1 | Lot of Land in the [illegible] district [illegible] County Ga No 211 containing 202½ acres | | | [illegible] |
| 4 | Town Lots in Dublin Nos 52 53, 60 and 61 | | | [illegible] |

THOMAS McCALL

**THE HUSBAND OF**
**ELIZABETH MARY ANN SMITH McCALL**

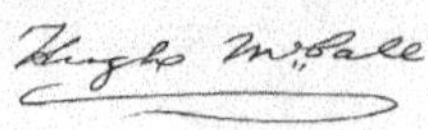

NOTICE
Please do not write in this
book or turn down the pages

## HUGH McCALL

IT is a matter of much regret that Georgia's first historian, who with such commendable efforts rescued from oblivion many of the early traditions of our State, should himself have left such scanty material for his own biographer. The life of this modest and worthy man has been too long neglected, and the reader must be content with only a brief sketch from the fragments gathered from various sources.

In the old Colonial Cemetery at Savannah, upon a plain marble slab level with the ground, may be read the following inscription:

"Sacred to the memory of
HUGH McCALL,
Brevet Major in the U. States army.
Born in N. Carolina
Feb. 17, 1767,
died
June 10, 1824.

He served the U. S. in various capacities 30 years; the last 20 years under severe bodily suffering, but with usefulness to himself, his country and his friends."

It is singular that so accurate a historian as Colonel C. C. Jones in his published address before the Georgia Historical Society, in 1881, refers to Hugh McCall, the historian, as an "officer in the army of the Revolution." As the subject of this sketch was only eight years old at the beginning of that memorable struggle, Colonel Jones obviously confounds the name of the historian with that of his father, James McCall, or of his uncle Hugh McCall, both of whom rendered valuable service in the Revolution.

The following sketch of the McCall family was written in 1829 by Thomas McCall, Esq., a brother of the historian, who lived on a plantation on the Oconee river near Dublin in Laurens county, Ga.

"The family of which I am a descendant were Scots, and in Scotland lived in the neighborhood of the family of Calhoun, properly Calquhun. The time of their migration is not known,



but the McCall, Harris and Calhoun families passed over from Scotland in the same ship to the northeast of Ireland, where they settled and remained two entire generations, when the three families migrated to Pennsylvania, where my grandfather James McCall was married to Janet Harris, the elder daughter of James Harris, and settled, as a farmer, on Canacocheque creek, where my father James McCall, Agnes, Hugh and Rachel were born, the former on the 11th of August, 1741. The three families removed from Canacocheque to New river, or little Kenhoway, in the western part of Virginia, where they remained for a number of years, and where Thomas McCall, Wm. McCall, and Jane (afterward married to Robert Harris) were born. The three families were driven away by the Indians after several of the Calhouns were killed. James Harris, my great-grandfather, remained on New river, and there died at the advanced age of 110 years. His children were Janet McCall Robertson, Isabell, Martha, and Wylly. James McCall, Robert Robertson and James Wylly settled in Mecklenburg county, North Carolina, where my father, James McCall, married Elizabeth, daughter of Thomas McCall, second cousin of my grandfather James McCall. John William and Patrick Calhoun removed into South Carolina and gave name to Calhoun's settlement on Little river, a branch of Long Cane. My grandfather James' family married in Mecklenburg, viz., my father James to Elizabeth McCall, Agnes to Elias Alexander, Rachel to Thomas McCall, son of Francis, a distant relation, not much liked by the family—ran away; Thomas married Jane, daughter of Samuel Harris; William married Elizabeth, daughter of Matthew Stewart; and Jane married Robert, son of John Harris. My maternal grandmother was Margaret Greenfield—had two sisters, Esther and ————, the former married Andrew Elliott and the latter married James Barr. My grandfather James had a brother Thomas, who settled at Wilmington in Delaware, and I think another brother William, of whom I know nothing. James Harris, my great-grandfather, was related to the family



of Livingstons, which went from Scotland to Holland, removed from Holland to New York (New Netherlands) and there remained. My grandfather, Thomas McCall, had children; viz., Elizabeth my mother, Margaret, Jane, Martha, and Ann and Mary who died in youth. Margaret married Thomas Harrison and had a number of children; Jane married John Luckie and had a number of children; Martha married Samuel Nelson and had several children. I know not what became of her or them. None of my family were men of letters except Thomas my uncle, who when at college changed his name to Thomas Harris McCaule. His posterity, Laird, Melinda Penelope, Leroy, Thomas 1st, and 2nd, and Jane, all died without issue, except Melinda, who married William Pinder and has two living children, viz., Thomas, and Jane who married Captain J. M. Russell, and later married Captain Phillips of Manchester, England, had a daughter (Melinda) and died. My father's descendants were Thomas, Hugh, Janet, Margaret, James, Harris, Elizabeth and William —all dead but Thomas, Janet and Margaret. Thomas married Henrietta Fall in 1787, and their issue were Eliza Henrietta, died young; Selina Mary Ann, married to Virgil H. Vivien who has many children in Florida; Louisa Freeman, married to George Gaines, has three children, and resides in Decatur county; Thomas William and James, both dead; and youngest still-born. He, in 1798, married Elizabeth Mary Ann Smith, by whom he had Sarah Georgiana, married to Colonel Spivey; Elizabeth Smith married to Doctor Thomas Moore; Harriet Moore, married to Major Mizell; Margaret, died young; Janet Harris married Ira Stanley; Margaret Sanders, married Jeremiah H. Yopp, Esq.

"Patrick Calhoun, father of John C. Calhoun, Vice-President of the United States, paid us a visit in 1794 or '93, and gave his benediction to three of my oldest children, and said to me: 'This is the fifth generation of your family that I have had by the hand and have intimately known,' and mentioned to me several of the above circumstances.

**Hugh McCall**

"My father was an adviser in what was called the Regulation in North Carolina about the year 1768 or '69, and that was the real beginning of the American Revolution. He, in 1771 or 1772, removed into the Calhoun settlement, South Carolina, and became an active officer in the Revolution. He was captain of minute men under the government in 1774, and rose in rank to that of colonel, and died of smallpox and a wound after having been in seventeen engagements against the enemy. Died in April, 1781.

"I was born 19th of March, 1764, old style, which was properly at the time 19th or 30th of March, 1765, new style, uncertain which day, as those old folks, all farmers, were not very learned and adhered to the old style and the old year for a number of years after the beginning of the year was altered from 25th of March to 1st of January."

From these facts it appears that while Major Hugh McCall, the historian, was himself too young to take an active part in the Revolution, he lived amid the stirring scenes of that great struggle, and upon his youthful memory were indelibly stamped the dramatic records and traditions which he so faithfully describes.

But little is known of his early life, but when quite a young man he became interested in military affairs, and for a long time he was connected with the United States army. On May 12th, 1794, he was ensign of the 3rd sub-legion, and May, 1796, he became first lieutenant. He was made deputy paymaster-general January 31st, 1800, and August of the same year, he was advanced to the position of captain. On the reorganization of the army, in 1802, he was retained in the second infantry, and on July 10th, 1812, he was breveted major. On July 15th, 1815, he was mustered out of service. On March 31st, 1818, he became military storekeeper at Savannah and in May, 1821, he served in the same capacity at Charleston, South Carolina. For eighteen months he lived at Point Peter. From 1806 to 1823, he was the jailer of Savannah, and it was during this



period that he wrote his History of Georgia. Many years before his death, his health failed and he became an invalid. He suffered much bodily pain, and when not actually confined to his bed, he had to use a roller chair to move about his room.

This was not an age of books and official records and the experiences and traditions of those who actually took part in the War of the Revolution were fast fading from memory. It was fortunate, indeed, for Georgia's early history, that Major Hugh McCall, at this crisis, though suffering from a painful disease, and in the face of great difficulties, undertook to rescue from oblivion the history of his State, and fix in imperishable record the deeds of her distinguished sons. From his own notes and experiences, and from the lips of many of the chief actors of the scenes he portrays, his materials were taken, and with wonderful patience and fortitude he prepared for the press the first volume of the History of Georgia, which was published in 1811. In the preface he says: "The occurrences of a new country, when dressed in their best attire are not very engaging, and it is to be expected that many interesting facts have escaped the author's notice, owing to the limited scope of his researches, in consequence of his affliction under a portion of disease and decrepitude almost without a parallel in the history of human life."

In 1816, he published the second volume of his History of Georgia, thus bringing down the record of the State to the end of the Revolution.

While his History of Georgia is not free from legitimate criticism as to style and historic treatment, still it is of inestimable value in the preservation of many of the important facts upon which are based the writings of later historians. He did not attempt a finished production, but he collected the material for the future historian, and in estimating the value of his work we must bear in mind what Jared Sparks says of it: "The work has its merits, but its author labored under disadvantages, and his materials were scanty."

Major McCall was never married, and his will, which is of



record in the office of the Ordinary in Savannah, shows that he lived in moderate circumstances. After a lingering illness and years of bodily suffering, he died in Savannah June 10th, 1824, and was buried in the old Colonial Cemetery, now in the midst of the city.

The only likeness of him in existence is an oil portrait in possession of the Georgia Historical Society at Savannah, from which the accompanying engraving is made.

As the years go by, his valuable work is more and more appreciated, and for all time he will be known and honored as Georgia's first historian. OTIS ASHMORE.

THE
# HISTORY OF GEORGIA.

## CHAPTER I.

IT is natural and right that we should feel a lively interest and concern in the lives and fortunes of our ancestors. When we behold them braving the horrors of the desert; surmounting the difficulties of an inhospitable climate; exploring forests infested with wild beasts, and surrounded by savages; their courage and perseverance inspire us with astonishment and admiration. We are pleased with a recital of the dangers they have escaped, and the difficulties they have encountered, in planning and executing the establishment of a country, where we are now in the enjoyment of liberty, peace and plenty. These reflections, justly fill us with enthusiastic esteem, respect and affection, for the stock from which we have descended.

From the best sources of information which can be resorted to at the present day, Sir Walter Raleigh is the reputed discoverer of that part of the United States, now denominated Georgia. This man, so greatly distinguished for his genius, courage, enterprise, and unmerited fate, under the government of a pusillanimous monarch, had been deeply interested in the adventures of his half brother, Sir Humphrey Gilbert; and anxious to complete the discoveries which he had commenced, determined to prosecute them with vigor. Accordingly Sir Walter made application to queen Elizabeth for a patent similar to the one granted to Gilbert, which was obtained on the 26th of March, 1584, to explore North-America, and take possession of such countries as he might discover; and on the 23d of April, he dispatched two ships under the command of captains Amadas

**Brother of Thomas McCall**

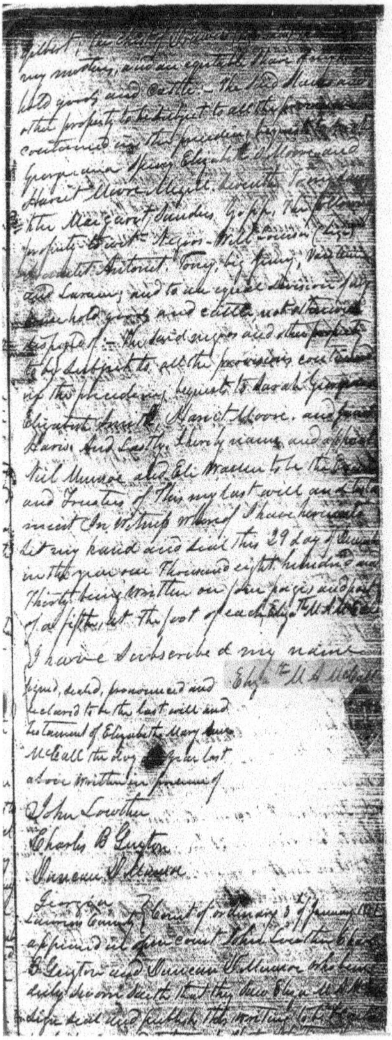

Seventh, to my daughter Margaret Sanders Yopp the following property - to wit - Negros - Will, Louisa ( Liza), HAMLET, Antonet, Tony, big Jimmy, Vincent, and Laurens, and to (her) an equal division of my household goods and cattle, not all herewith disposed of - the said Negros and other property to be subject to all the provisions contained in the preceding bequests to Sarah Georgiana, Elizabeth Smith, Harriet Moore, and Janet Harris. And lastly, I hereby name and appoint Neil Munroe, and Eli Warren to be the executors and trustees of this my last will and testament. In witness whereof I have hereunto set my hand and seal this 29th day of December in the year one thousand eight hundred and thirty being written on four pages and a part of a fifth, at the foot of each, Eliza th M. A. McCall

I have subscribed my name

signed, sealed, pronounced and ... Eliza th M. A. McCall

**THE 1830 WILL OF**
**ELIZABETH MARY ANN SMITH McCALL**

ancestry.com

## 1870 United States Federal Census

| | |
|---|---|
| Name: | **Hamlet Mccall** |
| Age in 1870: | 48 |
| Birth Year: | abt 1822 |
| Birthplace: | Georgia |
| Home in 1870: | Militia District 391, Laurens, Georgia |
| Race: | Black |
| Gender: | Male |
| Post Office: | Dublin |
| Value of real estate: | |

Household Members:

| Name | Age |
|---|---|
| Hamlet Mccall | 48 |
| Patsey Mccall | 47 |
| Ellen Mccall | 16 |
| Luisa Mccall | 14 |
| Norman Mccall | 12 |
| Tenner Mccall | 11 |
| Patsey Mccall | 9 |
| Mason Mccall | 6 |
| Julia Mccall | 5 |
| Peggy Mccall | 80 |

**Source Citation:** Year: *1870*; Census Place: *Militia District 391, Laurens, Georgia*; Roll: *M593_161*; Page: *333B*; Image: *54*; Family History Library Film: *545660*.

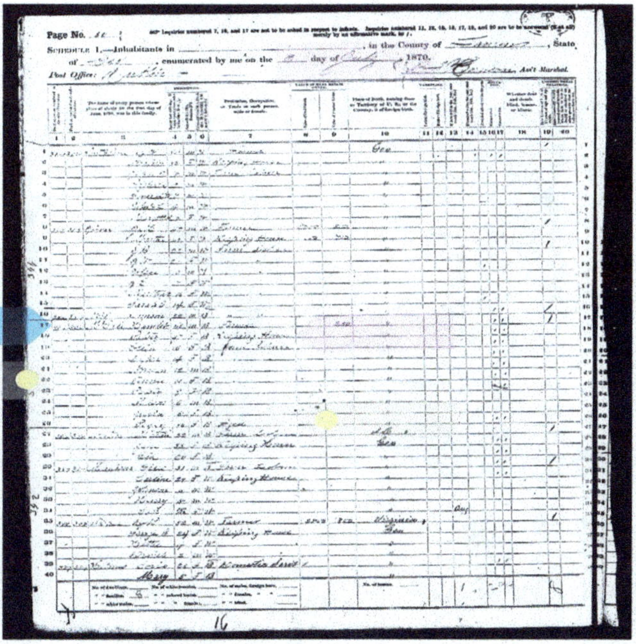

ancestry.com

## Georgia, Property Tax Digests, 1793-1893

| | |
|---|---|
| Name: | **Hamlet McCall** |
| Year: | 1871 |
| Militia District: | Smiths |
| Militia District Number: | 52 |
| County: | Laurens |

**Source Information:**
Ancestry.com. *Georgia, Property Tax Digests, 1793-1893* [database on-line]. Provo, UT, USA: Ancestry.com Operations, Inc., 2011.

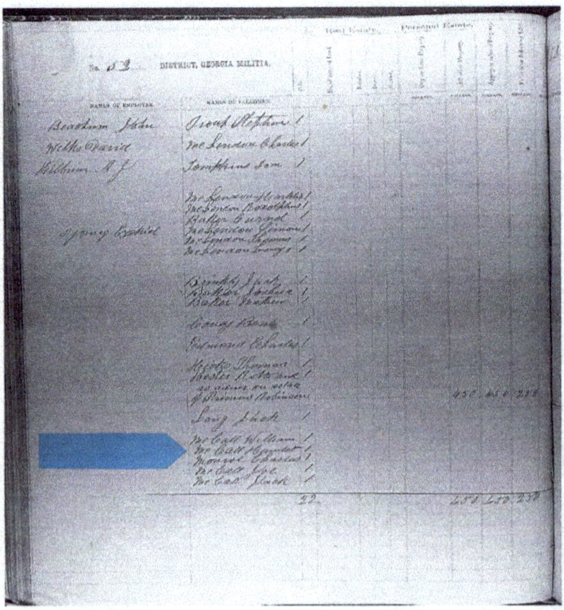

ancestry.com

## Georgia, Property Tax Digests, 1793-1893

| | |
|---|---|
| Name: | **Hamlet McCall** |
| Year: | 1872 |
| Militia District: | Smiths |
| Militia District Number: | 52 |
| County: | Laurens |

**Source Information:**
Ancestry.com. *Georgia, Property Tax Digests, 1793-1893* [database on-line]. Provo, UT, USA: Ancestry.com Operations, Inc., 2011.

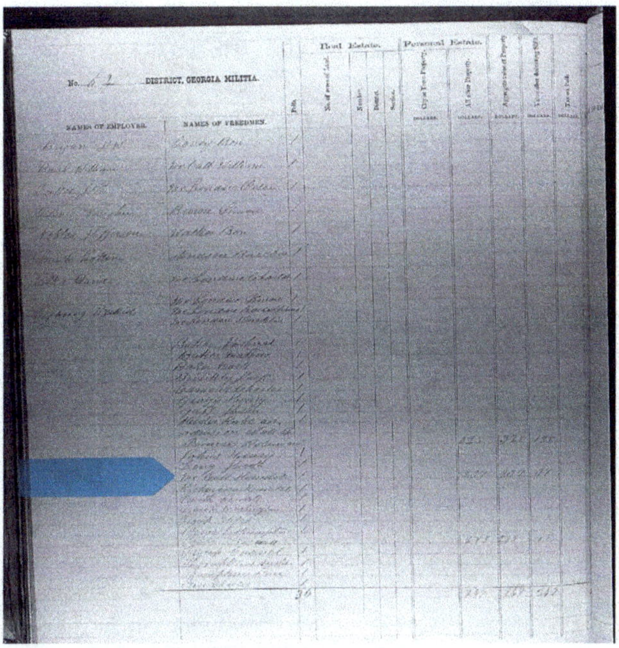
DISTRICT, GEORGIA MILITIA.

NAMES OF EMPLOYERS. | NAMES OF FREEDMEN.

Real Estate. | Personal Estate.

**Julia C. Hester**

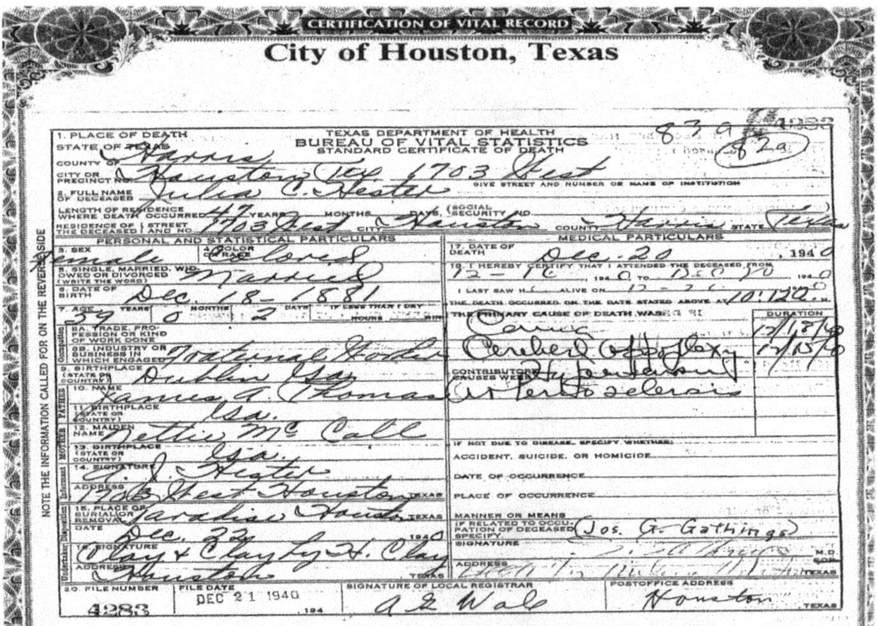

CERTIFICATION OF VITAL RECORD

**City of Houston, Texas**

TEXAS DEPARTMENT OF HEALTH
BUREAU OF VITAL STATISTICS
STANDARD CERTIFICATE OF DEATH

1. PLACE OF DEATH
STATE OF TEXAS
COUNTY OF Harris
CITY OR PRECINCT NO. Houston, Tex 1703 West
2. FULL NAME OF DECEASED Julia C. Hester
LENGTH OF RESIDENCE WHERE DEATH OCCURRED 47 YEARS
RESIDENCE OF THE DECEASED 1703 West CITY Houston COUNTY Harris STATE Texas

PERSONAL AND STATISTICAL PARTICULARS
3. SEX Female 4. COLOR OR RACE Colored
5. SINGLE, MARRIED, WIDOWED OR DIVORCED Married
6. DATE OF BIRTH Dec. 18-1881
7. AGE 59 YEARS 0 MONTHS 2 DAYS
8B. INDUSTRY OR BUSINESS IN WHICH ENGAGED Fraternal Worker
9. BIRTHPLACE Dublin Ga.
10. NAME James A. Thomas
11. BIRTHPLACE U.S.A.
12. MAIDEN NAME Nettie Mc Call
13. BIRTHPLACE U.S.A.
14. INFORMANT J. J. Hester
ADDRESS 1703 West Houston TEXAS
15. PLACE OF BURIAL OR REMOVAL Paradise Hous. TEXAS
DATE Dec. 22 1940
19. SIGNATURE Clay & Clay by H. Clay
ADDRESS Houston TEXAS
20. FILE NUMBER 4283 FILE DATE DEC 21 1940
SIGNATURE OF LOCAL REGISTRAR A. L. Wall

MEDICAL PARTICULARS
17. DATE OF DEATH Dec. 20, 1940
18. I HEREBY CERTIFY THAT I ATTENDED THE DECEASED FROM 12-16, 1940 TO Dec 20 1940
I LAST SAW H ALIVE ON 12-20
THE DEATH OCCURRED ON THE DATE STATED ABOVE AT 10:12 P.M.
THE PRIMARY CAUSE OF DEATH WAS: Coma / Cerebral Apoplexy — DURATION 12/18/40, 12/15/40
CONTRIBUTORY CAUSES WERE: Hypertension / Arteriosclerosis
IF NOT DUE TO DISEASE, SPECIFY WHETHER: ACCIDENT, SUICIDE, OR HOMICIDE
DATE OF OCCURRENCE
PLACE OF OCCURRENCE
MANNER OR MEANS
IF RELATED TO OCCUPATION OF DECEASED SPECIFY
SIGNATURE (Jos. G. Gathings) M.D.
ADDRESS
POSTOFFICE ADDRESS Houston TEXAS

NOTE THE INFORMATION CALLED FOR ON THE REVERSE SIDE

2461399

CERTIFIED COPY OF VITAL RECORDS
STATE OF TEXAS
COUNTY OF HARRIS
DATE ISSUED MAR 12 1996

This is a true and exact reproduction of the document officially registered and placed on file in the BUREAU OF VITAL STATISTICS, HOUSTON HEALTH AND HUMAN SERVICES DEPARTMENT.

R. W. Hanks
R. W. Hanks, Registrar
BUREAU OF VITAL STATISTICS

This copy not valid unless prepared on engraved border displaying seal and signature of Registrar.
LAMINATION MAY VOID CERTIFICATE.

ANY ALTERATION OR ERASURE VOIDS THIS CERTIFICATE

1880 United States Federal Census

| | |
|---|---|
| Name: | **Lucia Mc Call** |
| Age: | 3m |
| Birth Year: | abt 1880 |
| Birthplace: | Georgia |
| Home in 1880: | Dublin, Laurens, Georgia |
| Race: | Black |
| Gender: | Female |
| Relation to Head of House: | Daughter |
| Marital Status: | Single |
| Father's Name: | Calvin Johnson |
| Father's Birthplace: | Georgia |
| Mother's Name: | Alis Johnson |
| Mother's Birthplace: | Georgia |
| Neighbors: | |
| Cannot read/write: | |
| Blind: | |
| Deaf and dumb: | |
| Otherwise disabled: | |
| Idiotic or insane: | |

Household Members:

| Name | Age |
|---|---|
| Calvin Johnson | 24 |
| Alis Johnson | 20 |
| Julia Johnson | 11 |
| Elisabeth Johnson | 2 |
| Nittie Johnson | 5 |
| Julia Thompson | 14 |
| Tamer Mc Call | 22 |
| Lucia Mc Call | 3m |

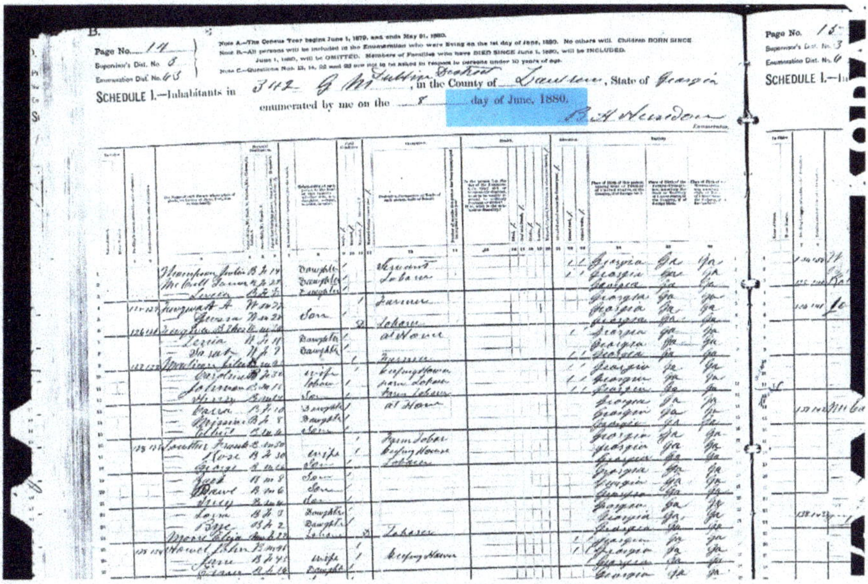
Page No. 14

Supervisor's Dist. No. 3

Enumeration Dist. No. 63

SCHEDULE 1.—Inhabitants in 3112 G M Dublin, in the County of Laurens, State of Georgia, enumerated by me on the 8 day of June, 1880.

ancestry.com

## 1880 United States Federal Census

| | |
|---|---|
| Name: | **Hamlet Mc Call** |
| Age: | 60 |
| Birth Year: | abt 1820 |
| Birthplace: | Georgia |
| Home in 1880: | Dublin, Laurens, Georgia |
| Race: | Black |
| Gender: | Male |
| Relation to Head of House: | Self (Head) |
| Marital Status: | Married |
| Spouse's Name: | Patsey Mc Call |
| Father's Birthplace: | Georgia |
| Mother's Birthplace: | Georgia |
| Neighbors: | |
| Occupation: | Farmer |
| Cannot read/write: | |
| Blind: | |
| Deaf and dumb: | |
| Otherwise disabled: | |
| Idiotic or insane: | |

Household Members:

| Name | Age |
|---|---|
| Hamlet Mc Call | 60 |
| Patsey Mc Call | 50 |
| Zena Mc Call | 20 |
| Mattie Mc Call | 17 |
| Mason Mc Call | 11 |
| Peggie Yopp | 100 |

**Source Citation:** Year: *1880*; Census Place: *Dublin, Laurens, Georgia*; Roll: *154*; Family History Film: *1254154*; Page: *513A*; Enumeration District: *063*; Image: *0791*.

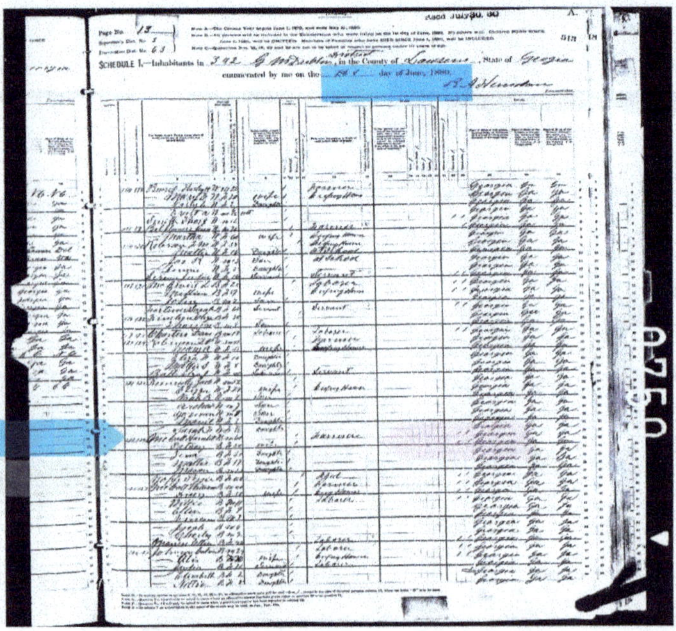

**1880 CENSUS & SOUNDEX OF HAMLET MCCALL**

Footnote: The history of Hamlet McCall is first recorded in 1830, when Hamlet was a boy of eight years old. He was listed as the property of Mrs. Thomas McCall in Dublin, Laurens County, Georgia. He was bequeathed to one of the daughters of the McCalls, Margaret Sanders McCall Yopp. Twenty-three years later, in 1853, 31 year-old Hamlet was valued at $1,200.00 on the inventory list of Judge Jeremiah Yopp, husband of the late Margaret Yopp. When Judge Yopp died that year, he bequeathed his property and 'Negros' to his children.

In 1870, the man, Hamlet McCall and his family were listed on the U.S. Decennial Census. His wife and six of their children were in the household. His granddaughter, Julia Thomas, and his mother-in-law, Peggy Yopp, were also listed with him. In 1871, Hamlet McCall was listed as a freedman in the Property Tax Digest. He paid a poll tax that year. In 1872, he was listed as a freedman in the same digest, and he paid a poll tax, and taxes on his personal property, which was valued at $239.00. On the 1880 census, Hamlet was listed with his wife and family, which included his mother-in-law, Peggy Yopp.

The Property Tax Digest of 1890 is the last known record of Hamlet McCall. He was listed as having no taxes paid on property or poll. It is likely that his property was turned over to his wife, Patsey, and he died by March of 1892, when her will was written.

ancestry.com™

## Georgia, Property Tax Digests, 1793-1893

| | |
|---|---|
| Name: | **Hamlet McCall** |
| Year: | 1890 |
| Militia District: | Dublin |
| Militia District Number: | 342 |
| County: | Laurens |

**Source Information:**

Ancestry.com. *Georgia, Property Tax Digests, 1793-1893* [database on-line]. Provo, UT, USA: Ancestry.com Operations, Inc., 2011.

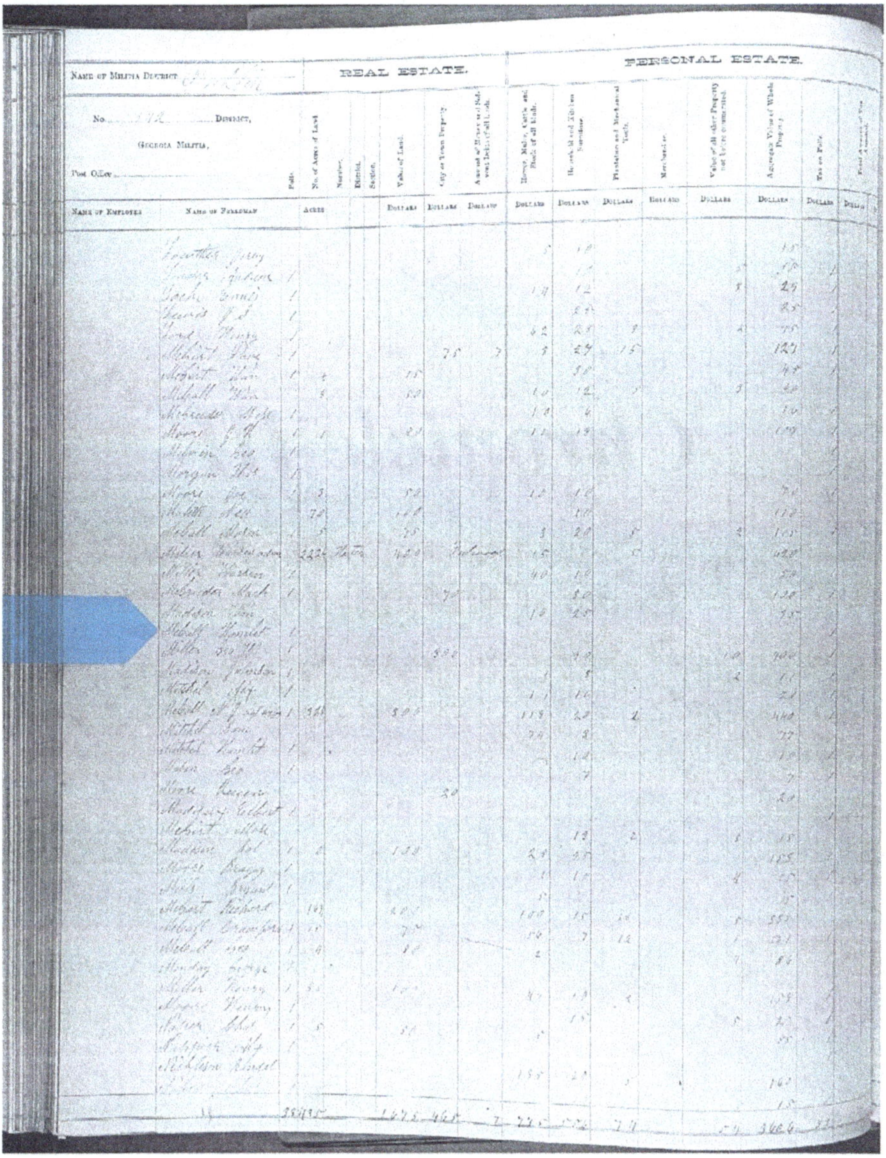
NAME OF MILITIA DISTRICT — REAL ESTATE. — PERSONAL ESTATE.

No. ______ DISTRICT, GEORGIA MILITIA, Post Office ______

NAME OF EMPLOYER — NAME OF FREEDMAN — ACRES — DOLLARS

**1890 Tax List of Hamlet McCall**

# *Chronicle III*

*... that we are the children of God: ...*
*Romans 8:14, 15, 16, 17*

*As arrows are in the hands of*
*a mighty man,*
*so are children of the youth.*
*Happy is the man*
*that has his quiver full of them.*

*Psalm 127:4-5*

**1907 christening photo of Ethel M. Walker**

**Ethel M. Walker Allen in early 1930s Chicago**

*Lo, children are an heritage of the Lord:*
*and the fruit of the womb is His reward.*
*Psalm 127:3*

As the spring of 1906 took full bloom in Atlanta, Milous and Lula were preparing themselves for the autumn arrival of a new addition to the family. Their daughter was born on Tuesday, October 9, 1906. They named her Ethel McCall Walker. The next year, their daughter, Martina Walker was born, and on Friday, February 12, 1909, Milous and Lula welcomed to the family their first and only male heir, Milous Wilburn Walker, Jr. The young couple couldn't have been more proud of their growing family, and Emma was extremely happy about being the grandmother of her youngest son's three children, and of her oldest son, John's first child, Martha, who was born a year before Milous, Jr.

Two more beautiful daughters were born to Lula and Milous. Mattie Walker was born on Monday, September 16, 1912, followed by Annie Walker, who was born on Saturday, June 13, 1914. Emma's oldest son, John, and his wife, Viola, had two more children. Elsie E. Walker was born around 1911, and in 1912, Viola gave birth to their only son, John Angus Walker III. Emma's granddaughter, Martina, died some time before 1920. Milous and Lula had four out of their seven children to survive to adulthood.

The Walker and McCall families were finally merged and growing. By the middle of the first decade of the 20th century, each family had migrated to and from several counties in Georgia. Lula's younger siblings, Mattie and Henry James McCall, made their home in the prominent Black community of Houston's Fifth Ward with their first cousin, Julia, and her husband, Mr. A. Z. Hester, who were their foster parents.

The McCalls were a family of educators. Julia taught several years in Dublin, Georgia before moving to Houston, Texas after her December 28, 1892 marriage to Mr. Hester. She also taught for many years in Houston, and her foster daughter/cousin, Mattie, was motivated to do the same. On the 1900 census, taken on June 4th, Mattie was listed as an absentee from the household of the Hesters. She was also listed as a student at the Prairie View Normal School, on the same day. Mattie's sister, Lula, taught school in Dublin, Georgia before migrating to Atlanta, where she worked in her home as mother and homemaker.

John Walker, Jr., the only brother of Milous, stayed in Macon, Bibb Co., Georgia and raised his family on the salary of a clothing store porter. Milous' older sister, Annie Walker, became the wife of Mr. Oscar Franklin Williams. Annie's mother, Emma Swift, moved in with Annie and Oscar around 1915. The Milous Walker Household was full with two adults and four children, so in her latter years, Emma opted to be in the care of her daughter. Annie was true to the calling that Emma had seen in her when she was a baby, playing "The Weeping Game" with her siblings. Annie would take care of Emma until her passing on Sunday, December 3, 1922.

By 1910, Milous was a preacher in The Church of God in Christ, and he was also listed on the 1910 census as a packer, employed by a pharmaceutical company. The company was known as Sharpe & Dohne Pharmaceutical. Lula was listed as a self-employed laundress (working her own account, as listed on the census form). On Thursday, September 12, 1918, Milous registered for the WWI Draft at Local Board Division No. 6 in Atlanta. His actual signature was written at the bottom of the registration card. He and his family lived at 8 Summit Street, at that time, and they were located at the same house on the 1920 census.

John A. Walker and his wife, Viola, were the parents of two daughters and a son, by the time the 1920 census was reported in January. John and his family were living at 256 Broad Street, in East Macon, and he was listed as an insurance sales agent for the Atlanta Mutual Insurance Company. He was at the same address in the 1920 and 1922 U.S. Macon City Directory. John's wife, Viola, worked as a domestic and was also listed in the Macon City Directory at 211 Green Street. This was the residence of the family who employed her. Milous' brother, John, died on Wednesday, November 1, 1922. His death was due to complications from toxemia. When Milous' mother, Emma Swift, died one month after John, Milous and his sister, Annie, were the only two family members to survive their nuclear family.

Lula's brother, Henry James McCall, was listed on the 1920 census as James C. McCall, with his foster parents, Julia and Alexander Z. Hester. He lived in their home at 1703 West Street, in Houston's Fifth Ward. He worked in a cotton factory as a cotton sampler. Mr. Hester also worked at the factory in the same capacity.

As the 1920s came to a close, Lula took a high school course of study at the Negro Evening Schools, and on Wednesday, May 29, 1929, Lula received her high school diploma for successfully completing what she set out to do. Later that same year, in Macon, Georgia, John's son, was arrested for the simple larceny of a cow, on Thursday, December 5, 1929. John A. Walker III was ordered by the Honorable Judge Malcolm D. Jones, to work on a Chain Gang for twelve months. That year, John was listed on the 1930 census as an inmate at the Bibb County Chain Gang.

By 1930, Lula and Milous Walker owned their home at 621 Houston Street in Atlanta. Milous continued his employment with the pharmaceutical company as a packer, and Lula was a public school teacher. Their daughters, Mattie and Annie, were 17 and 15 years old, and finishing their high school education. Their oldest daughter, Ethel, had moved to Chicago, Illinois a few years earlier, at the prompting of her aunt and uncle, Annie and Oscar Williams.

In the mid-1920s, Ethel frequently visited her Aunt Annie, and her Uncle Oscar. On one of her visits, a few years before locating there, Ethel was the maid of honor in a wedding, and she coyly said to the best man, "Why don't we get married?" That query was the beginning of the courtship between Maid of honor, Ethel McCall Walker and Best man, Edgar De Allen, Jr. Shortly after the wedding, Ethel returned to Atlanta, and for a year, the U.S. Postal Service was the vehicle for their courtship. Edgar proposed to Ethel, and sent her engagement ring by mail. On Thursday, July 21, 1927, they were married in Chicago. By census time in 1930, Lula and Milous were first-time grandparents to Ethel and Edgar's oldest son, and their only daughter.

The whereabouts of Milous, Jr. were not traceable on the census records of 1930. He was musically inclined, as was the entire Lula & Milous Walker Family. It is likely that he became a member of a band and ventured out in pursuit of a successful music career. His younger sister, Mattie, would soon follow in his footsteps and forge a fulfilling career in the music industry (see pp.165-180).

By April of 1932, Ethel had given birth to her fourth child, and third son. Lula left Atlanta to visit her daughter and help with the three toddlers. She never returned to Georgia. Her daughters, Mattie and Annie took the train to Chicago to be with their mother. The family story goes that Mattie put pony tails in Annie's hair, and dressed her down to appear as if she was about 12 years old, which was the age of a half-fare train ticket. It worked. Milous came to Chicago some time later in 1932 to win back his wife. He sent a letter before him, which he opened with, "My dearest

Lula... ", as his salutation. He returned to Atlanta without Lula, and later married Miss Georgette Nalls, after his divorce from Lula was finalized.

On the 1940 census, Milous and his wife, Georgette, were living at 441 Felton Drive in Atlanta. He continued as a packer at the pharmaceutical company, and Georgette was a homemaker. Lula was living in Chicago with her daughter, Ethel and her family, at 513 East 42nd Place. Lula worked as a sales woman in retail cosmetics. Ethel continued as a homemaker and a mother of their four children, with her husband, Edgar, working as a packer in a wholesale milleners' shop.

Ethel's third child, Darnell, was just under two years old when Lula arrived in Chicago. While Ethel was caring for the newborn baby, her middle children, Juanita and Darnell, became very ill. The oldest child, Edgar III, remained healthy. Little Darnell died on Sunday, May 8, 1932, just three weeks after the birth of Ethel's fourth child, David Rubinoff Allen, on Friday, April 15, 1932. Lula was a comfort to her daughter during that time, since she knew well the heartache of losing a child. Ten months later, on Wednesday, March 1, 1933, Ethel gave birth to her fifth child, Maurice Allen.

Milous Walker, Jr. showed up on the 1940 census as a Chicago resident, who was listed as a theater musician. The census stated that he lived at the same location at 3814 So. Calumet since 1935. Mattie had probably left Chicago for Los Angeles, California by 1940, since she didn't show up on Chicago's 1940 census. Her only child, Julie Ann, was born in Chicago on Tuesday, May 5, 1934, and was raised by Lula for a brief time, while Mattie launched her career.

Annie married Stephen Jackson, and they were a household of seven on the 1940 census of Chicago, Cook County, Illinois. Stephen had three daughters from his previous marriage, who were six, nine, and 13 years younger than his wife, Annie. He and Annie had four year-old daughter, Anita, and one year-old Betty.

In the meantime, the John A. Walker branch of the Walker family remained in Macon, Georgia. John Walker III, the nephew of Milous W. Walker, Sr., was listed on the 1940 census as the head of household, which included his wife, Susie, two daughters, and two sons. They lived at 209 Elliott Street since 1935, which was about the time their first daughter, Susie, Jr., was born. Essie Mae was born shortly afterwards, followed by Willie, and then Luther was born on Thursday, April 13, 1939. Also listed in the John Walker Household was a five year-old boy by the name of Richard Fanning. He was listed as John's brother-in-law, who resided in Wilkes County, Georgia in 1935.

John worked for the Marshall Lumber Company as a sawyer, and his wife, Susie, worked as a grader for a paper bag factory. John's mother, Viola McComb Walker, was listed in the Macon City Directory in 1934 and 1935. She resided at 338 Middle Street, and was listed as a cook for a private family. Viola died at the age of 50, on Tuesday, February 23, 1943. In the 1949 Macon City Directory, John was listed as a service salesman for the Huckabee Auto Company. John's son, Luther, carried on the Walker name from Milous' brother, John Angus Walker, Jr. Luther L. Walker died in Macon on Friday, September 12, 2008. It is very likely that Luther never had the opportunity to meet or know his grandfather's younger brother, Milous, who remained in Atlanta until his passing on Thursday, January 18, 1968. His wife, Georgette, was the informant on his death certificate. She correctly reported his birth date, but she didn't know the names of his parents. Milous lived to be 91 ½ years old.

Annie L. Walker Williams, the older sister of Milous, lived in Chicago until her passing on Wednesday, Decemer 5, 1956. Her husband, Oscar F.

Williams preceded her in death on Wednesday, May 17, 1944. Both were buried at The Burr Oak Cemetery in Alsip, Illinois.

Lula McCall Walker, the mother of Milous' four children, lived out her life in Chicago. Her brother, Henry James McCall, who was born on Thursday, July 13, 1885, preceded her in death. He died in Houston, Texas on Tuesday, January 18, 1953. Lula's only sister, Mattie Ellen McCall Martin, who was born on Thursday, January 25, 1883, lived in Houston, Texas, but she died in Natchez, Mississippi while staying with Henry's daughter, Tommie McCall Dumas. Mattie died on Monday, August 26, 1968. Mattie and Henry were both buried in the Hester Family Plot, at the Paradise West Cemetery, in Houston, Texas.

Lula McCall Walker, born Louisa Rebecca McCall in January of 1880, died in Chicago on Tuesday, September 27, 1960. Lula's youngest daughter, Annie, was the informant on her death certificate. It was recorded that Lula had lived in Chicago for 32 years at the time of her death. That would have placed her in Chicago in 1928. Lula was still in Atlanta in 1928, as she was listed on the 1930 census of Atlanta, Georgia. It is likely that the duration of 32 years in Chicago should have instead been the year, 1932, that she moved there, making her residence in Illinois 28 years.

*To every thing there is a season*
*and a time to every purpose under the heaven:*
*a time to be born, and a time to die; ...*
*Ecclesiastes 3:1-8*

36

Aug. 15, 1899

| To whom due | For what | Time | Amt. | |
|---|---|---|---|---|
| Harrell, A. A. | Teaching | 2 months | 28 | 18 |
| Freeman, Hattie | | | 39 | 20 |
| Smith, Annie | | | 37 | 28 |
| Methvin, T. C. | | | 28 | 24 |
| Harrill, John F. | | | 49 | 28 |
| Brown, Mabel | | | 36 | 64 |
| Stuckey, E. W. | | | 43 | 24 |
| Bedford, R. A. 1 asst. | | | 71 | 48 |
| Bryan, Agnes | | | 26 | 56 |
| Perry, B. D. | | | 44 | 96 |
| Eason, Mattie | | | 33 | 86 |
| Clark, Fannie | | | 33 | 56 |
| Griffin, F. D. | | | 42 | 24 |
| Fordham, L. P. | | | 31 | 48 |
| Morse, Emma F. | | | 48 | 48 |
| Fuller, Mattie | | | 30 | 00 |
| Grant, S. S. | | | 30 | 22 |
| Moses, Rosa A. | | | 48 | 64 |
| Hicks, T. H. | | | 69 | 96 |
| Harvard, Bessie | | | 65 | 04 |
| Pilcher, Laura | | | 25 | 50 |
| Jackson, Della 1 asst. | | | 62 | 20 |
| Boone, S. A. | | | 45 | 48 |
| Hilton, Mattie | | | 55 | 12 |
| Hilton, Mattie, S. F. | | | 48 | 88 |
| Whitaker, Rosa A. | | | 43 | 76 |
| McCall, Louisa R. | | | 41 | 45 |
| Cone, M. E. | | | 52 | 24 |
| Wimberly, H. B. | | 1 mo. | 18 | 56 |
| Scarborough Mrs. E. | | " " | 21 | 92 |
| Wood, Edna F. | | 2 months | 25 | 20 |
| Rutland, W. L. | | | 57 | 96 |
| Wynn, Jas. M. | | | 61 | 00 |
| Stokes, Minnie | | | 49 | 60 |
| Troup, Flora L. 1 asst. | | | 63 | 20 |
| Wright, C. D. | | | 54 | 92 |
| Moore, Fannie L. | | | 37 | 75 |
| Montford, H. D. | | | 36 | 64 |
| Daley, W. J. | | | 25 | 28 |
| Dunning, Dora | | | 31 | 04 |
| Burch, Nellie | | | 40 | 01 |
| Kerr, J. H. | | | 68 | 76 |

**1899 Pay Record of Louisa R. McCall**

ancestry.com

## 1910 United States Federal Census

| | |
|---|---|
| Name: | **John Walker**<br>**[John Mccombs]** |
| Age in 1910: | 57<br>[37] |
| Estimated Birth Year: | abt 1873<br>[1873] |
| Birthplace: | Georgia |
| Relation to Head of House: | Boarder |
| Father's Birth Place: | Georgia |
| Mother's Birth Place: | Georgia |
| Spouse's Name: | Viola M Walker |
| Home in 1910: | Macon Ward 3, Bibb, Georgia |
| Marital Status: | Married |
| Race: | Black |
| Gender: | Male |
| Neighbors: | |

Household Members:

| Name | Age |
|---|---|
| Mariah Mccombs | 57 |
| John Walker | 57<br>[37] |
| Viola M Walker | 28 |
| Matha M Walker | 2 |

**Source Citation:** Year: *1910*; Census Place: *Macon Ward 3, Bibb, Georgia*; Roll: *T624_173*; Page: *1B*; Enumeration District: *0040*; Image: *1068*; FHL Number: *1374186*.

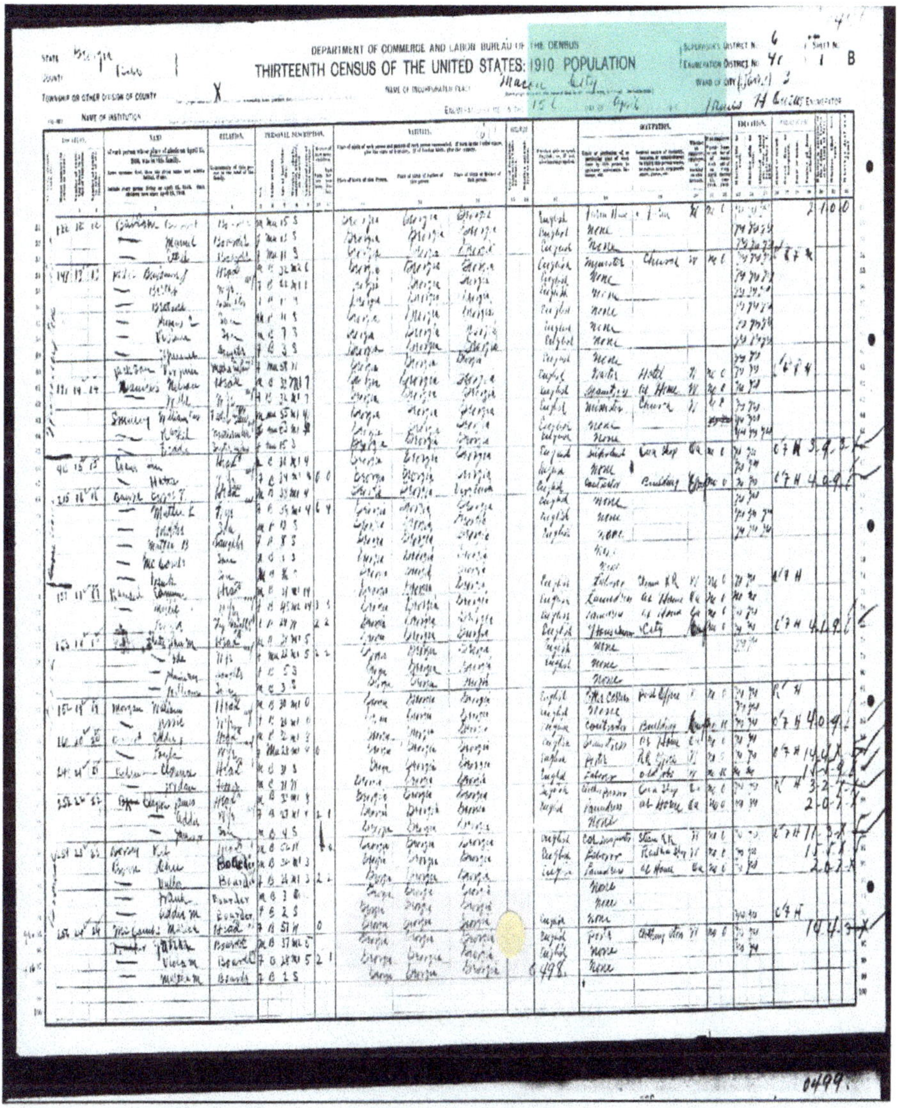
DEPARTMENT OF COMMERCE AND LABOR—BUREAU OF THE CENSUS

THIRTEENTH CENSUS OF THE UNITED STATES: 1910 POPULATION

0499

ancestry.com

## 1910 United States Federal Census

| | |
|---|---|
| Name: | **Milas Walker** |
| Age in 1910: | 33 |
| Estimated Birth Year: | 1877 |
| Birthplace: | Georgia |
| Relation to Head of House: | Head [Self (Head)] |
| Father's Birth Place: | Virginia |
| Mother's Name: | Emma Swift |
| Mother's Birth Place: | Georgia |
| Spouse's Name: | Lulu Walker |
| Home in 1910: | Atlanta Ward 4, Fulton, Georgia |
| Marital Status: | Married |
| Race: | Black |
| Gender: | Male |
| Neighbors: | |

Household Members:

| Name | Age |
|---|---|
| Milas Walker | 33 |
| Lulu Walker | 32 |
| Ethel Walker | 3 |
| Martina Walker | 2 |
| Milas Walker Jr. | 1 |
| Emma Swift | 60 |

**Source Citation:** Year: *1910*; Census Place: *Atlanta Ward 4, Fulton, Georgia*; Roll: *T624_191*; Page: *2A*; Enumeration District: *0070*; Image: *664*; FHL Number: *1374204*.

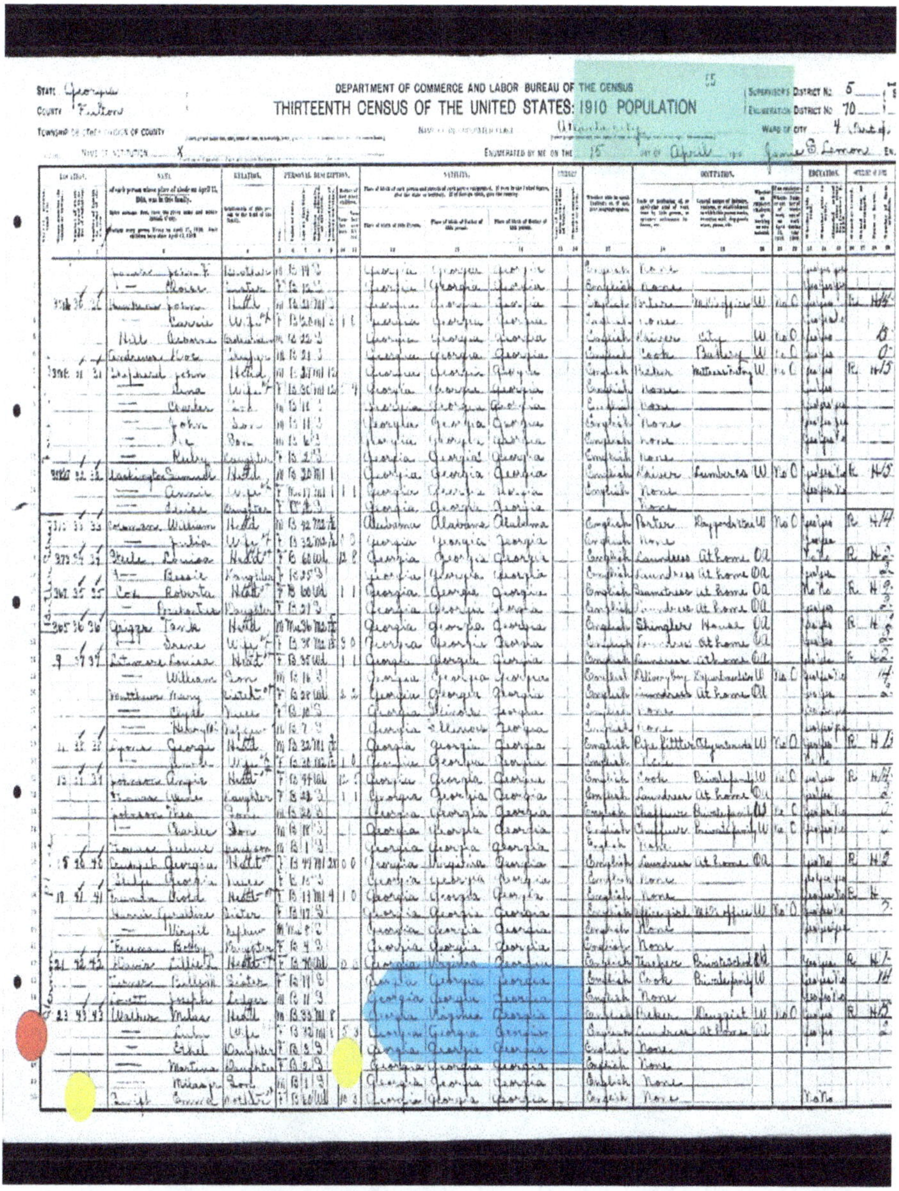

STATE Georgia  
COUNTY Fulton  
TOWNSHIP OR OTHER DIVISION OF COUNTY  
NAME OF INSTITUTION X

DEPARTMENT OF COMMERCE AND LABOR—BUREAU OF THE CENSUS  
THIRTEENTH CENSUS OF THE UNITED STATES: 1910—POPULATION

SUPERVISOR'S DISTRICT No. 5  
ENUMERATION DISTRICT No. 70  
NAME OF INCORPORATED PLACE Atlanta city  
WARD OF CITY 4  
ENUMERATED BY ME ON THE 15 DAY OF April, 1910. James E. Lemons, Enumerator.

| Name | Relation | Sex | Race | Age | Marital | Birthplace | Father's birthplace | Mother's birthplace | Language | Occupation | Industry |
|---|---|---|---|---|---|---|---|---|---|---|---|
| [illegible] John F. | Brother | M | B | 19 | S | Georgia | Georgia | Georgia | English | None | |
| — Eloise | Sister | F | B | 12 | S | Georgia | Georgia | Georgia | English | None | |
| Henderson John | Head | M | B | 21 | M1 | Georgia | Georgia | Georgia | English | Porter | Mill office |
| — Carrie | Wife | F | B | 20 | M1 | Georgia | Georgia | Georgia | English | None | |
| Hill Osborne | Brother-in-law | M | B | 22 | S | Georgia | Georgia | Georgia | English | Driver | City |
| Anderson Roe | Lodger | M | B | 21 | S | Georgia | Georgia | Georgia | English | Cook | Bakery |
| Shepherd John | Head | M | B | 37 | M1 | Georgia | Georgia | Georgia | English | Baker | Mattress factory |
| — Lina | Wife | F | B | 30 | M1 | Georgia | Georgia | Georgia | English | None | |
| — Charles | Son | M | B | 11 | S | Georgia | Georgia | Georgia | | | |
| — John | Son | M | B | 11 | S | Georgia | Georgia | Georgia | English | None | |
| — Ira? | Son | M | B | 6 | S | Georgia | Georgia | Georgia | English | None | |
| — Ruby | Daughter | F | B | 2 | S | Georgia | Georgia | Georgia | English | None | |
| Washington Samuel | Head | M | B | 20 | M1 | Georgia | Georgia | Georgia | English | Driver | Lumber co. |
| — Annie | Wife | F | Mu | 17 | M1 | Georgia | Georgia | Georgia | English | None | |
| — Lizzie? | Daughter | F | B | [illegible] | S | Georgia | Georgia | Georgia | | None | |
| Simmons? William | Head | M | B | 42 | M2 | Alabama | Alabama | Alabama | English | Porter | Dry goods store |
| — Julia | Wife | F | B | 32 | M2 | Georgia | Georgia | Georgia | English | None | |
| Steele Louisa | Head | F | B | 60 | Wd | Georgia | Georgia | Georgia | English | Laundress | At home |
| — Bessie | Daughter | F | B | 25 | S | Georgia | Georgia | Georgia | English | Laundress | At home |
| Cox Roberta | Head | F | B | 60 | Wd | Georgia | Georgia | Georgia | English | Seamstress | At home |
| — [illegible] | Daughter | F | B | 21 | S | Georgia | Georgia | Georgia | English | Laundress | At home |
| Griggs Tank? | Head | M | Mu | 36 | M2 | Georgia | Georgia | Georgia | English | Shingler | House |
| — Irene | Wife | F | B | 38 | M2 | Georgia | Georgia | Georgia | English | Laundress | At home |
| Latimore Louisa | Head | F | B | 35 | Wd | Georgia | Georgia | Georgia | English | Laundress | At home |
| — William | Son | M | B | 16 | S | Georgia | Georgia | Georgia | English | Delivery boy | Department store |
| Matthews Mary | Sister | F | B | 28 | Wd | Georgia | Georgia | Georgia | English | Laundress | At home |
| — Clyde | Niece | F | B | 10 | S | Georgia | Illinois | Georgia | | None | |
| — Henry? | Nephew | M | B | 7 | S | Georgia | Illinois | Georgia | | None | |
| Spires? George | Head | M | B | 32 | M1 | Georgia | Georgia | Georgia | English | Pipe fitter | [illegible] |
| — [illegible] | Wife | F | B | 30 | M2 | Georgia | Georgia | Georgia | English | None | |
| Johnson Angie | Head | F | B | 44 | Wd | Georgia | Georgia | Georgia | English | Cook | Private family |
| Thomas Annie | Daughter | F | B | 22 | S | Georgia | Georgia | Georgia | English | Laundress | At home |
| Johnson [illegible] | Son | M | B | 20 | S | Georgia | Georgia | Georgia | English | Chauffeur | Private family |
| — Charlie | Son | M | B | 18 | S | Georgia | Georgia | Georgia | English | Chauffeur | Private family |
| Thomas Julius | Grandson | M | B | 1 | S | Georgia | Georgia | Georgia | English | None | |
| Campbell Georgia | Head | F | B | 44 | M1 | Georgia | Virginia | Georgia | English | Laundress | At home |
| [illegible] Georgia | Niece | F | B | 15 | S | Georgia | Georgia | Georgia | English | None | |
| [illegible] | Head | F | B | 19? | M1 | Georgia | Georgia | Georgia | English | None | |
| [illegible] Geraldine | Sister | F | B | 17 | S | Georgia | Georgia | Georgia | English | Office girl | Mill office |
| — Virgil | Nephew | M | Mu | 8 | S | Georgia | Georgia | Georgia | English | None | |
| Freeman Betty | Daughter | F | B | 4 | S | Georgia | Georgia | Georgia | English | None | |
| Harris Lillie L. | Head | F | B | 30? | Wd | Georgia | Virginia | Georgia | English | Teacher | Private school |
| Turner Pollie? | Sister | F | B | 11 | S | Georgia | Georgia | Georgia | English | Cook | Private family |
| Scott Joseph | Lodger | M | B | 11 | S | Georgia | Georgia | Georgia | English | None | |
| Walker Miles | Head | M | B | 33 | M1 | Georgia | Virginia | Georgia | English | Baker | [illegible] |
| — Lula? | Wife | F | B | 32 | M1 | Georgia | Georgia | Georgia | English | Laundress | At home |
| — Ethel | Daughter | F | B | 3 | S | Georgia | Georgia | Georgia | English | None | |
| — Martina | Daughter | F | B | 2 | S | Georgia | Georgia | Georgia | English | None | |
| — Miles Jr. | Son | M | B | 1 | S | Georgia | Georgia | Georgia | English | None | |
| [illegible] | Mother-in-law | F | B | 60 | Wd | Georgia | Georgia | Georgia | English | None | |

ancestry library edition

## U.S., World War I Draft Registration Cards, 1917-1918

| | |
|---|---|
| Name: | **Milous Walker** |
| City: | Atlanta |
| County: | Fulton |
| State: | Georgia |
| Birth Date: | 7 Jul 1876 |
| Race: | Black |
| Draft Board: | 6 |
| Age: | |
| Occupation: | |
| Nearest Relative: | |
| Height/Build: | |
| Color of Eyes/Hair: | |
| Signature: | |

**Source Citation:** Registration State: *Georgia*; Registration County: *Fulton*; Roll: *1556954*; Draft Board: 6.

**WWI Marching Band**

## World War I Draft Registration Card C—(12 September 1918)

### REGISTRATION CARD

| SERIAL NUMBER | | | ORDER NUMBER | |
|---|---|---|---|---|

1

First name | Middle name | Family name

2 PERMANENT HOME ADDRESS

(No.) (Street or R.F.D. number) (City or town) (County) (State)

| Age by Years 3 | Date of Birth 4 (Month) (Day) (Year) |
|---|---|

RACE

| White | Negro | Oriental | Indian | |
|---|---|---|---|---|
| | | | Citizen | Non-Citizen |
| 5 | 6 | 7 | 8 | 9 |

| U.S. CITIZEN | | | ALIEN | |
|---|---|---|---|---|
| Native Born | Naturalized | Citizen by Father's Naturalization before Registrant's Majority | Declarant | Non-declarant |
| 10 | 11 | 12 | 13 | 14 |

15
If not a citizen of the U.S., of what nation are you a citizen or subject? ____________

| PRESENT OCCUPATION | EMPLOYER'S NAME |
|---|---|
| 16 | 17 |

18 PLACE OF EMPLOYMENT OR BUSINESS

(No.) (Street or R.F.D. number) (City or town) (County) (State)

| NEAREST RELATIVE | Name | 19 |
|---|---|---|
| | Address | 20 |
| | | (No.) (Street or R.F.D. number) (City or town) (County) (State) |

I AFFIRM THAT I HAVE VERIFIED ABOVE ANSWERS AND THAT THEY ARE TRUE.

P.M.G.O.
Form No. 1

(Registrant's signature or mark)

MyFamily.com, Inc. © 2002

### REGISTRAR'S REPORT

DESCRIPTION OF REGISTRANT

| HEIGHT | | | BUILD | | | COLOR OF EYES | COLOR OF HAIR |
|---|---|---|---|---|---|---|---|
| Tall | Medium | Short | Slender | Medium | Stout | | |
| 21 | 22 | 23 | 24 | 25 | 26 | 27 | 28 |

29 Has person lost arm, leg, hand, eye, or is he obviously physically disqualified? (SPECIFY.)

30 I certify that my answers are true, that the person registered has read or has had read to him his own answers, that I have witnessed his signature or mark and that all of his answers of which I have knowledge are true, except as follows:

Signature of Registrar

Date of Registration ____________

(The stamp of the local board having jurisdiction of the area in which the registrant has his permanent home shall be placed in this box)

Ancestry.com

*For more helpful family history charts and forms visit www.ancestry.com/save/charts./ancchart.htm*

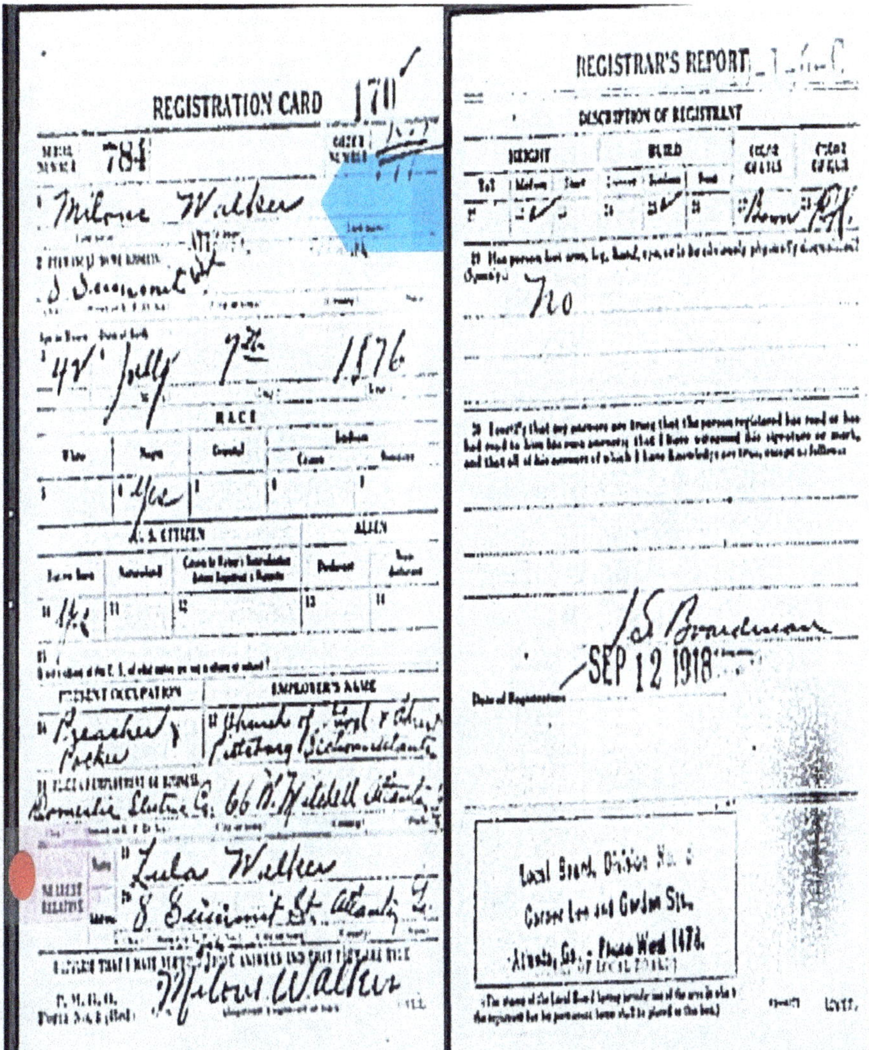
REGISTRATION CARD 170

SERIAL NUMBER 784

Milone Walker

S. Simmons St.

48 July 7th 1876

RACE

Negro: Yes

U. S. CITIZEN

Native Born: Yes

PRESENT OCCUPATION: Preacher & Porter

EMPLOYER'S NAME: Church of God & Christ, Pittsburg, Richmond, Atlanta

PLACE OF EMPLOYMENT OR BUSINESS: Commercial Electric Co. 66 W. Mitchell Atlanta

NEAREST RELATIVE: Lula Walker, 8 Simmons St. Atlanta Ga.

I AFFIRM THAT I HAVE VERIFIED ABOVE ANSWERS AND THAT THEY ARE TRUE

Milone Walker

P. M. G. O. Form No. 1 (Red)

REGISTRAR'S REPORT

DESCRIPTION OF REGISTRANT

| HEIGHT | | | BUILD | | | COLOR OF EYES | COLOR OF HAIR |
|---|---|---|---|---|---|---|---|
| Tall | Medium | Short | Slender | Medium | Stout | | |
| | ✓ | | | ✓ | | Brown | Blk |

Has person lost arm, leg, hand, eye, or is he obviously physically disqualified? (Specify.) No

I certify that my answers are true; that the person registered has read or has had read to him his own answers; that I have witnessed his signature or mark, and that all of his answers of which I have knowledge are true, except as follows:

J. S. Boardman

Date of Registration SEP 12 1918

Local Board, Division No. ... Corner Lee and Gordon Sts. Atlanta, Ga. - Phone West 1478.

ancestry.com

## 1910 United States Federal Census

| | |
|---|---|
| Name: | **Emma Swift** |
| Age in 1910: | 60 |
| Estimated Birth Year: | 1850 |
| Birthplace: | Georgia |
| Relation to Head of House: | Mother |
| Father's Birth Place: | Georgia |
| Mother's Birth Place: | Georgia |
| Home in 1910: | Atlanta Ward 4, Fulton, Georgia |
| Marital Status: | Widowed |
| Race: | Black |
| Gender: | Female |
| Neighbors: | |

Household Members:

| Name | Age |
|---|---|
| Milas Walker | 33 |
| Lulu Walker | 32 |
| Ethel Walker | 3 |
| Martina Walker | 2 |
| Milas Walker Jr. | 1 |
| Emma Swift | 60 |

**Source Citation:** Year: *1910*; Census Place: *Atlanta Ward 4, Fulton, Georgia*; Roll: *T624_191*; Page: *2A*; Enumeration District: *0070*; Image: *664*; FHL Number: *1374204*.

ancestry.com

## 1920 United States Federal Census

| | |
|---|---|
| Name: | **Emma Swift** |
| Home in 1920: | Atlanta Ward 4, Fulton, Georgia |
| Age: | 74 |
| Estimated Birth Year: | abt 1846 |
| Birthplace: | Georgia |
| Relation to Head of House: | Mother-in-Law |
| Father's Birth Place: | Georgia |
| Mother's Birth Place: | Georgia |
| Marital Status: | Widowed [Widow] |
| Race: | Black |
| Sex: | Female |
| Able to read: | No |
| Able to Write: | No |
| Neighbors: | |

Household Members:

| Name | Age |
|---|---|
| Oscar F Williams | 45 |
| Annie L Williams | 42 |
| Emma Swift | 74 |

**Source Citation:** Year: *1920*;Census Place: *Atlanta Ward 4, Fulton, Georgia*; Roll: *T625_250*; Page: *15A*; Enumeration District: *87*; Image: *794*.

ancestry library edition

## 1920 United States Federal Census

| | |
|---|---|
| Name: | **Annie L Williams [Annie L Swift]** |
| Age: | 42 |
| Birth Year: | abt 1878 |
| Birthplace: | Georgia |
| Home in 1920: | Atlanta Ward 4, Fulton, Georgia |
| Race: | Black |
| Gender: | Female |
| Relation to Head of House: | Wife |
| Marital Status: | Married |
| Spouse's Name: | Oscar F Williams |
| Father's Birthplace: | Georgia |
| Mother's Name: | Emma Swift |
| Mother's Birthplace: | Georgia |
| Able to Read: | Yes |
| Able to Write: | Yes |
| Neighbors: | |

Household Members:

| Name | Age |
|---|---|
| Oscar F Williams | 45 |
| Annie L Williams | 42 |
| Emma Swift | 74 |

**Source Citation:** Year: *1920*; Census Place: *Atlanta Ward 4, Fulton, Georgia*; Roll: *T625_250*; Page: *15A*; Enumeration District: *87*; Image: *794*.

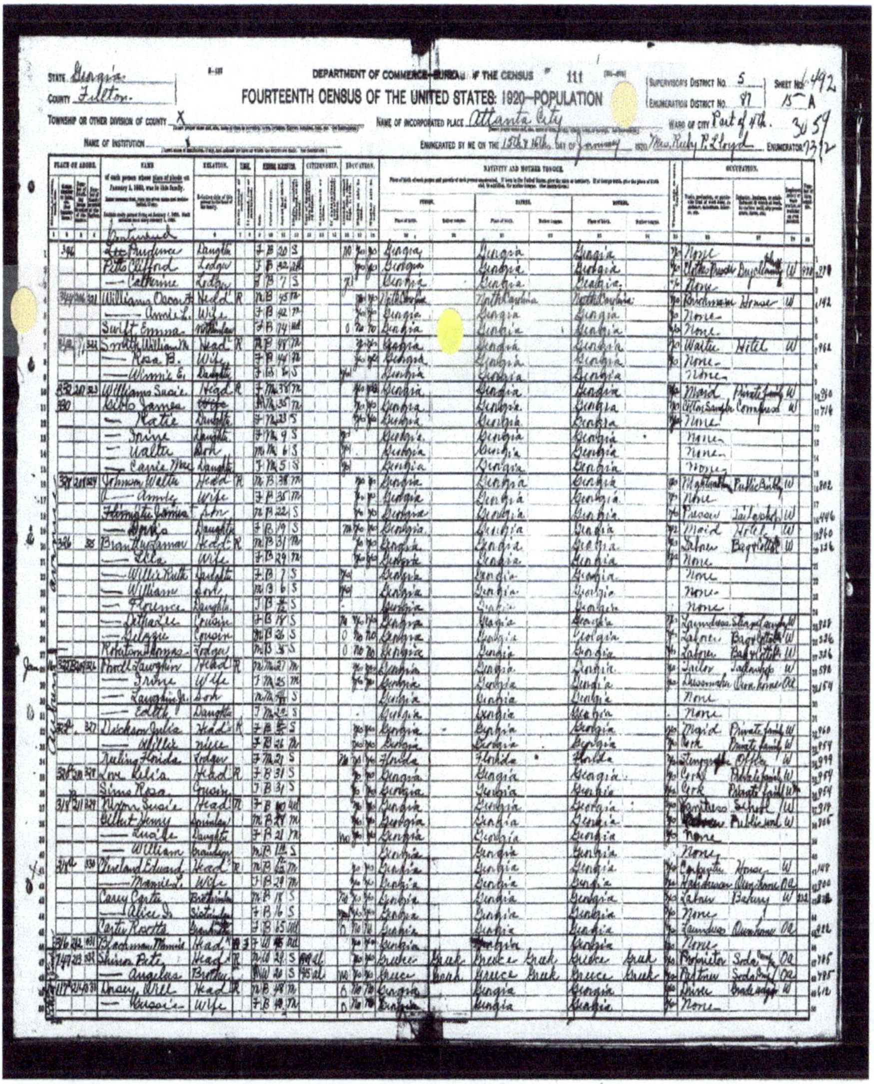

DEPARTMENT OF COMMERCE—BUREAU OF THE CENSUS

FOURTEENTH CENSUS OF THE UNITED STATES: 1920—POPULATION

State: Georgia. County: Fulton. Township or other division of county: X. Name of incorporated place: Atlanta City. Ward of city: Part of 4th. Name of institution: —

Supervisor's District No. 5. Enumeration District No. 87. Sheet No. 15 A.

Enumerated by me on the 15th & 16th day of January 1920. Mrs. Ruby P. Lloyd, Enumerator.

| Line | Name | Relation | Sex | Race | Age | Marital | Birthplace | Father's birthplace | Mother's birthplace | Occupation | Industry |
|---|---|---|---|---|---|---|---|---|---|---|---|
| | Continued | | | | | | | | | | |
| 1 | Lee Prudence | Daughter | F | B | 20 | S | Georgia | Georgia | Georgia | None | |
| 2 | Pitts Clifford | Lodger | F | B | 32 | Wd | Georgia | Georgia | Georgia | Clothes Presser | Dry cleaning |
| 3 | — Catherine | Lodger | F | B | 7 | S | Georgia | Georgia | Georgia | None | |
| 4 | Williams Oscar H. | Head | M | B | 45 | M | North Carolina | North Carolina | North Carolina | Brickman | House |
| 5 | — Annie L. | Wife | F | B | 42 | M | Georgia | Georgia | Georgia | None | |
| 6 | Swift Emma | Mother-in-law | F | B | 74 | Wd | Georgia | Georgia | Georgia | None | |
| 7 | Smith William M. | Head | M | B | 48 | M | Georgia | Georgia | Georgia | Waiter | Hotel |
| 8 | — Rosa B. | Wife | F | B | 44 | M | Georgia | Georgia | Georgia | None | |
| 9 | — Winnie E. | Daughter | F | B | 6 | S | Georgia | Georgia | Georgia | None | |
| 10 | Williams Susie | Head | F | Mu | 38 | M | Georgia | Georgia | Georgia | Maid | Private family |
| 11 | Gibbs James | Wife | M | Mu | 35 | M | Georgia | Georgia | Georgia | Cotton Sampler | Compress |
| 12 | — Hattie | Daughter | F | Mu | 23 | S | Georgia | Georgia | Georgia | None | |
| 13 | — Irine | Daughter | F | Mu | 9 | S | Georgia | Georgia | Georgia | None | |
| 14 | — Walter | Son | M | Mu | 6 | S | Georgia | Georgia | Georgia | None | |
| 15 | — Carrie Mae | Daughter | F | Mu | 5 | S | Georgia | Georgia | Georgia | None | |
| 16 | Johnson Walter | Head | M | B | 38 | M | Georgia | Georgia | Georgia | Nightwatchman | Public Building |
| 17 | — Annie | Wife | F | B | 35 | M | Georgia | Georgia | Georgia | None | |
| 18 | Harrington James | Son | M | B | 22 | S | Georgia | Georgia | Georgia | Presser | Tailorshop |
| 19 | — Doris | Daughter | F | B | 19 | S | Georgia | Georgia | Georgia | Maid | Hotel |
| 20 | Brantley Lamar | Head | M | B | 31 | M | Georgia | Georgia | Georgia | Laborer | Bag factory |
| 21 | — Lila | Wife | F | B | 29 | M | Georgia | Georgia | Georgia | None | |
| 22 | — Willie Ruth | Daughter | F | B | 7 | S | Georgia | Georgia | Georgia | None | |
| 23 | — William | Son | M | B | 6 | S | Georgia | Georgia | Georgia | None | |
| 24 | — Florence | Daughter | F | B | 7/12 | S | Georgia | Georgia | Georgia | None | |
| 25 | — Letha Lee | Cousin | F | B | 18 | S | Georgia | Georgia | Georgia | Laundress | Steam laundry |
| 26 | — Gelagie | Cousin | M | B | 26 | S | Georgia | Georgia | Georgia | Laborer | Bag factory |
| 27 | Robertson Thomas | Lodger | M | B | 35 | S | Georgia | Georgia | Georgia | Laborer | Bag factory |
| 28 | Powell Laughlin | Head | M | Mu | 27 | M | Georgia | Georgia | Georgia | Tailor | Tailorshop |
| 29 | — Irene | Wife | F | Mu | 25 | M | Georgia | Georgia | Georgia | Dressmaker | Own home |
| 30 | — Laughlin Jr. | Son | M | Mu | 4 | S | Georgia | Georgia | Georgia | None | |
| 31 | — Edith | Daughter | F | Mu | 2 | S | Georgia | Georgia | Georgia | None | |
| 32 | Dickson Julia | Head | F | B | [illegible] | S | Georgia | Georgia | Georgia | Maid | Private family |
| 33 | — Willie | Niece | F | B | 26 | M | Georgia | Georgia | Georgia | Cook | Private family |
| 34 | Kerling Florida | Lodger | F | Mu | 21 | S | Florida | Florida | Florida | Stenographer | Office |
| 35 | Love Lelia | Head | F | B | 31 | S | Georgia | Georgia | Georgia | Cook | Private family |
| 36 | Sims Rosa | Cousin | F | B | 31 | S | Georgia | Georgia | Georgia | Cook | Private family |
| 37 | Nixon Susie | Head | F | B | 40 | Wd | Georgia | Georgia | Georgia | Janitress | School |
| 38 | Gilbert Henry | Son-in-law | M | B | 27 | M | Georgia | Georgia | Georgia | [illegible] | Public works |
| 39 | — Lucile | Daughter | F | B | 21 | M | Georgia | Georgia | Georgia | None | |
| 40 | — William | Grandson | M | B | 1 | S | Georgia | Georgia | Georgia | None | |
| 41 | Cleveland Edward | Head | M | B | 65 | M | Georgia | Georgia | Georgia | Carpenter | House |
| 42 | — Mamie L. | Wife | F | B | 29 | M | Georgia | Georgia | Georgia | Hairdresser | Own home |
| 43 | Carey Carter | Brother-in-law | M | B | 18 | S | Georgia | Georgia | Georgia | Laborer | Bakery |
| 44 | — Alice J. | Sister-in-law | F | B | 16 | S | Georgia | Georgia | Georgia | None | |
| 45 | Carter Rosetta | Grandmother | F | B | 65 | Wd | Georgia | Georgia | Georgia | Laundress | Own home |
| 46 | Blackman Mamie | Head | F | W | 45 | Wd | Georgia | Georgia | Georgia | None | |
| 47 | Shinos Pete | Head | M | W | 29 | S | Greece (Greek) | Greece (Greek) | Greece (Greek) | Proprietor | Soda fountain |
| 48 | — Angelus | Brother | M | W | 20 | S | Greece (Greek) | Greece (Greek) | Greece (Greek) | Partner | Soda fountain |
| 49 | Dorsey Will | Head | M | B | 48 | M | Georgia | Georgia | Georgia | Driver | Grade wagon |
| 50 | — Bessie | Wife | F | B | 40 | M | Georgia | Georgia | Georgia | None | |

ancestry library edition

## 1920 United States Federal Census

| | |
|---|---|
| Name: | **James C Mccall** |
| Age: | 31 |
| Birth Year: | abt 1889 |
| Birthplace: | Georgia |
| Home in 1920: | Houston Ward 5, Harris, Texas |
| Race: | Mulatto |
| Gender: | Male |
| Relation to Head of House: | Cousin |
| Marital Status: | Single |
| Father's Birthplace: | Texas |
| Mother's Birthplace: | Texas |
| Able to Read: | Yes |
| Able to Write: | Yes |
| Neighbors: | |

Household Members:

| Name | Age |
|---|---|
| Alisa Z Hester | 52 |
| Julia C Hester | 44 |
| James C Mccall | 31 |

**Source Citation:** Year: *1920*; Census Place: *Houston Ward 5, Harris, Texas*; Roll: *T625_1814*; Page: *13A*; Enumeration District: *86*; Image: *734*.

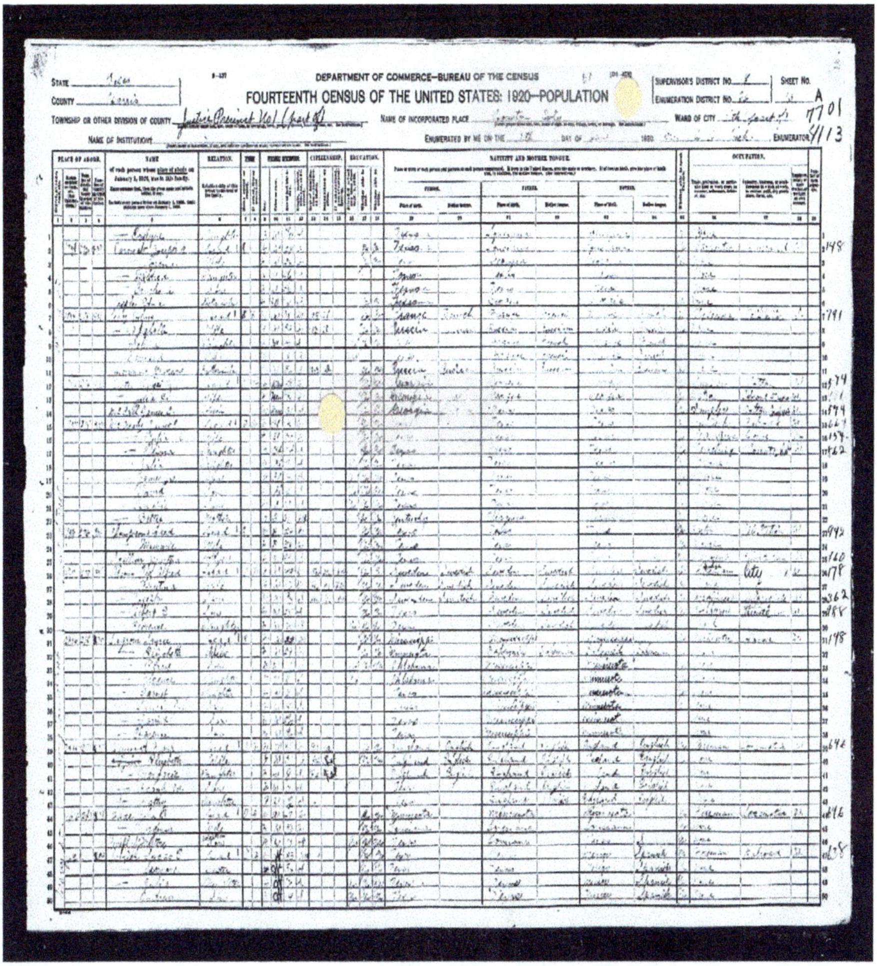
DEPARTMENT OF COMMERCE—BUREAU OF THE CENSUS

FOURTEENTH CENSUS OF THE UNITED STATES: 1920—POPULATION

STATE

COUNTY

TOWNSHIP OR OTHER DIVISION OF COUNTY

NAME OF INSTITUTION

NAME OF INCORPORATED PLACE

ENUMERATED BY ME ON THE DAY OF 1920.

SUPERVISOR'S DISTRICT NO.

ENUMERATION DISTRICT NO.

SHEET NO.

WARD OF CITY

ENUMERATOR

PLACE OF ABODE. NAME. RELATION. TENURE. PERSONAL DESCRIPTION. CITIZENSHIP. EDUCATION. NATIVITY AND MOTHER TONGUE. OCCUPATION.

ancestry.com

## 1920 United States Federal Census

| | |
|---|---|
| Name: | **Milas Waller** **[Thelas Walter]** **[Milas Wallar]** |
| Home in 1920: | Atlanta Ward 10, Fulton, Georgia |
| Age: | 42 |
| Estimated Birth Year: | abt 1878 |
| Birthplace: | Georgia |
| Relation to Head of House: | Self (Head) [Head] |
| Spouse's Name: | Lula Waller |
| Father's Birth Place: | Georgia |
| Mother's Birth Place: | Georgia |
| Marital Status: | Married |
| Race: | Black [Colored (Black)] |
| Sex: | Male |
| Home owned: | Rent |
| Able to read: | Yes |
| Able to Write: | Yes |
| Neighbors: | |

Household Members:

| Name | Age |
|---|---|
| Milas Waller | 42 |
| Lula Waller | 37 |
| Ethel Waller | 13 |
| Milas Waller | 10 |
| Mattie Waller | 7 |
| Annie Waller | 5 |

**Source Citation:** Year: *1920*;Census Place: *Atlanta Ward 10, Fulton, Georgia*; Roll: *T625_250*; Page: *5B*; Enumeration District: *143*; Image: *983*.

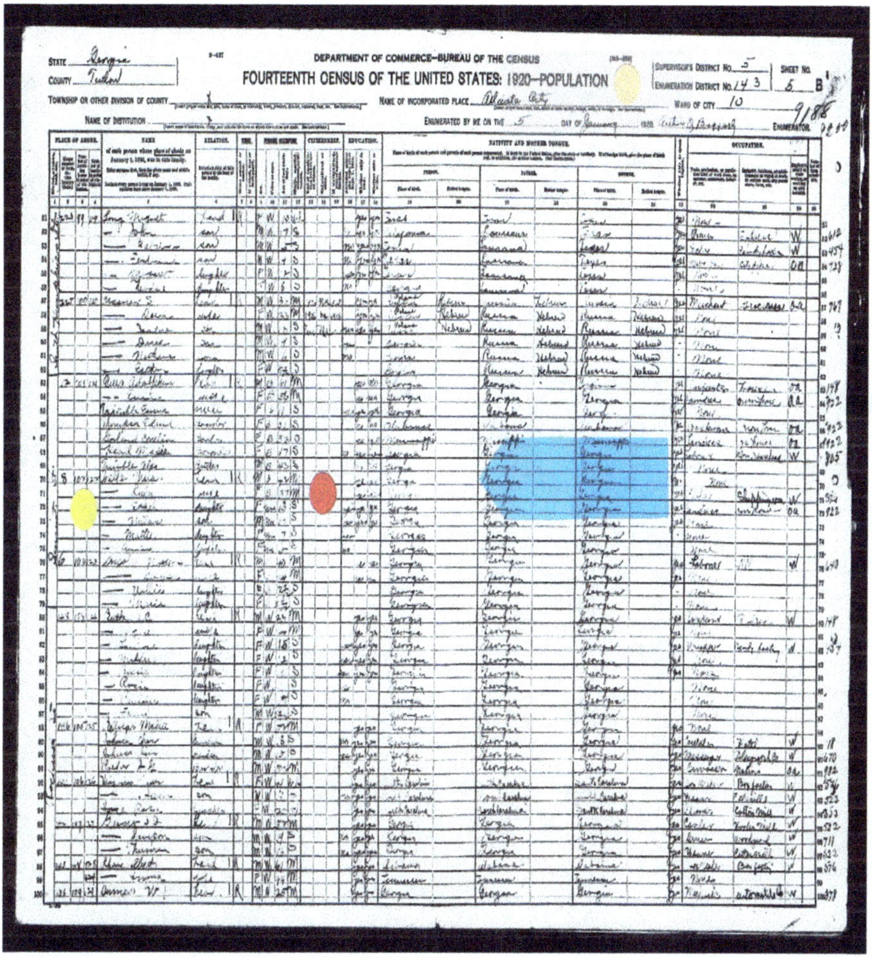
STATE Georgia
COUNTY Fulton
TOWNSHIP OR OTHER DIVISION OF COUNTY
NAME OF INSTITUTION
DEPARTMENT OF COMMERCE—BUREAU OF THE CENSUS
FOURTEENTH CENSUS OF THE UNITED STATES: 1920—POPULATION
NAME OF INCORPORATED PLACE Atlanta City
ENUMERATED BY ME ON THE 5 DAY OF January, 1920.
SUPERVISOR'S DISTRICT NO. 5
ENUMERATION DISTRICT NO. 143
SHEET NO. 5 B
WARD OF CITY 10
ENUMERATOR.
PLACE OF ABODE. NAME. RELATION. TENURE. PERSONAL DESCRIPTION. CITIZENSHIP. EDUCATION. NATIVITY AND MOTHER TONGUE. OCCUPATION.

ancestry.com

## 1920 United States Federal Census

| | |
|---|---|
| Name: | **John A Walker** |
| Home in 1920: | Macon Ward 1, Bibb, Georgia |
| Age: | 38 |
| Estimated Birth Year: | abt 1882 |
| Birthplace: | Georgia |
| Relation to Head of House: | Self (Head) [Head] |
| Spouse's Name: | Viola M Walker |
| Father's Birth Place: | Georgia |
| Mother's Birth Place: | Georgia |
| Marital Status: | Married |
| Race: | Black |
| Sex: | Male |
| Home owned: | Own |
| Able to read: | Yes |
| Able to Write: | Yes |
| Neighbors: | |
| Household Members: | |

| Name | Age |
|---|---|
| John A Walker | 38 |
| Viola M Walker | 34 |
| Martha M Walker | 11 |
| Elsie E Walker | 8 |
| John A Walker | 7 |

**Source Citation:** Year: *1920*;Census Place: *Macon Ward 1, Bibb, Georgia*; Roll: *T625_235*; Page: *6B*; Enumeration District: *16*; Image: *617*.

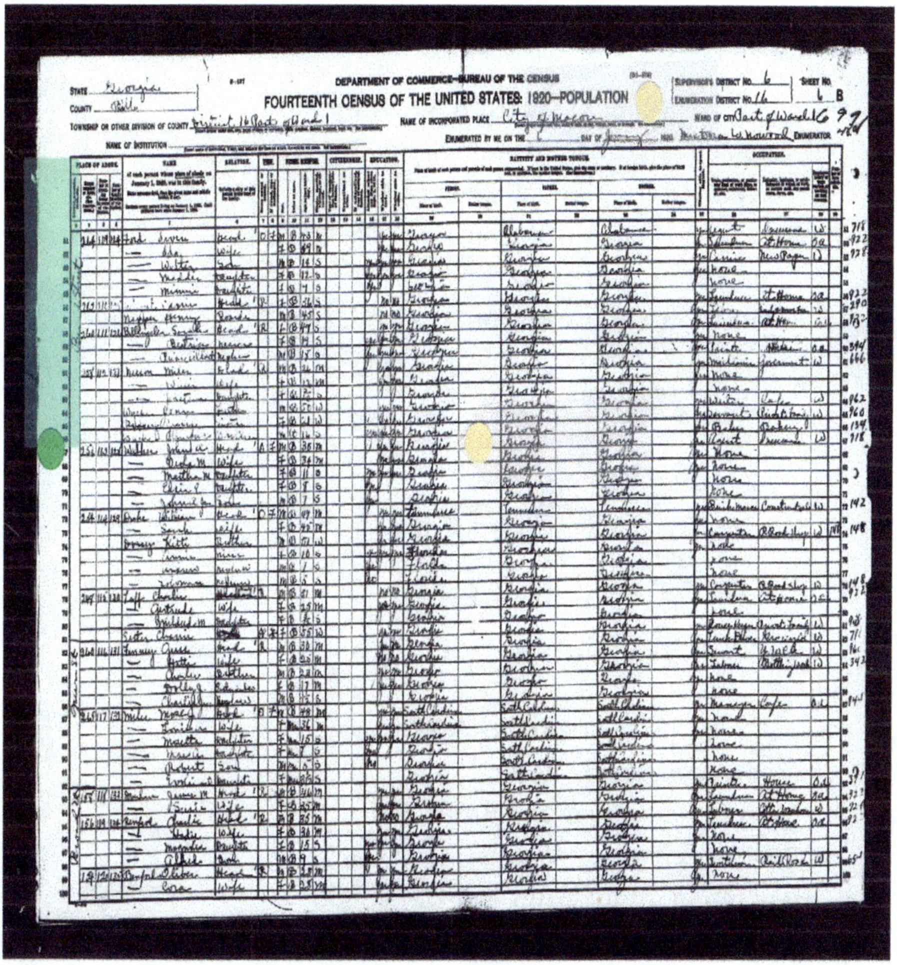

DEPARTMENT OF COMMERCE—BUREAU OF THE CENSUS

FOURTEENTH CENSUS OF THE UNITED STATES: 1920—POPULATION

STATE Georgia

COUNTY Bibb

TOWNSHIP OR OTHER DIVISION OF COUNTY District 16 Part of Ward 1

NAME OF INCORPORATED PLACE City of Macon

NAME OF INSTITUTION

SUPERVISOR'S DISTRICT NO. 6

ENUMERATION DISTRICT NO. 16

SHEET NO. 6 B

WARD OF CITY Part of Ward 1

ENUMERATED BY ME ON THE 6 DAY OF January 1920 ENUMERATOR

ancestry.com

U.S. City Directories, 1821-1989 (Beta)

| | |
|---|---|
| Name: | **John A Walker** |
| Residence Year: | 1920 |
| Street Address: | 256 Broad EM |
| Residence Place: | Macon, Georgia |
| Occupation: | Agt |
| Publication Title: | Macon, Georgia, City Directory, 1920 |

**Source Information:**
Ancestry.com. *U.S. City Directories, 1821-1989 (Beta)* [database on-line]. Provo, UT, USA: Ancestry.com Operations, Inc., 2011.

ancestry.com

U.S. City Directories, 1821-1989 (Beta)

| | |
|---|---|
| Name: | **John A Walker** |
| Residence Year: | 1922 |
| Street Address: | 256 Broad EM |
| Residence Place: | Macon, Georgia |
| Occupation: | Agt |
| Publication Title: | Macon, Georgia, City Directory, 1922 |

**Source Information:**
Ancestry.com. *U.S. City Directories, 1821-1989 (Beta)* [database on-line]. Provo, UT, USA: Ancestry.com Operations, Inc., 2011.

BARRON & REAGAN
FEDERAL TAX COUNSELLORS
Income and Estate Tax Returns Given Special Attention
519-520 Bibb Realty Bldg.—Telephone 213

851 (1922) R. L. POLK & CO.'S

MACON SEWER PIPE WORKS Telephone 617
MANUFACTURERS OF SEWER PIPE, FLUE LINING, WALL COPING, DRAIN TILE

*Walker Frank, porter, h 161 Grant av
*Walker Freddie, lab, h 234 Bostick's al
*Walker Frederick, lab, h 410 Mitchell's al
*Walker Garfield, lab, r 80 Wilder, SM
*Walker Geddie, maid 587 College
*Walker George (m), carp, h 255 4th av, V
Walker George S, mach, r 603 Plum
Walker Gladys, r 103 Latta pl
Walker Gladys, nurse Oglethorpe Private Infirmary
Walker G Albert (Fannie), tchr, h 115 Crescent av
*Walker Henrietta, cook, r 70 Schofield
*Walker Henrietta, lndrs, h 261 Chestnut
*Walker Henry D Rev, h 238 1st av, V
Walker Homer, mill opr, r 27 Adams B
Walker Horace D (Lelia), route agt Am Ry Express, h 36 Arlington pl
*Walker Ida, lndrs, h 436 Hammond
*Walker Irene, dom, r 193 Ellis av
*Walker Jacob W, lab, h 162 Paradise al
*Walker James, driver, h 1 Smith's al
*Walker James, lab, r 220 Daley's Ditch

A 75c Bottle Makes a Quart
PYORAL
THE BEST MOUTH WASH
If your gums are not a healthy pink, firm, and elastic. If they bleed on slight provocation, THEY ARE UNHEALTHY. This is a danger signal. See your dentist AND USE PYORAL DAILY. For sale at your Druggist's.

*Walker James (m), lab, h 534 Kahn's al
*Walker James (m), lab, h 46 Massee la
*Walker James jr, lab Cherokee Brick Co, r 46 Massee la
*Walker James (m), lab, h 25 Reid
*Walker James E (m), carp, h 115 Jones
*Walker James H (m), farmer, h 460 Clinton
Walker James N (Laura), coppersmith, h 1520 3d
*Walker Janie, lndrs, r 1236 Broadway
Walker Jarrell (Elizabeth), insp, r 1331 Broadway
*Walker Jefferson (m), watchmn W R Richardson, h 780 Lexington av
*Walker Jessie, presser Union Dry Goods Co, r 168 2d av
*Walker John (m), lab, h 214 Edison, EM
*Walker John (m), lab, h 193 Ellis av
*Walker John A, agt Atlanta Mutual Ins Co, r 256 Broad, EM
Walker John H (Ruth; Macon Cycle Co), h 121 Garden

Morgan & Morgan Insurance Agency
GENERAL INSURANCE
601 BIBB BUILDING
TELEPHONE 4147

A Trip To ENGLAND
THE CHIROPRACTOR
Will Remove the CAUSE of Your Disease
815 BIBB REALTY BLDG. PHONE 4557

MACON CITY DIRECTORY 855

*WALKER JOHN H (m), Pres Peoples Drug Co and V-Pres Liberty Savings & Real Estate Corporation, h 380 Monroe
Walker John R jr, student, r 210 Coleman av
*Walker Jonas (m), lab, h 522 Elbert
*Walker Joseph, lab, r 46 Massee la
*Walker Joseph (m), lab, h 416 Stein's al
*Walker Josephine M, tchr Pleasant Hill School, r 320 Middle
Walker Julia (wid John C), h 667 Oak
*Walker Julia, lndrs, r 4 Stewart's la
Walker J Clay (Analou), prof Mercer University, h same
Walker J Edward (Ruth), dentist 904 Casualty bldg, res Rivoli, Ga
Walker Katherine, student, r 750 2d
*Walker Laura J, lndrs, r 211 Green
*Walker Lee (m), mill wkr, h 339 Elbert
Walker Lewis A (May), pres Macon Cigar & Tobacco Co, h 336 Napier av
*Walker Lillian, r 46 Massee la
*Walker Lillian, lndrs, h 1226 1st
*Walker Lizzie, cook, h 116 Wood's al

CABINET MANTELS, TILE, GRATES, ETC.,
Willingham Sash & Door Co.
OFFICE, 457 THIRD STREET TELEPHONES 278 AND 3976

*Walker Loda, lndrs, h 21 Holt's al
*Walker Lula, lndrs, h 1229 Tracey's al
*Walker Lurinda, cook, 314 College
*Walker Mamie, cook, h 904 Hazel
Walker Marie, student, r 1520 3d
Walker Marie E, r 852 Orange
Walker Marion, mill opr, r 27 Adams B
*Walker Mary, cook, h 149 Lincoln
*Walker Mary, dom, 515 Napier av
*Walker Mary, lndrs, r 424 Long's la
Walker Mary S (wid Sanders), h 213 High
Walker Maud Mrs, mill opr, r 862 3d
*Walker Maxie, maid Y R Coleman
Walker Minnie, mill opr, r 27 Adams, B
*Walker Minnie, lndrs, r 80 Wilder SM
*Walker Minnie, maid, r 1064 Cole's al
Walker Olin, r 1520 3d
*Walker Pearl, dom, r 216 Lynwood av
*Walker Peter (m), lab, h 442 Gilmer
*Walker Pomp (m), porter, h 114 Roosevelt
Walker Raymond, student, r 1356 Edgewood av
*Walker Richard F (m), brk mason, h 132 Jones
*Walker Robert, butler, r 367 College

**1922 Macon City Directory Listing of John A. Walker**

# Georgia Deaths, 1914-1927 for John Walker

| | |
|---|---|
| Name: | John Walker |
| Titles and Terms: | |
| Death Date: | 01 Nov 1922 |
| Estimated Death Year: | |
| Age at Death: | 45 years |
| Death Place: | Macon, Bibb, Georgia, United States |
| Birth Date: | |
| Estimated Birth Year: | 1877 |
| Birthplace: | Houston Ga. |
| Gender: | Male |
| Marital Status: | Married |
| Race or Color (Expanded): | Negro |
| Race: | Black |
| Ethnicity: | American |
| Spouse's Name: | Viola Walker |
| Spouse's Titles & Terms: | |
| Fathers Name: | J A Walker |
| Father's Titles & Terms: | Sr |
| Mother's Name: | Emma |
| Mother's Titles & Terms: | |
| Film Number: | 2320111 |
| Digital Folder Number: | 4176528 |
| Image Number: | 00841 |
| Reference Number: | 28070 |

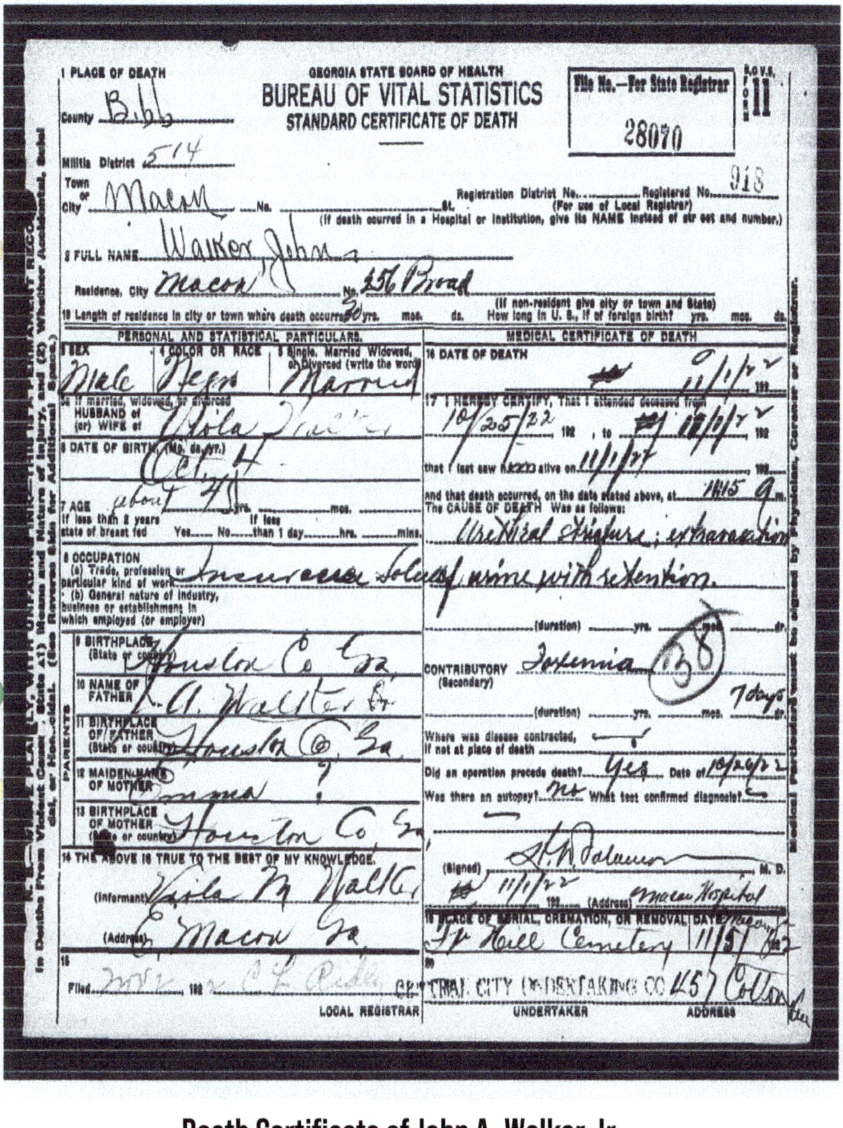

1 PLACE OF DEATH

GEORGIA STATE BOARD OF HEALTH
BUREAU OF VITAL STATISTICS
STANDARD CERTIFICATE OF DEATH

File No.—For State Registrar 28070

County Bibb

Militia District 514

Town or City Macon No. St. Registration District No. Registered No. 918 (For use of Local Registrar)
(If death occurred in a Hospital or Institution, give its NAME instead of street and number.)

2 FULL NAME Walker, John

Residence, City Macon No. 256 Broad (If non-resident give city or town and State)

18 Length of residence in city or town where death occurred 30 yrs. mos. ds. How long in U. S., if of foreign birth? yrs. mos. ds.

PERSONAL AND STATISTICAL PARTICULARS

3 SEX Male

4 COLOR OR RACE Negro

5 Single, Married, Widowed, or Divorced (write the word) Married

5a If married, widowed, or divorced HUSBAND of (or) WIFE of Viola Walker

6 DATE OF BIRTH (Mo., day, yr.) Oct. 4

7 AGE about 45 yrs. mos. ds. If less than 2 years state of breast fed Yes No If less than 1 day hrs. mins.

8 OCCUPATION (a) Trade, profession or particular kind of work Insurance Solicitor (b) General nature of industry, business or establishment in which employed (or employer)

9 BIRTHPLACE (State or country) Houston Co. Ga.

10 NAME OF FATHER J. A. Walker Sr.

11 BIRTHPLACE OF FATHER (State or country) Houston Co. Ga.

12 MAIDEN NAME OF MOTHER Emma ?

13 BIRTHPLACE OF MOTHER (State or country) Houston Co. Ga.

14 THE ABOVE IS TRUE TO THE BEST OF MY KNOWLEDGE.
(Informant) Viola M. Walker
(Address) E. Macon Ga.

Filed 11/1/22 192 C. L. Ridley LOCAL REGISTRAR

MEDICAL CERTIFICATE OF DEATH

16 DATE OF DEATH 11/1/22

17 I HEREBY CERTIFY, That I attended deceased from 10/25/22 192 , to 11/1/22 192
that I last saw him alive on 11/1/22 192
and that death occurred, on the date stated above, at 11:15 a.m.
The CAUSE OF DEATH was as follows:
Urethral Stricture; extravasation of urine with retention.
(duration) yrs. mos. ds.
CONTRIBUTORY (Secondary) Toxemia
(duration) yrs. mos. 7 days
Where was disease contracted, if not at place of death —
Did an operation precede death? Yes Date of 10/26/22
Was there an autopsy? No What test confirmed diagnosis? —
(Signed) A. W. Palmer M. D.
11/1/22 192 (Address) Macon Hospital

19 PLACE OF BURIAL, CREMATION, OR REMOVAL Ft. Hill Cemetery DATE OF BURIAL 11/5/22

20 UNDERTAKER Central City Undertaking Co. ADDRESS 457 Cotton Ave.

Death Certificate of John A. Walker, Jr.

ancestry.com

## U.S. City Directories, 1821-1989 (Beta)

| | |
|---|---|
| Name: | **Viola Walker** |
| Residence Year: | 1922 |
| Street Address: | 211 Green |
| Residence Place: | Macon, Georgia |
| Occupation: | Dom |
| Publication Title: | Macon, Georgia, City Directory, 1922 |

**Source Information:**
Ancestry.com. *U.S. City Directories, 1821-1989 (Beta)* [database on-line]. Provo, UT, USA: Ancestry.com Operations, Inc., 2011.

**Widow Viola Walker by Nov 1922**

A natural by-product of the Directory business is the compilation of Mailing Lists. If interested, ask for our Free "List of Mailing Lists." R. L. POLK & CO., Detroit

856 (1922) R. L. POLK & CO.'S

*Walker Robert (m), fireman, h 241 Jackson
Walker Robert L (Alice V), grocer 1020 Ash, h same
Walker Robert L, mus tchr, h 506 Orange
*Walker Ruby, lndrs, h 1 Alabama
*Walker Rufus, lab, r 46 Massee la
*Walker Samuel A, grocer, r 460 Clinton
*Walker Sansie, lab, r 780 Lexington av
*Walker Solomon (m), lab, h 124 Edison, EM
*Walker Stephen (m), lab, h 112 4th av, V
Walker Thomas D jr (Margaret T), phys 1019 Ga Casualty bldg, h 253 Boulevard, NH
Walker Thomas L, pharm Chapman's Pharmacy, r Y M C A
Walker Thomas M (Vesta), architect, r 412 Walnut
*Walker Viola, dom, r 211 Green
Walker Watson (Eunice), asst county engineer, h 215 Carling av
Walker Wm B, shipper Armour & Co, r 280 Orange
Walker Wm F (Minnie L), slsmn McCommon Bros, h 1525 3d
*Walker Willie, lndrs, h 604 May av, U
*Walker Wilson (m), lab, r 240 Concord, SM
*Walker Winston (m), lab, h 211 Green

LIFE INSURANCE ONLY J. G. JACKSON LIFE INSURANCE COUNSELOR 208 Cits. & Sou. Bk. Blg. Tels. 3987-2000-W

*Walker Winston (m), mason, h 140 Roosevelt
*Walker Winston (m), porter Union Dry Goods Co, h 1232 2d
*Walker & Green (Arthur Walker, Edgar Green), shoemkrs 363½ Broadway
Wall Allan B Rev (Mattie), pastor East Macon Methodist Church, h 104 Church, EM
Wall Alonzo L, r 106 Latta pl
Wall Benjamin F (Bessie), mill opr, r 321 Shamrock
Wall Harris C, plmbr, r 206 Hydrola
*Wall John H (Lottie), lab, h 410 Railroad av
Wall Joseph A (Sarah B), flagmn, h 106 Latta pl
WALL J "BRAD" (Zeta), V-Pres Peacock Auto Supply Co, h 142 Pierce
Wall J Lowe (Lillian), sslmn, h 129 Pierce av
*Wall Lucy, dom, h 152 Clara
*Wall Sydney, lab, r 410 Railroad
*Wall Thomas, agt North Carolina Mutual Life Ins Co
Wall Wm (Mollie), com trav, r 742 Walnut
Wall Wm C (Cyntha A), carp, h 2344 2d
Wall Wm L, baker Barker System of Bakeries, r 2344 2d
Wallace see also Wallis

THE MORE PRINTING YOU BUY OF US THE BETTER WE WILL BOTH BE SATISFIED THE J. W. BURKE COMPANY MACON, GEORGIA "The South's Most Modern Print Shop"

MACON CITY DIRECTORY 857

*Wallace Alonzo (m), chauf, h 1 Carling av
*Wallace Anna, h 156 Madison
Wallace Bailey (Edna), mill opr, h 20 Shell av
*Wallace Benjamin, lab, r Monroe Hill
Wallace Carrie W (wid Ludrick H), r 552 1st
Wallace David C (Lorena), sec-treas C H Bateman Co, h 227 Chappell
Wallace Edgar B (Mary B), mech, h 115 Feb av
Wallace Edith, sten, r 862 Cherry
*Wallace Edna, cook, r 455 4th av, V
*Wallace Edna M, dom, r 142 Middle
Wallace Edna P, student, r 115 Feb av
Wallace Elise, clk of Ga Ry, r 28 Arlington pl
Wallace Essie B, mill wkr, r 114 (631) Holt av Napier Hts
*Wallace Fannie, cook, r Monroe Hill
Wallace George F, mach, r 121 Broadway
*Wallace Glenn (m), lab, r 156 College
*Wallace Gussie, lndrs, h 218 Jones
*Wallace Henry, porter, h 313 Hazel
Wallace John T (Mary), carp, r 104 American blvd, B
Wallace Laura M, r 552 1st
*Wallace Mary, h 4 Dasher's al

Chero-Cola MACON Chero-Cola Bottling Co. F. E. Land J. J. Willa

*Wallace Mary, lndrs, r 10 Cole's al
Wallace Milton K, student, r 1356 Edgewood av
Wallace Nora, dom, r 739 Hawthorne
Wallace Otis B (Bennie), formn, h 102 Park av, CP
*Wallace Rufus (m), lab, h 349 Craft la
*Wallace Rufus (m), lab, h Monroe Hill
Wallace Vernon, student, r 20 (1421) Lawton av
Wallace Walter E (Ruth), boilermkr, h 215 Chappell
Wallace Wm H (Sophia S), eng, r 771 Oak
Wallace Wm W, cond Sou Ry, r 161 Broadway
Wallenstein Stanley (Deborah), slsmn, h 324 Hill Crest av
*Waller Anthony (m), lab, h 15 Glenn
Waller Benjamin I (Caroline), eng, h 1518 Broadway
Waller Bryan, clk, r 604 1st
*Waller Caroline, lndrs, r 614 Ross
Waller Ella F Mrs, r 717 1st
Waller Garrett H (Sidney L), cond, h 1045 College
Waller George (Annie), millwright, h 419 Hazel
Waller Harry H, student, r 1518 Broadway
Waller John K (Belle), opr Dixie Roll & Cot Co Inc, r 623 Main, EM
Waller Mattie, student, r 419 Hazel

# Georgia Deaths, 1914-1927 for Emma Swift

| | |
|---|---|
| Name: | Emma Swift |
| Titles and Terms: | |
| Death Date: | 03 Dec 1922 |
| Estimated Death Year: | |
| Age at Death: | 76 years |
| Death Place: | Atlanta, Fulton, Georgia, United States |
| Birth Date: | |
| Estimated Birth Year: | 1846 |
| Birthplace: | Ga |
| Gender: | Female |
| Marital Status: | Married |
| Race or Color (Expanded): | Colored |
| Race: | Black |
| Ethnicity: | American |
| Spouse's Name: | Jefferson Swift |
| Spouse's Titles & Terms: | |
| Fathers Name: | Alex Nixon |
| Father's Titles & Terms: | |
| Mother's Name: | Grace Felder |
| Mother's Titles & Terms: | |
| Film Number: | 2320114 |
| Digital Folder Number: | 4176522 |
| Image Number: | 00936 |

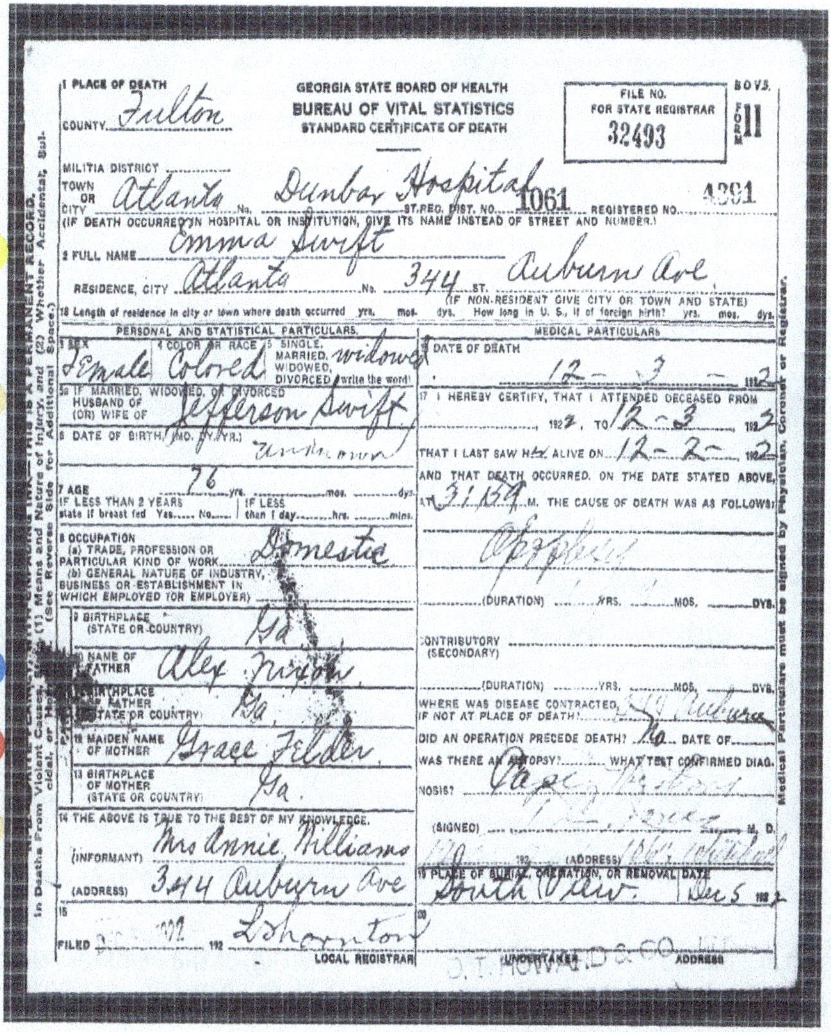

1 PLACE OF DEATH
COUNTY Fulton

GEORGIA STATE BOARD OF HEALTH
BUREAU OF VITAL STATISTICS
STANDARD CERTIFICATE OF DEATH

FILE NO. FOR STATE REGISTRAR 32493

MILITIA DISTRICT
TOWN OR CITY Atlanta No. Dunbar Hospital ST. REG. DIST. NO. 1061 REGISTERED NO. 4391
(IF DEATH OCCURRED IN HOSPITAL OR INSTITUTION, GIVE ITS NAME INSTEAD OF STREET AND NUMBER.)

2 FULL NAME Emma Swift
RESIDENCE, CITY Atlanta No. 344 ST. Auburn Ave
(IF NON-RESIDENT GIVE CITY OR TOWN AND STATE)
18 Length of residence in city or town where death occurred yrs. mos. dys. How long in U. S., if of foreign birth? yrs. mos. dys.

PERSONAL AND STATISTICAL PARTICULARS

3 SEX Female
4 COLOR OR RACE Colored
5 SINGLE, MARRIED, WIDOWED, DIVORCED (write the word) widow
5a IF MARRIED, WIDOWED, OR DIVORCED HUSBAND OF (OR) WIFE OF Jefferson Swift
6 DATE OF BIRTH (MO. DY. YR.) Unknown
7 AGE 76 yrs. mos. dys.
IF LESS THAN 2 YEARS state if breast fed Yes No IF LESS than 1 day hrs. mins.
8 OCCUPATION (a) TRADE, PROFESSION OR PARTICULAR KIND OF WORK Domestic
(b) GENERAL NATURE OF INDUSTRY, BUSINESS OR ESTABLISHMENT IN WHICH EMPLOYED (OR EMPLOYER)
9 BIRTHPLACE (STATE OR COUNTRY) Ga
10 NAME OF FATHER Alex Nixon
11 BIRTHPLACE OF FATHER (STATE OR COUNTRY) Ga
12 MAIDEN NAME OF MOTHER Grace Felder
13 BIRTHPLACE OF MOTHER (STATE OR COUNTRY) Ga.
14 THE ABOVE IS TRUE TO THE BEST OF MY KNOWLEDGE.
(INFORMANT) Mrs Annie Williams
(ADDRESS) 344 Auburn Ave
15
FILED 192 L Thornton
LOCAL REGISTRAR

MEDICAL PARTICULARS

16 DATE OF DEATH 12 - 3 - 1922
17 I HEREBY CERTIFY, THAT I ATTENDED DECEASED FROM 1922, TO 12 - 3 1922
THAT I LAST SAW HER ALIVE ON 12 - 2 - 1922
AND THAT DEATH OCCURRED, ON THE DATE STATED ABOVE, AT 3:15 P M. THE CAUSE OF DEATH WAS AS FOLLOWS:
[illegible]
(DURATION) YRS. MOS. DYS.
CONTRIBUTORY (SECONDARY)
(DURATION) YRS. MOS. DYS.
WHERE WAS DISEASE CONTRACTED, IF NOT AT PLACE OF DEATH? 344 Auburn
DID AN OPERATION PRECEDE DEATH? No DATE OF
WAS THERE AN AUTOPSY? WHAT TEST CONFIRMED DIAGNOSIS? [illegible]
(SIGNED) [illegible] M. D.
192 (ADDRESS) [illegible]
19 PLACE OF BURIAL, CREMATION, OR REMOVAL South View DATE Dec 5 1922
20
UNDERTAKER D. T. HOWARD & CO. ADDRESS

BOVS. FORM 11

In Deaths From Violent Causes, State (1) Means and Nature of Injury, and (2) Whether Accidental, Suicidal, or Homicidal. (See Reverse Side for Additional Space.)

Medical Particulars must be signed by Physician, Coroner or Registrar.

DAY AGE LOT RANGE GRAVE SECTION BLOCK PLATT MORTUARY

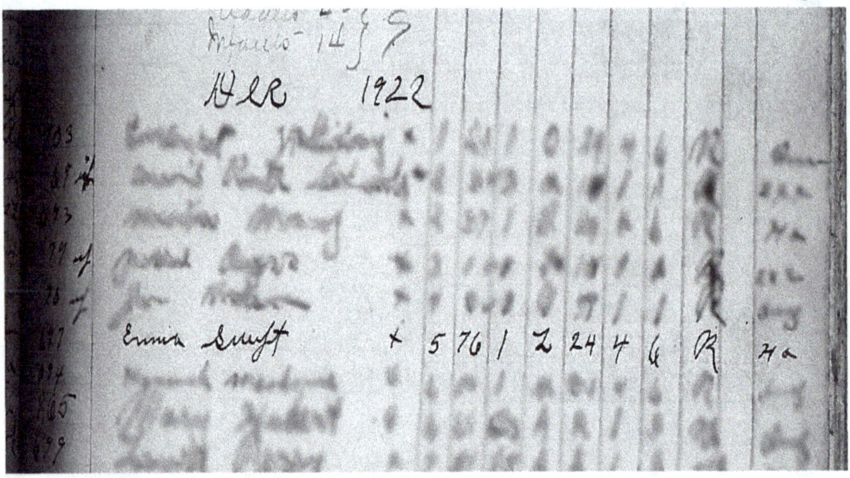


**Emma Felder Swift & her son, Milous Wilburn Walker, Sr.**

**Both are buried on PUBLIC GROUND. This is a section of the cemetery donated to families to bury their loved ones without any cost. The exception to this is that it is the responsibility of the families to remember the location and maintain the area. The cemetery charges a $20 per year fee if you are trying to locate the gravesite.**

**South View Cemetery Atlanta, Fulton Co., Georgia**

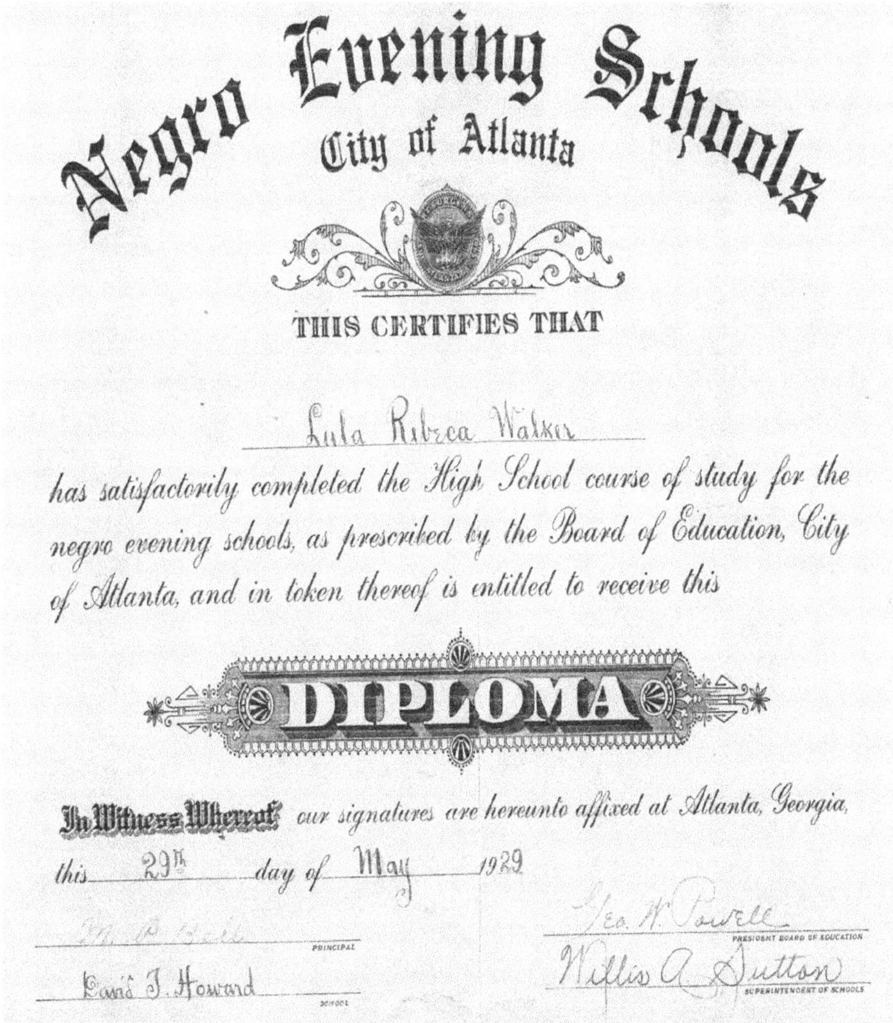

Negro Evening Schools

City of Atlanta

THIS CERTIFIES THAT

Lula Ribeca Walker

has satisfactorily completed the High School course of study for the negro evening schools, as prescribed by the Board of Education, City of Atlanta, and in token thereof is entitled to receive this

DIPLOMA

In Witness Whereof our signatures are hereunto affixed at Atlanta, Georgia, this 29th day of May 1929

[illegible] PRINCIPAL

David T. Howard SCHOOL

Geo. W. Powell PRESIDENT BOARD OF EDUCATION

Willis A. Sutton SUPERINTENDENT OF SCHOOLS

Criminal Minutes Superior Court, Bibb County, NOVEMBER Term, 1929

THE STATE : NO. 933 NOVEMBER TERM, 1929
VS : BIBB SUPERIOR COURT
QUINNET SANDERS : BURGLARY

Lee Battle, Prosecutor Witnesses: Lee Battle, Off. Bowden, Off. Carroll

J. E. Yates, Foreman Chas. H. Garrett, Sol.General

------------oOo------------

THE STATE : NO. 935NOVEMBER TERM, 1929
VS : BIBB SUPERIOR COURT
JOHN WALKER : SIMPLE LARCENY

Dalton Lucas, Prosecutor Witnesses: Dalton Lucas, Off. Branan

J. E. Yates, Foreman Chas. H. Garrett, Sol. General

------------oOo------------

THE STATE : NO. 935 NOVEMBER TERM, 1929
VS : BIBB SUPERIOR COURT
JOHN WALKER : PLEA & SENTENCE

Plea.

1. The Defendant waives being arraigned, and pleads guilty.

This 5th day of Dec. 1929.

Chas. H. Garrett, Sol.General

Sentence.

Indictment for Simple Larceny of Cow.

Tried at November Term, 1929 and Plea of Guilty.

The Defendant being before the Bar of the Court and showing no reason why the sentence of the Court should not be pronounced,

It is Ordered and Adjudged by the Court

That the said John Walker do work in the Chain Gang, on the Public Works of said County, for the term of Twelve months, to be computed from the date he is received by the Superintendent of Public Works,

It is Further Ordered, That the said defendant be committed to the common Jail of said County, there to be kept in close custody, until he shall be demanded by the Superintendent of Public Works of said County.

In Open Court, this 5th day of December, 1929.

Malcolm D. Jones, Judge SCMC

------------oOo------------

ancestry library edition

## 1930 United States Federal Census

| | |
|---|---|
| Name: | **John Walker** |
| Gender: | Male |
| Birth Year: | abt 1911 |
| Birthplace: | Georgia |
| Race: | Negro (Black) [Black] |
| Home in 1930: | Macon, Bibb, Georgia |
| Marital Status: | Single |
| Relation to Head of House: | Inmate |
| Father's Birthplace: | Georgia |
| Mother's Birthplace: | Georgia |

Household Members:

| Name | Age |
|---|---|
| Sam Robinson | 19 |
| Wesley Robinson | 27 |
| Elbert Ross | 28 |
| Hubert Sanders | 23 |
| H Sherley | 47 |
| Eddie Smith | 23 |
| W M Smith | 29 |
| Blanton Stuckey | 30 |
| Joe Thomas | 26 |
| A J Turner | 42 |
| Jim Vinson | 38 |
| John Walker | 19 |
| Charlie Williams | 47 |

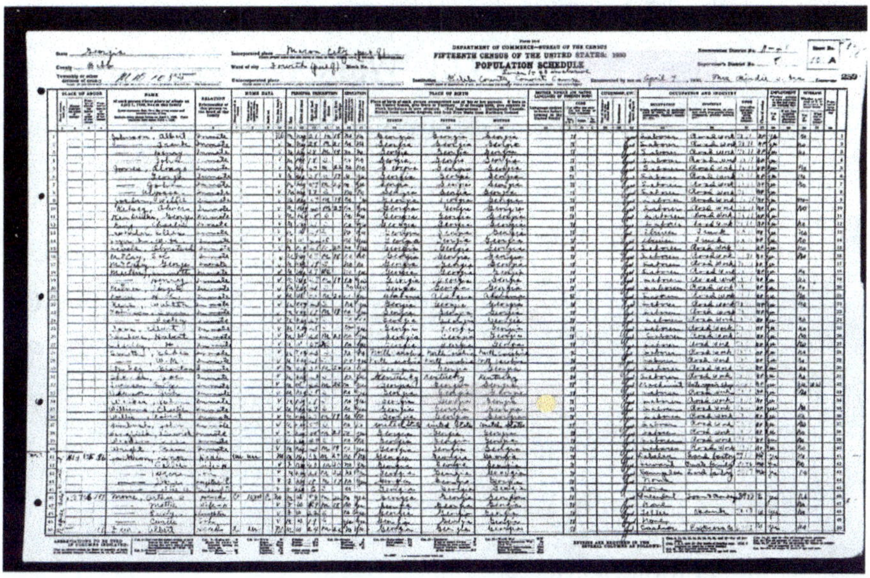
DEPARTMENT OF COMMERCE—BUREAU OF THE CENSUS
FIFTEENTH CENSUS OF THE UNITED STATES: 1930
POPULATION SCHEDULE

ancestry.com

## 1930 United States Federal Census

| | |
|---|---|
| Name: | **Milos Walker** |
| Home in 1930: | Atlanta, Fulton, Georgia |
| Age: | 53 |
| Estimated Birth Year: | abt 1877 |
| Birthplace: | Georgia |
| Relation to Head of House: | Head |
| Spouse's Name: | Lula Walker |
| Race: | Negro (Black) |

Household Members:

| Name | Age |
|---|---|
| Milos Walker | 53 |
| Lula Walker | 50 |
| Annie Walker | 15 |
| Mattie Walker | 17 |

**Source Citation:** Year: *1930*;
Census Place: *Atlanta, Fulton, Georgia*; Roll: *361*; Page: *5A*;
Enumeration District: *64*; Image: *842.0*.

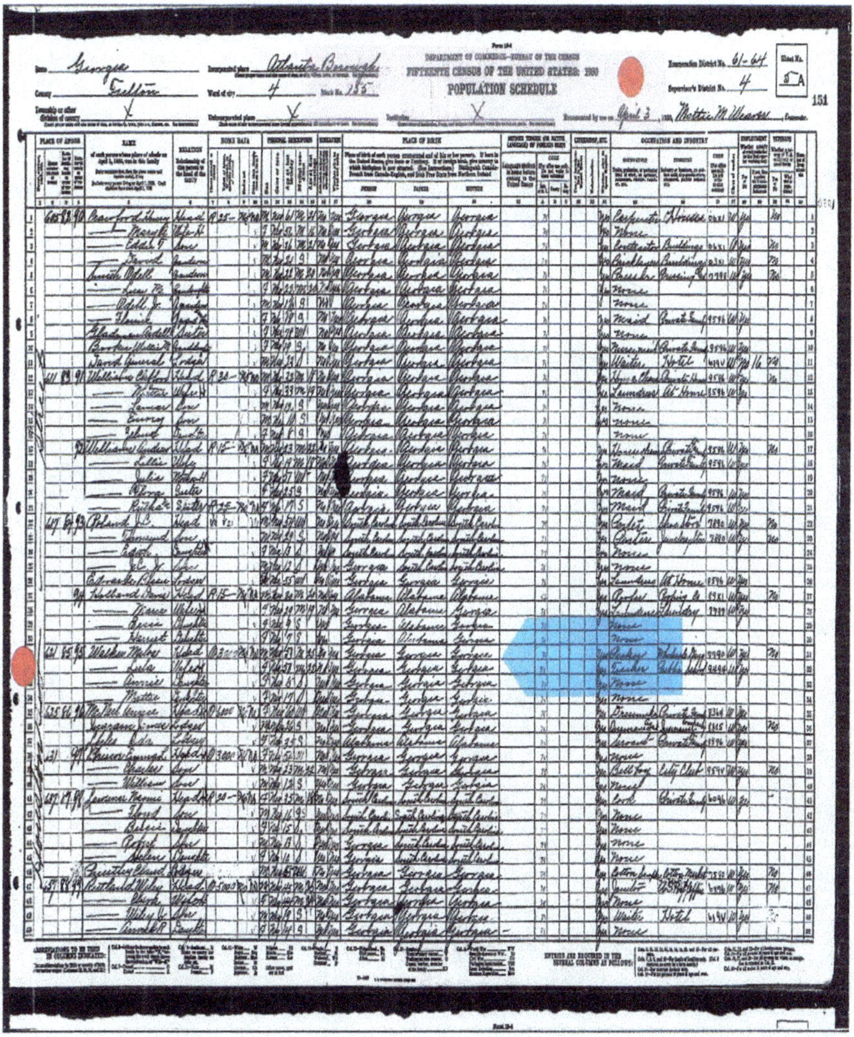
DEPARTMENT OF COMMERCE—BUREAU OF THE CENSUS

FIFTEENTH CENSUS OF THE UNITED STATES: 1930

POPULATION SCHEDULE

State: Georgia

County: Fulton

Incorporated place: Atlanta Borough

Ward of city: 4

Block No.: 155

Enumeration District No. 61-64

Supervisor's District No. 4

Sheet No. 5A

151

Enumerated by me on April 3, 1930, Mattie M Weaver, Enumerator.

ancestry library edition

## 1930 United States Federal Census

| | |
|---|---|
| Name: | **Ethel Allen** |
| Gender: | Female |
| Birth Year: | abt 1907 |
| Birthplace: | Georgia |
| Race: | Negro (Black) |
| Home in 1930: | Chicago, Cook, Illinois |
| Marital Status: | Married |
| Relation to Head of House: | Wife |
| Spouse's Name: | Edgar Allen |
| Father's Birthplace: | Georgia |
| Mother's Birthplace: | Georgia |
| Household Members: | Name / Age |
| | Edgar Allen / 25 |
| | Ethel Allen / 23 |
| | Edgar Allen / 1 |
| | Juanita Allen / 0 [6/12] |

**Source Citation:** Year: *1930*; Census Place: *Chicago, Cook, Illinois*; Roll: *419*; Page: *5A*; Enumeration District: *91*; Image: *288.0*; FHL microfilm: *2340154*.

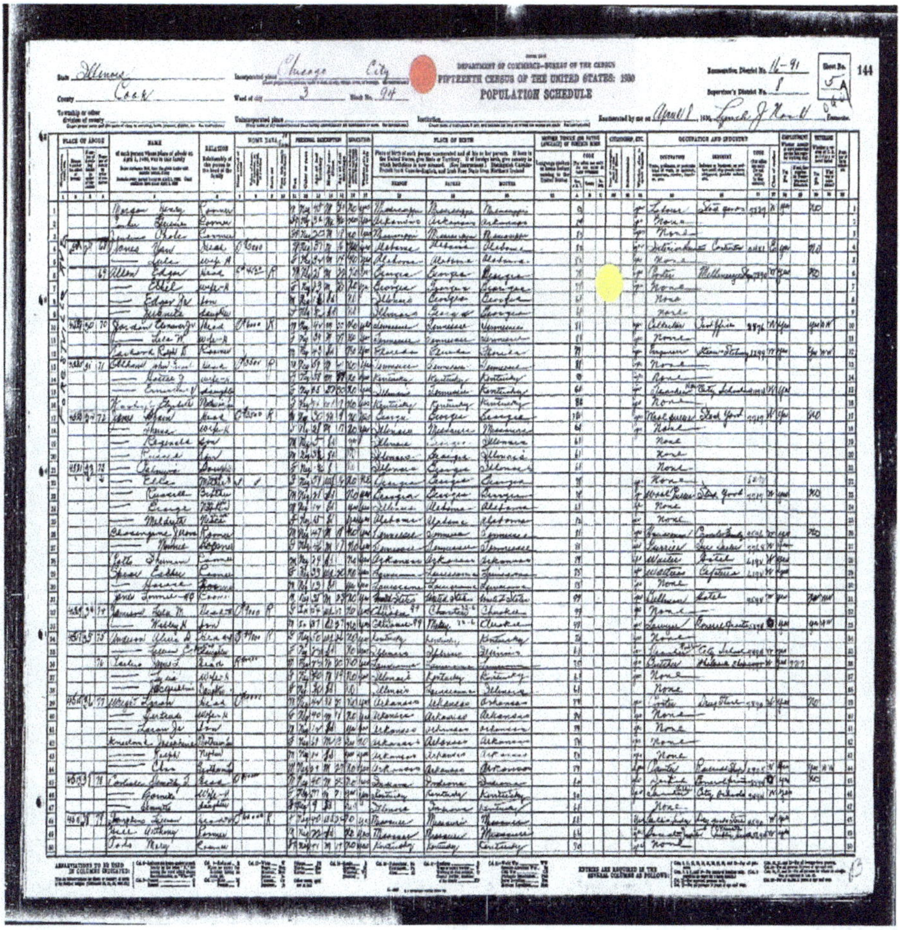
DEPARTMENT OF COMMERCE—BUREAU OF THE CENSUS
FIFTEENTH CENSUS OF THE UNITED STATES: 1930
POPULATION SCHEDULE
144

Edgar @ 1920s

Ethel Walker & Edgar Allen, Jr. @ 1935

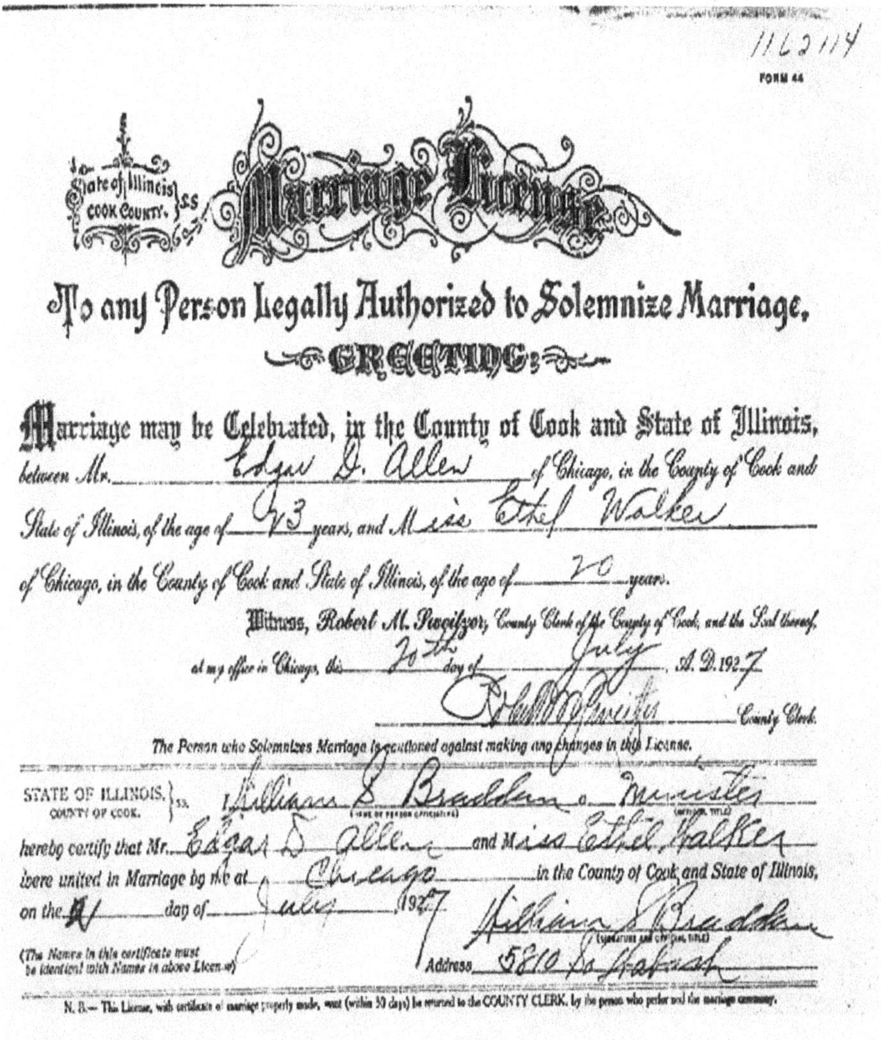

1162114

FORM 44

State of Illinois, Cook County, } ss.

# Marriage License

To any Person Legally Authorized to Solemnize Marriage,

GREETING:

Marriage may be Celebrated, in the County of Cook and State of Illinois, between Mr. Edgar D. Allen of Chicago, in the County of Cook and State of Illinois, of the age of 23 years, and Miss Ethel Walker of Chicago, in the County of Cook and State of Illinois, of the age of 20 years.

Witness, Robert M. Sweitzer, County Clerk of the County of Cook, and the Seal thereof, at my office in Chicago, this 20th day of July A. D. 1927

Robert M. Sweitzer County Clerk.

The Person who Solemnizes Marriage is cautioned against making any changes in this License.

STATE OF ILLINOIS, } ss.
COUNTY OF COOK.

I, William S. Braddan a Minister (NAME OF PERSON OFFICIATING) (OFFICIAL TITLE) hereby certify that Mr. Edgar D. Allen and Miss Ethel Walker were united in Marriage by me at Chicago in the County of Cook and State of Illinois, on the 21 day of July 1927

William S. Braddan (SIGNATURE AND OFFICIAL TITLE)

(The Names in this certificate must be identical with Names in above License)

Address 5810 So Wabash

N. B.— This License, with certificate of marriage properly made, must (within 30 days) be returned to the COUNTY CLERK, by the person who performed the marriage ceremony.

**Marriage License of Ethel & Edgar Allen, Jr.**

Ethel Allen w/Edgar III, Juanita & Darnell @ 1931

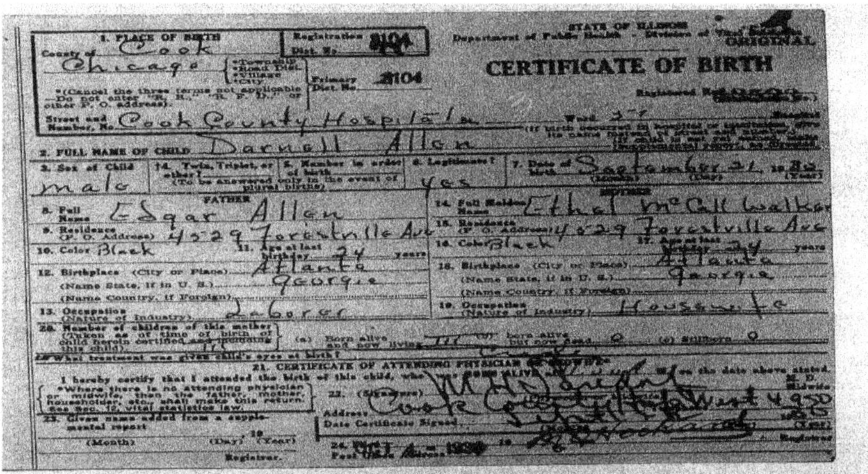

STATE OF ILLINOIS
Department of Public Health - Division of Vital Statistics
ORIGINAL
CERTIFICATE OF BIRTH

1. PLACE OF BIRTH
County of Cook
Chicago
Registration Dist. No. 3104
Primary Dist. No. 3104
Street and Number, No. Cook County Hospital
2. FULL NAME OF CHILD Darnell Allen
3. Sex of Child male
6. Legitimate? yes
7. Date of birth September 21, 1930
FATHER
8. Full Name Edgar Allen
9. Residence 4529 Forestville Ave
10. Color Black
11. Age at last birthday 24 years
12. Birthplace Atlanta Georgia
13. Occupation Laborer
MOTHER
14. Full Maiden Name Ethel McCall Walker
15. Residence 4529 Forestville Ave
16. Color Black
17. Age at last birthday 24 years
18. Birthplace Atlanta Georgia
19. Occupation Housewife
20. Number of children of this mother (a) Born alive and now living 3 (b) Born alive but now dead 0 (c) Stillborn 0
21. CERTIFICATE OF ATTENDING PHYSICIAN OR MIDWIFE
I hereby certify that I attended the birth of this child, who was born alive at on the date above stated.
22. (Signature) M.D.
Address Cook County Hospital
Date Certificate Signed
24. Filed OCT 4 - 1930

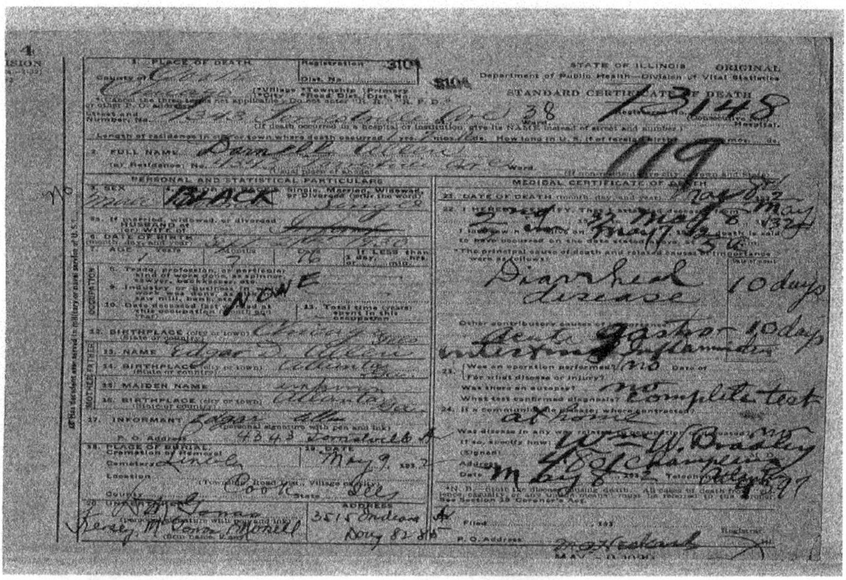

STATE OF ILLINOIS
Department of Public Health—Division of Vital Statistics
ORIGINAL
STANDARD CERTIFICATE OF DEATH
Registration Dist. No. 3104
13148
1. PLACE OF DEATH
County of Cook
Chicago
Street and Number, No. 4343 Forestville Ave
2. FULL NAME Darnell Allen
119
PERSONAL AND STATISTICAL PARTICULARS
3. SEX Male
4. Color or Race BLACK
5. Single, Married, Widowed, or Divorced Single
6. DATE OF BIRTH Sept 21 1930
7. AGE 1 Years 7 Months
OCCUPATION NONE
12. BIRTHPLACE Chicago Ill
FATHER
13. NAME Edgar D. Allen
14. BIRTHPLACE Atlanta Ga
MOTHER
15. MAIDEN NAME unknown
16. BIRTHPLACE Atlanta Ga
17. INFORMANT Edgar Allen
P. O. Address 4343 Forestville Av
18. PLACE OF BURIAL Lincoln
Date May 9, 1932
Cook Ills
19. UNDERTAKER 3515 Indiana Av
MEDICAL CERTIFICATE OF DEATH
21. DATE OF DEATH May 8 1932
22. I HEREBY CERTIFY, That I attended deceased from May 1 1932 to May 8 1932
The principal cause of death and related causes of importance were as follows:
Diarrheal disease 10 days
Other contributory causes of importance:
Acute gastro intestinal inflammation 10 days
23. Was an operation performed? no
Was there an autopsy? no
What test confirmed diagnosis? complete test
24. at home
(Signed) W. W. Bradley
Address 4851 Champlain
Date May 8 1932

**Birth & Death Certificates of Darnell Allen I**

**Ethel & Edgar De Allen II and children**

**Maurice Allen @ 1934**

ancestry library edition

## 1940 United States Federal Census

| | |
|---|---|
| Name: | **Ethel M Allen** |
| Respondent: | Yes |
| Age: | 33 |
| Estimated Birth Year: | abt 1907 |
| Gender: | Female |
| Race: | Negro (Black) |
| Birthplace: | Georgia |
| Marital Status: | Married |
| Relation to Head of House: | Wife |
| Home in 1940: | Chicago, Cook, Illinois |
| Street: | E 42nd Place |
| House Number: | 513 |
| Farm: | No |
| Inferred Residence in 1935: | Chicago, Cook, Illinois |
| Residence in 1935: | Same Place |
| Resident on farm in 1935: | No |
| Sheet Number: | 5A |
| Attended School or College: | No |
| Highest Grade Completed: | College, 2nd year |
| Weeks Worked in 1939: | 0 |
| Income: | 0 |
| Income Other Sources: | No |
| Neighbors: | |

Household Members:

| Name | Age |
|---|---|
| Edgar D Allen | 36 |
| Ethel M Allen | 33 |
| Edgar Allen | 11 |
| Jaunita L Allen | 9 |
| David R Allen | 7 |
| Maurice Allen | 7 |
| Lula Walker | 62 |

**Source Citation:** Year: *1940*; Census Place: *Chicago, Cook, Illinois*; Roll: *T627_924*; Page: *5A*; Enumeration District: *103-107*.

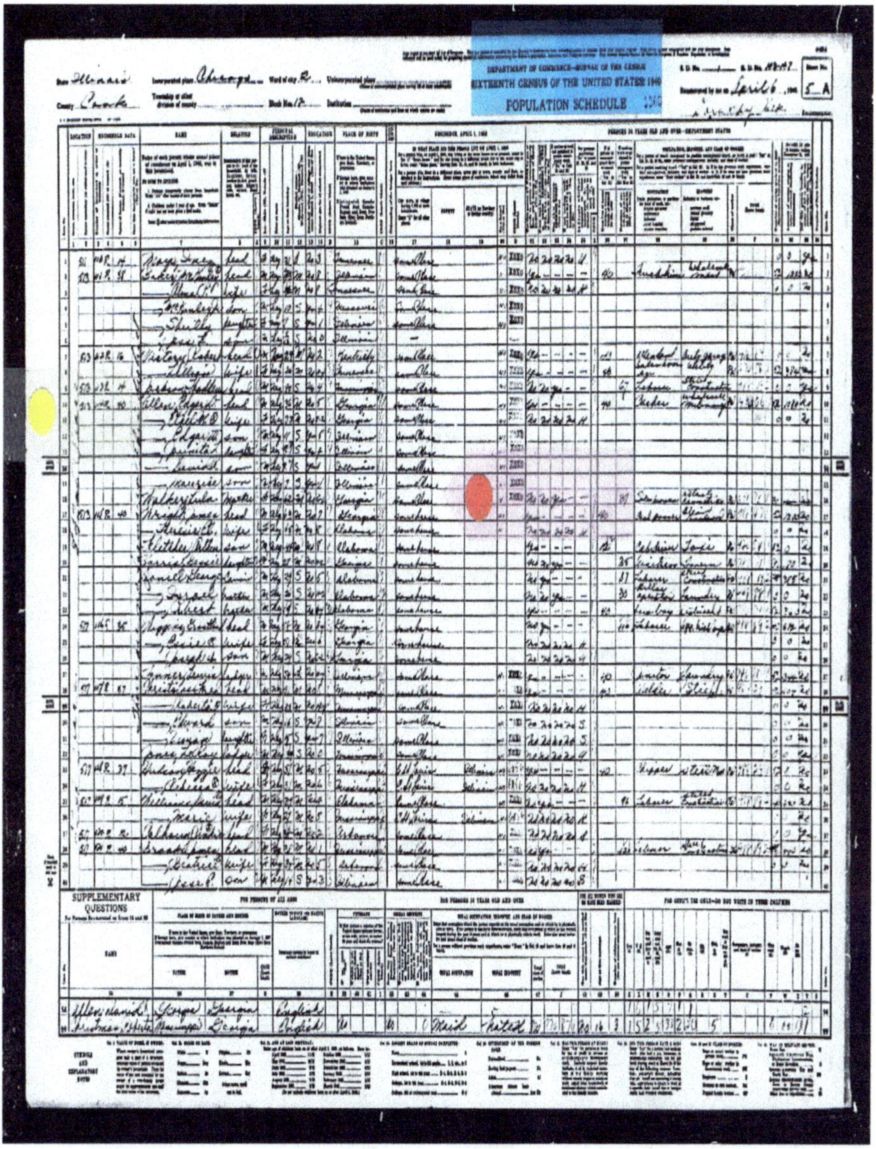

DEPARTMENT OF COMMERCE—BUREAU OF THE CENSUS
SIXTEENTH CENSUS OF THE UNITED STATES 1940
POPULATION SCHEDULE

SUPPLEMENTARY QUESTIONS

ancestry

1940 United States Federal Census

| | |
|---|---|
| Name: | **Miles Walker** **[*Milous Wilburn Walker*]** |
| Respondent: | Yes |
| Age: | 31 |
| Estimated Birth Year: | abt 1909 |
| Gender: | Male |
| Race: | Negro (Black) |
| Birthplace: | Georgia |
| Marital Status: | Married |
| Relation to Head of House: | Lodger |
| Home in 1940: | Chicago, Cook, Illinois |
| House Number: | 3814 |
| Inferred Residence in 1935: | Chicago, Cook, Illinois |
| Residence in 1935: | Same Place |
| Resident on farm in 1935: | No |
| Sheet Number: | 61A |
| Occupation: | Musician |
| Attended School or College: | No |
| Highest Grade Completed: | High School, 4th year |
| Duration of Unemployment: | 17 |
| Class of Worker: | Wage or salary worker in private work |
| Weeks Worked in 1939: | 52 |
| Income: | 1000 |
| Income Other Sources: | No |
| Neighbors: | |

Household Members:

| Name | Age |
|---|---|
| Minnia Mc Cay | 42 |
| Emerson Dover | 55 |
| Miles Walker | 31 |
| Cora Gerner | 39 |
| Alberta Rose | 30 |
| Mary Rosy | 38 |
| William A Yarber | 40 |
| Tom Ross | 69 |
| Lizzie Ross | 68 |

**Source Citation:** Year: *1940*; Census Place: *Chicago, Cook, Illinois*; Roll: *T627_923*; Page: *61A*; Enumeration District: *103-88B*.

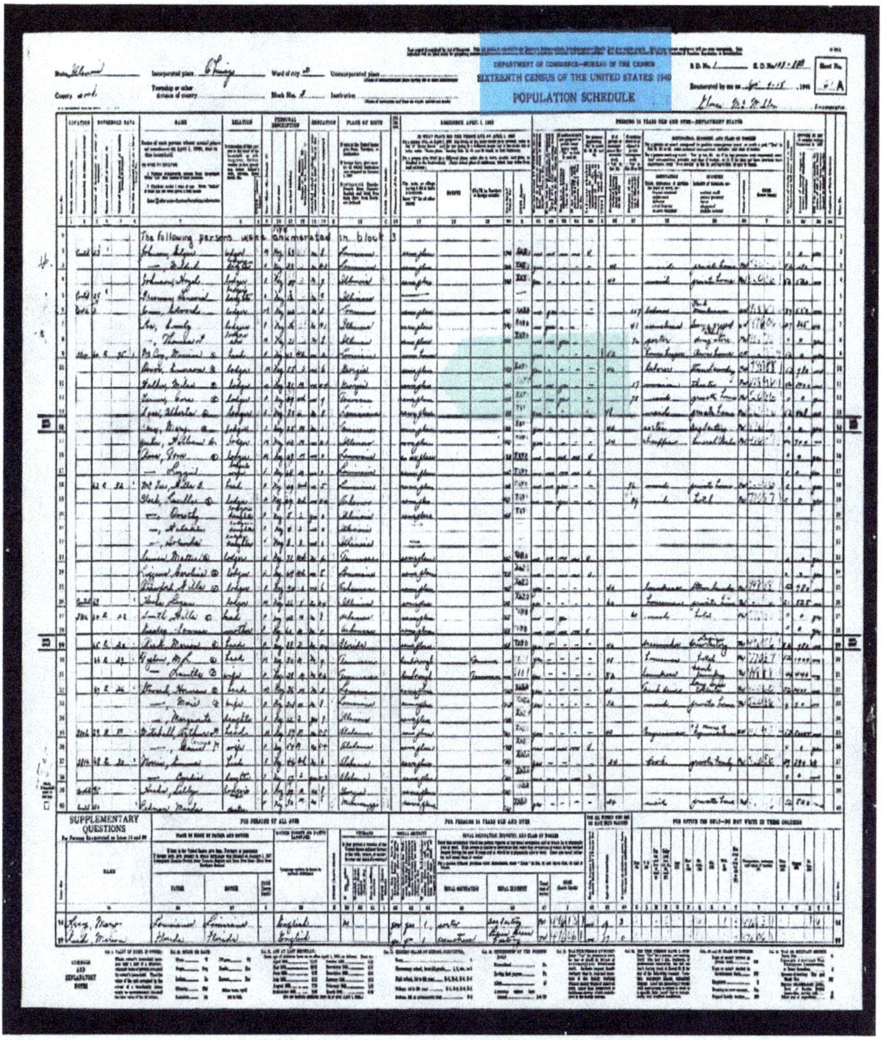
DEPARTMENT OF COMMERCE—BUREAU OF THE CENSUS
SIXTEENTH CENSUS OF THE UNITED STATES: 1940
POPULATION SCHEDULE
The following persons were enumerated in block 3
SUPPLEMENTARY QUESTIONS

**Milous Walker, Jr.*Musician Extraordinaire**

# The Three Brown Notes

**Piano Player Unknown "Mike" Walker on clarinet June Walker on organ**

**Milous Walker & sister, Mattie Walker**

**Wife of Milous Walker * June Walker**

**Mattie Walker w/ Three Brown Notes**

**Mattie Walker a.k.a. Mata & Musician**

# The Sepia Tones

**Mata on piano Nina on guitar Ginger on organ**

# The Four Vs

**From the movie I Love A Bandleader 1945**

**Mattie Walker *Accomplished Pianist**

DON AND MATA DUO

PERSONAL DIRECTION
ARTISTS CORPORATION OF AMERICA
Hotel Wisconsin - Milwaukee, Wisconsin
Broadway 2-2772

**Don and Mata Duo in later years**

Mata Roy * The Latter Years

*Introducing...*

# MATA ROY

**ORGANIST ★ PIANIST ★ SONG STYLIST**

Mata started her career in the 1940's with Jimmy Noone's Dixieland Combo playing piano. After Noone's passing in 1944, Mata worked with several combos before taking bookings as a solo performer. She has often been compared to Pearl Bailey, for her wit and voice and personality; to Ethel Waters for her looks, and to Jimmy Smith as she triggers her swinging organ. She plays popular, modern, rhythm and blues. Mata gives a outstanding performance on a production number titled "Time Marches On" in which she gives impressions of some of the nations most popular pianists and their style of playing. It has been proclaimed by all critics as outstanding.

Mata plays a jazz organ (Hammond) with a jazz feeling combining piano, vocals, novelties, together with an electronic rhythm instrument that echoes a full band sound suitable for dancing.

Mata has appeared in several movies for Paramount Studios - notably ""A Tale of Two Cities" and "I Love a Bandleader" featuring Phil Harris and Rochester. She has appeared in countless night spots, Holiday Inn Lounges and supper clubs from Key West and Miami Florida to Hollywood and San Francisco, plus New York, Chicago, Wisconsin, Arizona, Oregon, Washington State and Canada.

Mata Roy is the act for smart rooms, supper clubs, piano and organ bars and lounges

HOME ADDRESS:
MATA ROY
R. R. No. 5, Box 1111
Fox Lake
Angola, Indiana 46703
Phone (219) 665-5985

CURRENTLY APPEARING:

______________________

______________________

**Mata Roy * The Veteran Entertainer**

# As a child she pretended black sticks, white stones were her imaginary piano

**Story and photo by Joan D. LaGuardia**

Mata Roy is a performer, singer, pianist. In 1957, she got fed up with poorly tuned pianos and became an organist.

"Bad pianos made me take up the organ," she said, recalling 1957 when she was performing in a string of hotels.

Her picture albums are filled with newspaper column tidbits and advertisements that trace her performing career from Chicago to the west coast, to Canada and through the midwest. Today, she is still Mata Roy, the performer, but also, Mata Roy Pryor, Fox Lake resident of Steuben County.

The daughter of musicians, her life is a wave of transition between two solid shores, her Atlanta upbringing and her life here with Albert Pryor. In between, she travelled first with Jimmy Noone's Dixieland Combo, with several small groups, and later as a single.

During her Atlanta childhood, her father taught guitar, mandolin, saxophone, clarinet.

"But he didn't teach piano, so he sent us all out to learn," she recalled.

Her mother was a school teacher who may have given her father his start in the music.

"She supposedly taught him the lines and spaces years ago. She was a teacher."

"We had a musical library that took up a whole wall."

Although Mata Roy has had two years of formal training at the American Conservatory in Chicago, her education began at home with her parents' influence and her own desire to learn.

No piano in their home, she envied the other children who did have pianos. When they would go home to practice, she would line up black sticks and white rocks and pretend to be a pianist.

"Music has a great meaning for me. When I started out, we didn't have a piano."

Finally, the family acquired a piano when her father was asked to keep one for a friend. Anxious to play, she rushed her lessons, studying ahead in the book.

"It's a gift," she explained of talent. "It's inside you. You have no control over it."

After her parents divorced, she left Atlanta and moved to Chicago in the 1930's. It was there her formal musical education began and she first went on the road as a performer with Jimmy Noone. She moved to the west coast and began to work out of Los Angeles.

Her mother wanted her to stay home and finish school. "But I didn't finish," she said, "because I wanted to go on the road."

She moved to the west coast and worked out of Los Angeles with Jimmy Noone. The music was dixieland, but her sound has been characterized as popular, modern, rhythm and blues.

"I started out in that big band era."

She later joined a small group of women called the Four V's and appeared with them in Paramount Studios movies including, "Tale of Two Cafes" and "I Love a Band Leader."

Later she wanted to work as a single. The advice she received from music world masters was to take bits and pieces of all her former acts and blend them together in a single. She began working for hotel chains, living and performing from hotel to hotel in Michigan and later Indiana and Illinois.

It was in Ishpeming, Michigan, that she came up with the successful idea for an education type of medley, "Time Marches On, A Cavalcade of Pianists," which remains the foundation of her act.

In the Michigan iron town, she performed to large crowds, but noticed no one was really listening to her. One man explained that the people of the iron mills were not too knowledgeable of music, and liked what they heard on the juke boxes, tunes like, "Your Cheating Heart."

Not to be defeated, she set about learning the country style song and a variety of others that would capture the attention of her audience. Then she would introduce herself, and tell the story of music in America, beginning with Scott Joplin's ragtime right up to the rhythm and blues sound of the 1950's.

Now, she recalls that town fondly for the friends she made there, especially

Page 3 Wed., January 24, 1979 Steuben Republican

**Involved performance**

At the Holiday Inn in Angola, Mata Roy performs on weekends. She uses her own organ and the house piano. Her own piano is at her Fox Lake home where she gives lessons.

--Photo by Joan D. LaGuardia

the man who gave her the tip. He was Judge Robert Vaulkner of Michigan, a writer, who later penned the popular book and screenplay, "Anatomy of a Murder," under the name of Robert Travis.

In the 1960's, she returned to the west coast, this time working out of San Francisco. She had been in Chicago for a time in the 1950's and worked for the Chicago park system for two years coordinating children's music programs.

In 1969, she returned to Chicago for the opening of the Holiday O'Hare, a Holiday Inn. In the 1970's she again began working for the district managers of Holiday Inn in Indiana and Illinois as well as some Ramada Inns.

It was on a visit to the Holiday Inn in Angola that she met Albert Pryor, a Fox Lake resident. Mutual friends of theirs in Chicago suggested that Pryor show Mata Roy around the lakes in Steuben County during her stay here.

**B**efore leaving, she attempted to introduce him to a friend of hers in Kendallville, however, Albert Pryor wasn't interested. Instead, he visited her at her next performance in Illinois and later saw her in Coldwater. It was in Coldwater that he asked her to marry him and she accepted.

"It's just been a beautiful experience," she said. "He's the greatest thing that ever happened to me."

They had the wedding at Fox Lake. She remarked that it was probably the biggest party the lake had ever had.

"I work out of here now. I teach three days a week and perform at this Holiday Inn."

Her contract at the Holiday Inn of Angola has recently been extended into March.

It feels good to be settled again, she said, after so many years of travel.

"You want to feel that you belong. You want to be the people that live next door."

"It did get very lonely at times," she admitted of the travel. "But it was such an experience. It showed you how people live."

Most of all, she enjoyed experiencing the different pockets of ethnic communities in the midwest, the Flemmish, Italian, Polish and others. She learned their customs, traditions, and especially their cooking.

"I learned how to make real good spaghetti," she joked.

"I still get Christmas cards from them."

One of her fondest memories is of performing in Canada where it was extremely cold, 15 degrees below zero. It was lonely and the piano was poorly tuned.

"The music sounded just awful to me," she said.

She decided to get down off the stage and talk to the people. "The Canadian people love to talk to you. They'd send me fan mail and write what a wonderful time they had."

Today, these memories are tucked away in her mind to be brought out as she pages through her albums filled with write-ups.

"I'd like to play more and I'd like to learn more. I'd like to go back to school."

"You never stop learning music. I don't know everything there is to know about music. If there was a big music school around here, I'd be like Pearl Bailey, I'd be right there back in college."

Although she sometimes longs for the schools and concerts of the big city, she enjoys Steuben County because of its setting, but mostly because Albert Pryor is here.

She has weathered a great deal of loneliness in order to be a performer. A Christian Scientist, she often called the practitioners of her faith when she was alone on the road and needed advice.

She would get self conscious performing to all-white audiences who were not familiar with black women.

"Sometimes," she said, "I'd go into restaurants and people would stop eating and stare at me. I felt that coldness."

Remembering those times, she said, "Anything I can do for lonely people, I'll do it."

Mr. and Mrs. Arden Tubbs recently

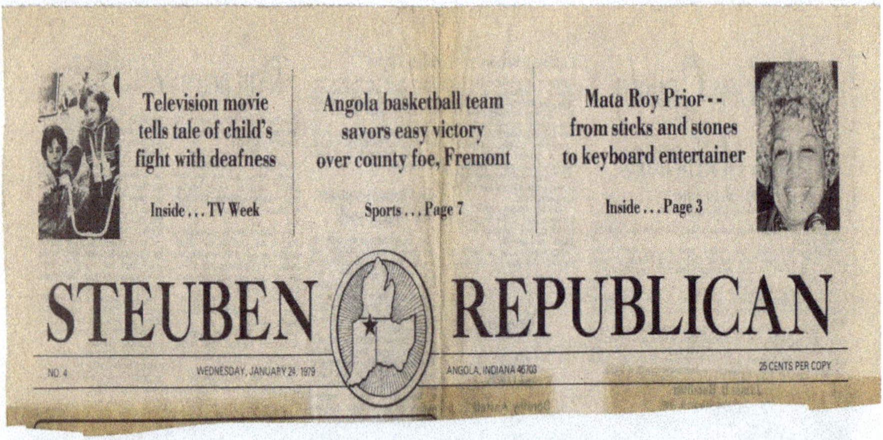

Television movie tells tale of child's fight with deafness

Inside . . . TV Week

Angola basketball team savors easy victory over county foe, Fremont

Sports . . . Page 7

Mata Roy Prior - - from sticks and stones to keyboard entertainer

Inside . . . Page 3

STEUBEN REPUBLICAN

NO. 4 WEDNESDAY, JANUARY 24, 1979 ANGOLA, INDIANA 46703 25 CENTS PER COPY

**Mattie Walker @ mid 1930s in Chicago**

**Mattie Walker in 1930s Glamour Shot**

ancestry library edition

## 1940 United States Federal Census

| | |
|---|---|
| Name: | **Annie L Jackson** |
| Respondent: | Yes |
| Age: | 26 |
| Estimated Birth Year: | abt 1914 |
| Gender: | Female |
| Race: | Negro (Black) |
| Birthplace: | Georgia |
| Marital Status: | Married |
| Relation to Head of House: | Wife |
| Home in 1940: | Chicago, Cook, Illinois |
| Street: | South Parkway |
| House Number: | 3147 |
| Inferred Residence in 1935: | Chicago, Cook, Illinois |
| Residence in 1935: | Same House |
| Sheet Number: | 12A |
| Attended School or College: | No |
| Highest Grade Completed: | High School, 4th year |
| Weeks Worked in 1939: | 0 |
| Income: | 0 |
| Income Other Sources: | No |
| Neighbors: | |

Household Members:

| Name | Age |
|---|---|
| Stephen Jackson | 41 |
| Annie L Jackson | 26 |
| Verna Jackson | 20 |
| Ruby Jackson | 17 |
| Rose Jackson | 13 |
| Annita Jackson | 4 |
| Betty Jackson | 1 |
| Phillip Gibson | 65 |
| Harrison Miller | 60 |

**Source Citation:** Year: *1940*; Census Place: *Chicago, Cook, Illinois*; Roll: *T627_922*; Page: *12A*; Enumeration District: *103-59*.

**Picture of Annie Walker with Nephew David, Sister Ethel, & Bro-in-law Edgar @ 1935**

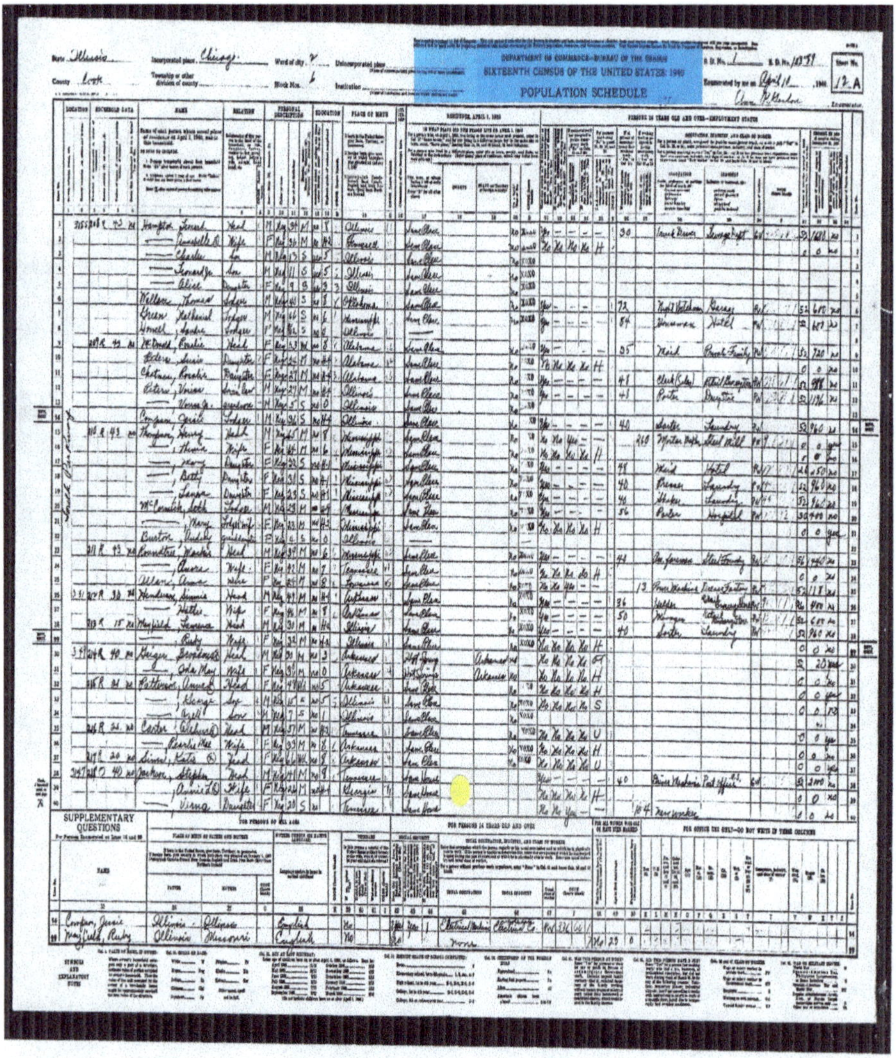
State Illinois
County Cook
Incorporated place Chicago
DEPARTMENT OF COMMERCE—BUREAU OF THE CENSUS
SIXTEENTH CENSUS OF THE UNITED STATES: 1940
POPULATION SCHEDULE
Sheet No. 12 A
SUPPLEMENTARY QUESTIONS

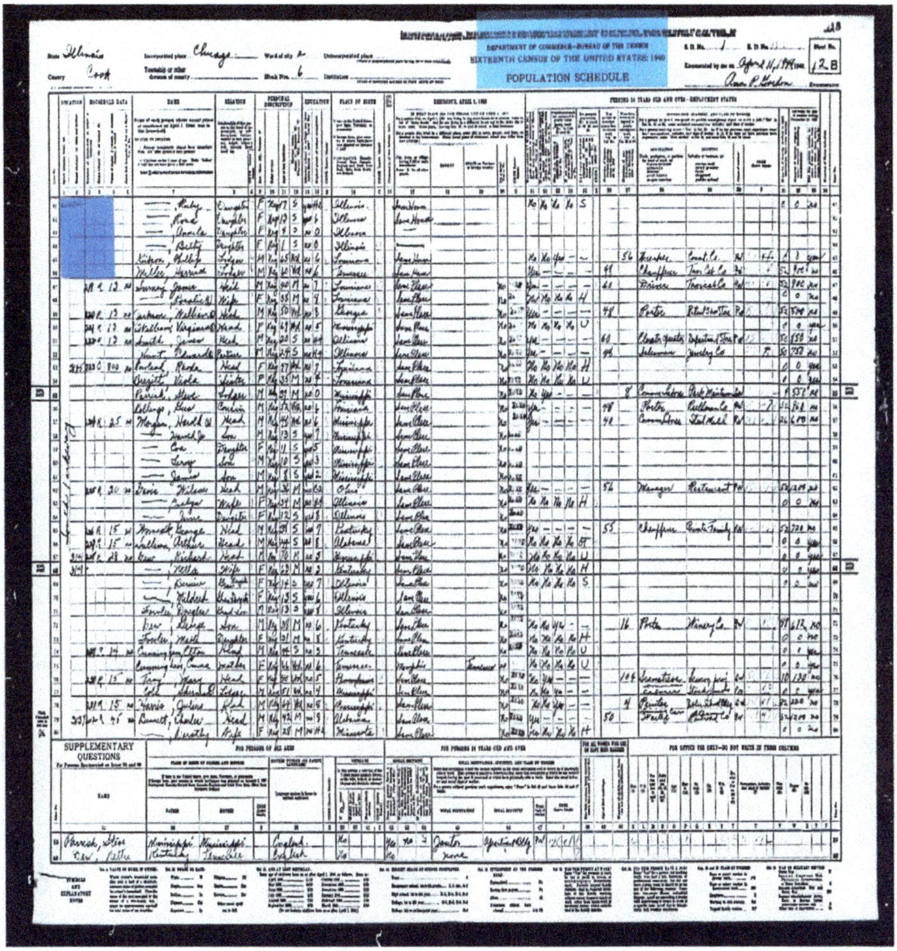
DEPARTMENT OF COMMERCE—BUREAU OF THE CENSUS
SIXTEENTH CENSUS OF THE UNITED STATES: 1940
POPULATION SCHEDULE

State Illinois
County Cook
Incorporated place Chicago

SUPPLEMENTARY QUESTIONS

ancestry.com

1940 United States Federal Census

| | |
|---|---|
| Name: | **John Walker** |
| Age: | 30 |
| Estimated Birth Year: | abt 1910 |
| Gender: | Male |
| Race: | Negro (Black) |
| Birthplace: | Georgia |
| Marital Status: | Married |
| Relation to Head of House: | Head |
| Home in 1940: | Macon, Bibb, Georgia |
| Street: | Elliott Street |
| House Number: | 209 |
| Farm: | No |
| Inferred Residence in 1935: | Macon, Bibb, Georgia |
| Residence in 1935: | Same Place |
| Resident on farm in 1935: | No |
| Sheet Number: | 17A |
| Number of Household in Order of Visitation: | 435 |
| Occupation: | Sawer |
| House Owned or Rented: | Rented |
| Value of Home or Monthly Rental if Rented: | 5 |
| Attended School or College: | No |
| Highest Grade Completed: | Elementary school, 3rd grade |
| Hours Worked Week Prior to Census: | 42 |
| Class of Worker: | Wage or salary worker in private work |
| Weeks Worked in 1939: | 23 |
| Income: | 276 |
| Income Other Sources: | No |
| Neighbors: | |

Household Members:

| Name | Age |
|---|---|
| John Walker | 30 |
| Susie Walker | 27 |
| Susie L Walker | 5 |
| Essie Mae Walker | 4 |
| Willie L Walker | 2 |
| Luther L Walker | 11/12 |
| Richard Fanning | 5 |

**Source Citation:** Year: *1940*; Census Place: *Macon, Bibb, Georgia*; Roll: *T627_640*; Page: *17A*; Enumeration District: *11-5*.

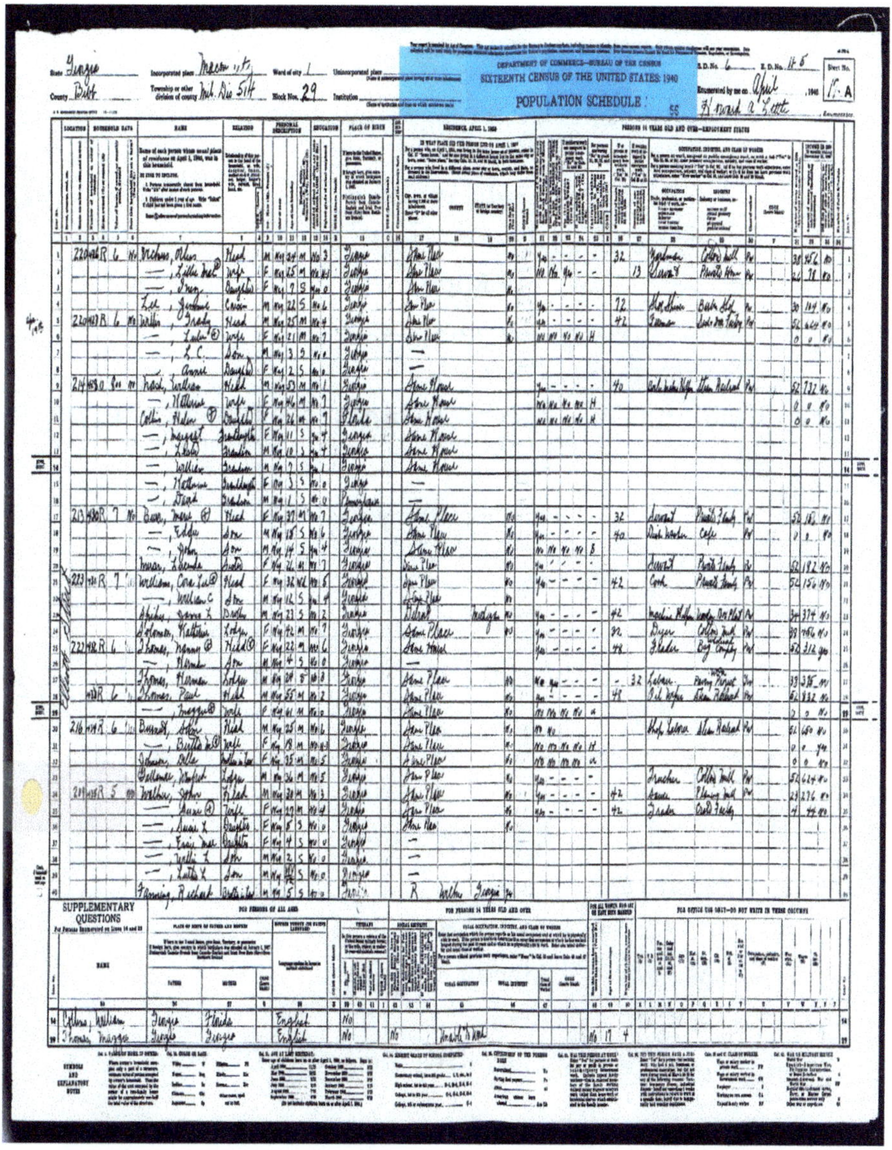
DEPARTMENT OF COMMERCE—BUREAU OF THE CENSUS

SIXTEENTH CENSUS OF THE UNITED STATES: 1940

POPULATION SCHEDULE

SUPPLEMENTARY QUESTIONS

ancestry.com

## U.S. City Directories, 1821-1989 (Beta)

| | |
|---|---|
| Name: | **Viola Walker** |
| Residence Year: | 1934 |
| Street Address: | 338 Middle V |
| Residence Place: | Macon, Georgia |
| Occupation: | Cook |
| Publication Title: | Macon, Georgia, City Directory, 1934 |

**Source Information:**
Ancestry.com. *U.S. City Directories, 1821-1989 (Beta)* [database on-line]. Provo, UT, USA: Ancestry.com Operations, Inc., 2011.

ancestry.com

## U.S. City Directories, 1821-1989 (Beta)

| | |
|---|---|
| Name: | **Viola Walker** |
| Residence Year: | 1935 |
| Street Address: | 338 Middle V |
| Residence Place: | Macon, Georgia |
| Occupation: | Cook |
| Publication Title: | Macon, Georgia, City Directory, 1935 |

**Source Information:**
Ancestry.com. *U.S. City Directories, 1821-1989 (Beta)* [database on-line]. Provo, UT, USA: Ancestry.com Operations, Inc., 2011.

# Georgia, Death Index, 1933-1998 for Viola Walker

| | |
|---|---|
| Name: | Viola Walker |
| Event: | Death |
| Event Date: | 23 Feb 1943 |
| Event Place: | Bibb, Georgia |
| Registration Date: | |
| Residence: | |
| Gender: | Female |
| Age: | 50 |
| Race: | C |
| Estimated Birth Year: | 1893 |
| Registration Note: | |
| Certificate Number: | 2090 |

ancestry.com

U.S. City Directories, 1821-1989 (Beta)

| | |
|---|---|
| Name: | **John A Walker Jr** |
| Gender: | M (Male) |
| Residence Year: | 1949 |
| Street Address: | Rd 6 |
| Residence Place: | Macon, Georgia |
| Occupation: | Serv Slsmn |
| Spouse: | Sally Walker |
| Publication Title: | Macon, Georgia, City Directory, 1949 |

**Source Information:**
Ancestry.com. *U.S. City Directories, 1821-1989 (Beta)* [database on-line]. Provo, UT, USA: Ancestry.com Operations, Inc., 2011.

MID-STATE PAINT CO.

McNAIR LUMBER & SUPPLY CO.

Cement
Lime
Plaster
Metal Lath
Wallboard
Water-proofing Materials
Weather-wood
Glass Wool

Tel. 5200

READY-MIXED CONCRETE
CORNELL-YOUNG COMPANY

JOHN ALDEN MOTORS, INC.

Atlantic Ice Company

ATLANTIC ALE AND BEER

Phone 3636 90-5th

Hotel Grady

Eat in Our Coffee Shop

100 Rooms
100 Baths

301 Cherry

Tel. 1228

Fickling & Walker, Inc.
Realtors — Insurors

**John A. Walker III / nephew of Milous Walker, Sr.**

ancestry.com

1940 United States Federal Census

| | |
|---|---|
| Name: | **Milous W Walker** |
| Age: | 63 |
| Estimated Birth Year: | abt 1877 |
| Gender: | Male |
| Race: | Negro (Black) |
| Birthplace: | Georgia |
| Marital Status: | Married |
| Relation to Head of House: | Head |
| Home in 1940: | Atlanta, Fulton, Georgia |
| Street: | Angier Av, NE |
| House Number: | 441 |
| Farm: | No |
| Inferred Residence in 1935: | Atlanta, Fulton, Georgia |
| Residence in 1935: | Same Place |
| Resident on farm in 1935: | No |
| Sheet Number: | 4B |
| Number of Household in Order of Visitation: | 69 |
| Father's Birthplace: | Georgia |
| Mother's Birthplace: | Georgia |
| Occupation: | Packer |
| House Owned or Rented: | Rented |
| Value of Home or Monthly Rental if Rented: | 18 |
| Attended School or College: | No |
| Highest Grade Completed: | Elementary school, 7th grade |
| Hours Worked Week Prior to Census: | 48 |
| Class of Worker: | Wage or salary worker in private work |
| Weeks Worked in 1939: | 52 |
| Income: | 1236 |
| Income Other Sources: | No |
| Native Language: | English |
| Social Security Number: | Yes |
| Usual Occupation: | Packer |
| Usual Industry: | Wholesale Dauggist |
| Usual Class of Worker: | Wage or salary worker in private work |
| Neighbors: | |

Household Members:

| Name | Age |
|---|---|
| Milous W Walker | 63 |
| Georgette Walker | 38 |

**Source Citation:** Year: *1940*; Census Place: *Atlanta, Fulton, Georgia*; Roll: *T627_733*; Page: *4B*; Enumeration District: *160-228*

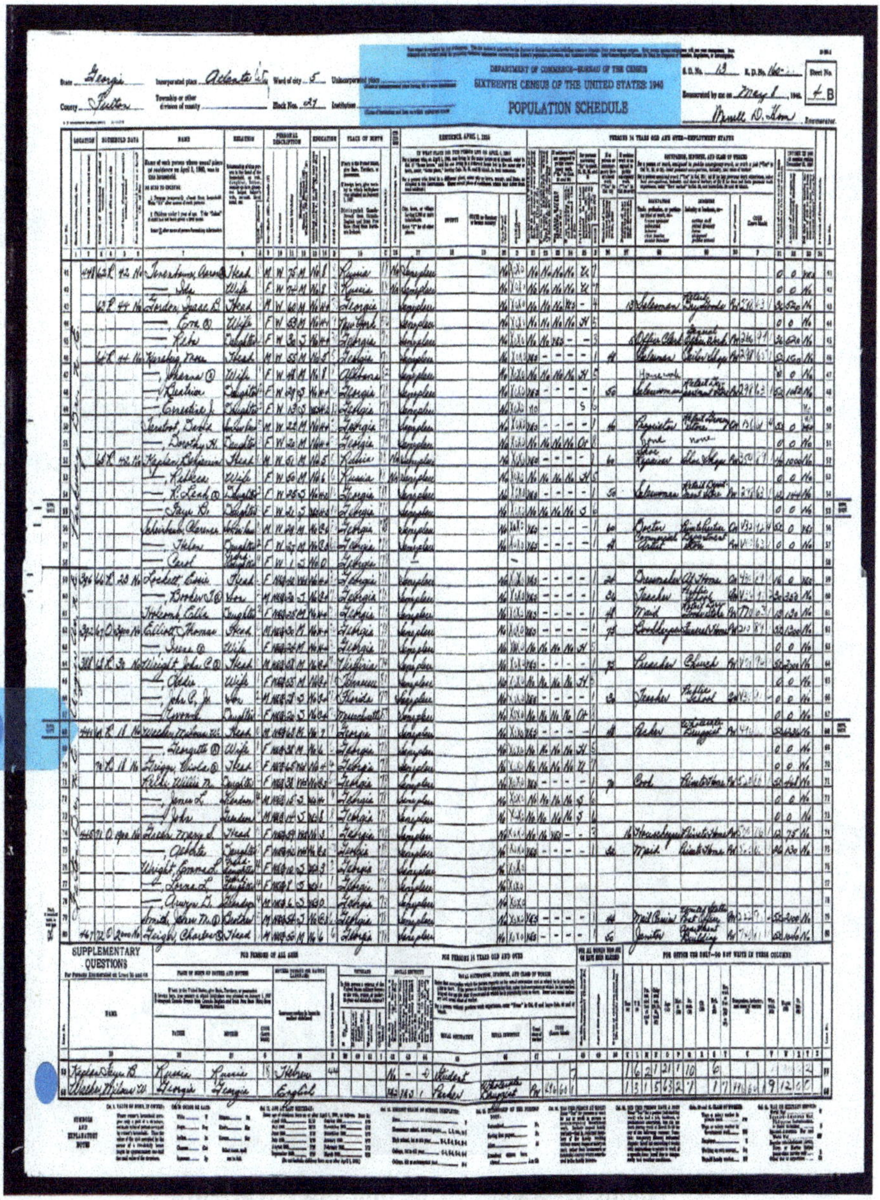

DEPARTMENT OF COMMERCE—BUREAU OF THE CENSUS
SIXTEENTH CENSUS OF THE UNITED STATES: 1940
POPULATION SCHEDULE

State: Georgia — County: Fulton — Incorporated place: Atlanta City — Ward of city: 5 — Block No.: 29 — S.D. No.: 13 — E.D. No.: 160 — Sheet No.: 4 B — Enumerated by me on May 1, 1940 — Merrill D. Horn, Enumerator

| Line | Name | Relation | Sex | Race | Age | Marital status | Place of birth |
|---|---|---|---|---|---|---|---|
| 41 | Tenenbaum, Aaron | Head | M | W | 75 | M | Russia |
| 42 | —, Ida | Wife | F | W | 74 | M | Russia |
| 43 | Gordon, Isaac B. | Head | M | W | 60 | M | Georgia |
| 44 | —, Eva | Wife | F | W | 53 | M | New York |
| 45 | —, Reba | Daughter | F | W | 30 | S | Georgia |
| 46 | Hershberg, Max | Head | M | W | 55 | M | Georgia |
| 47 | —, Johanna | Wife | F | W | 48 | M | Alabama |
| 48 | —, Beatrice | Daughter | F | W | 29 | S | Georgia |
| 49 | —, Ernestine J. | Daughter | F | W | 13 | S | Georgia |
| 50 | [illegible], [illegible] | Son-in-law | M | W | 22 | M | Georgia |
| 51 | —, Dorothy H. | Daughter | F | W | 20 | M | Georgia |
| 52 | Kaplan, Benjamin | Head | M | W | 61 | M | Russia |
| 53 | —, Rebecca | Wife | F | W | 60 | M | Russia |
| 54 | —, R. Leah | Daughter | F | W | 25 | S | Georgia |
| 55 | —, Faye B. | Daughter | F | W | 21 | S | Georgia |
| 56 | [illegible], Clarence | Son-in-law | M | W | 29 | M | Georgia |
| 57 | —, Helen | Daughter | F | W | 27 | M | Georgia |
| 58 | —, Carol | Grand-daughter | F | W | 1 | S | Georgia |
| 59 | Lockett, Essie | Head | F | Neg | [illegible] | Wd | Georgia |
| 60 | —, Brooker T. | Son | M | Neg | 20 | S | Georgia |
| 61 | Holcomb, Ella | Daughter | F | Neg | 25 | M | Georgia |
| 62 | Elliott, Thomas | Head | M | Neg | 30 | M | Georgia |
| 63 | —, Irene | Wife | F | Neg | 24 | M | Georgia |
| 64 | Wright, John C. | Head | M | Neg | 57 | M | Virginia |
| 65 | —, Addie | Wife | F | Neg | 55 | M | Tennessee |
| 66 | —, John C., Jr. | Son | M | Neg | 21 | S | Florida |
| 67 | —, [illegible] | Daughter | F | Neg | 20 | S | Massachusetts |
| 68 | Washer, Wilson W. | Head | M | Neg | [illegible] | M | Georgia |
| 69 | —, Georgette | Wife | F | Neg | 38 | M | Georgia |
| 70 | Griggs, Viola | Head | F | Neg | 65 | Wd | Georgia |
| 71 | [illegible], Willie M. | Daughter | F | Neg | 38 | Wd | Georgia |
| 72 | —, James L. | Grandson | M | Neg | 15 | S | Georgia |
| 73 | —, John | Grandson | M | Neg | 14 | S | Georgia |
| 74 | [illegible], Mary L. | Head | F | Neg | [illegible] | Wd | Georgia |
| 75 | —, [illegible] | Daughter | F | Neg | [illegible] | Wd | Georgia |
| 76 | Wright, [illegible] L. | Grand-daughter | F | Neg | 10 | S | Georgia |
| 77 | —, Lorene L. | Grand-daughter | F | Neg | 7 | S | Georgia |
| 78 | —, [illegible] D. | Grandson | M | Neg | 6 | S | Georgia |
| 79 | Smith, John M. | Brother | M | Neg | 54 | S | Georgia |
| 80 | Haight, Charles | Head | M | Neg | 56 | M | Georgia |

SUPPLEMENTARY QUESTIONS

**Milous W. Walker, Sr. @ mid 1940 in Atlanta**

## *STEWARDESS BOARD*

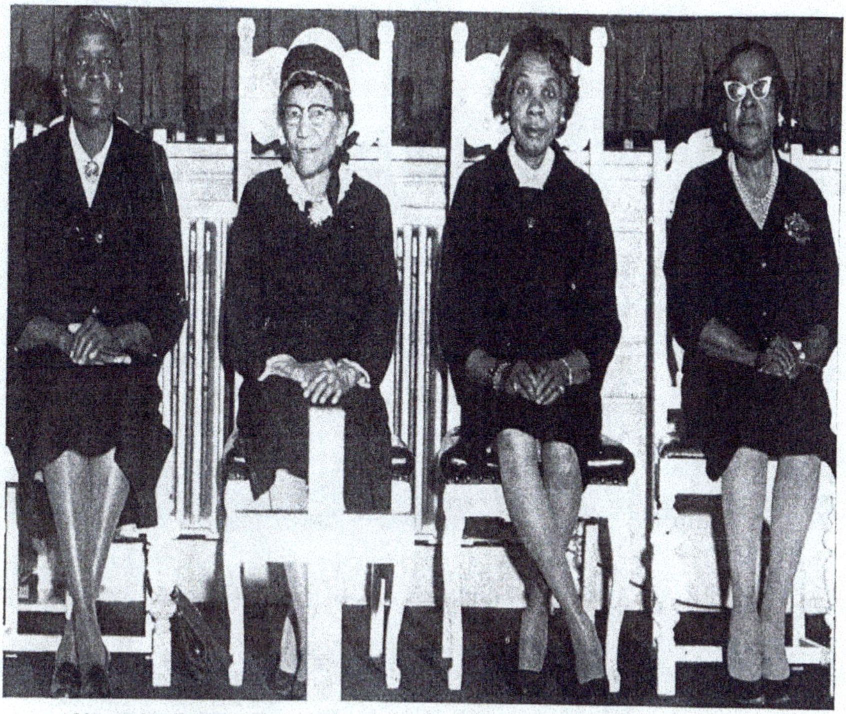

*Mrs. Mable Kellam, Mrs. Lettie Crawford, Mrs. Georgette Walker, Mrs. Addie Giles*

**Georgette/Last wife of Milous W. Walker, Sr.**

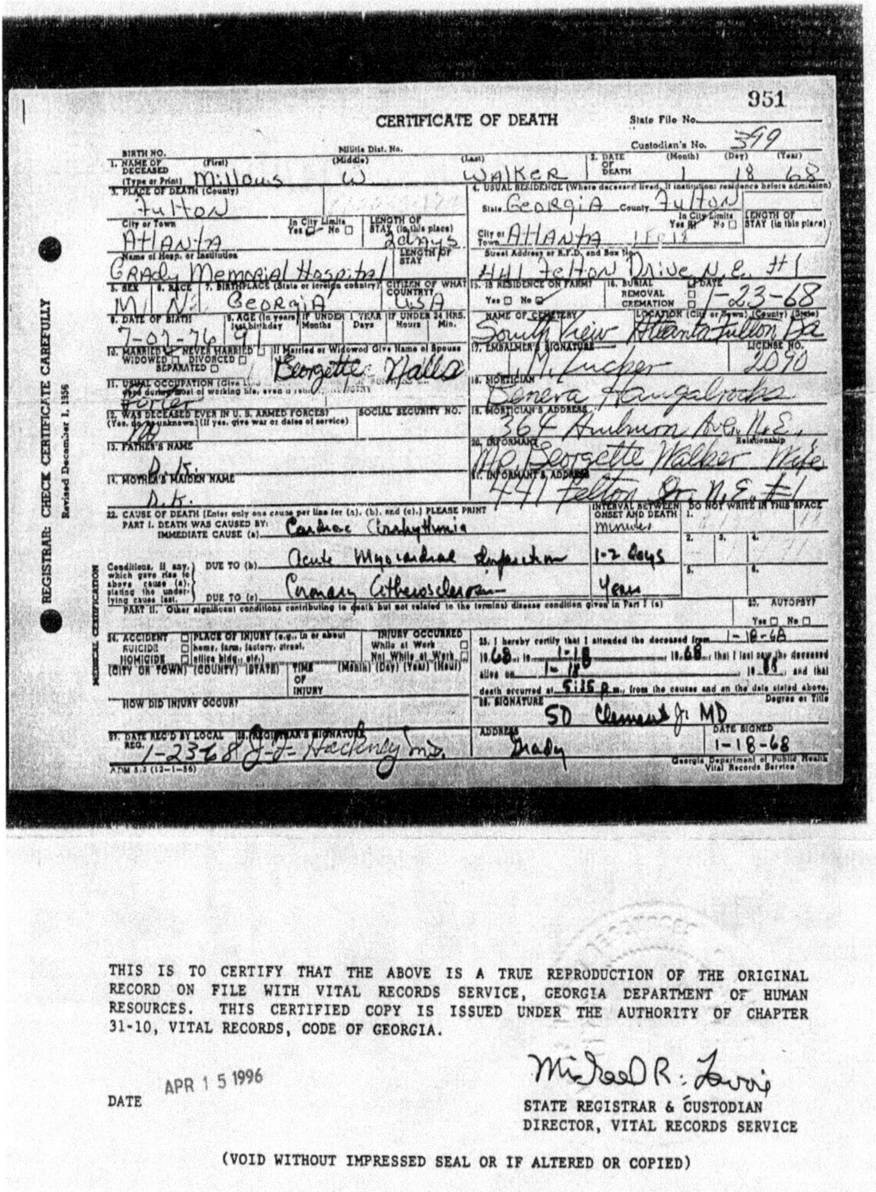

951

CERTIFICATE OF DEATH

State File No.

Custodian's No. 399

1. NAME OF DECEASED (Type or Print) (First) Millous (Middle) W. (Last) WALKER

2. DATE OF DEATH (Month) 1 (Day) 18 (Year) 68

3. PLACE OF DEATH (County) Fulton; City or Town Atlanta; In City Limits Yes; Length of Stay 2 days; Name of Hosp. or Institution Grady Memorial Hospital

4. USUAL RESIDENCE: State Georgia; County Fulton; City or Town Atlanta; Street Address 441 Felton Drive N.E. #1; Is Residence on Farm? No

5. SEX M; 6. RACE N; 7. BIRTHPLACE Georgia; CITIZEN OF WHAT COUNTRY USA

8. DATE OF BIRTH 7-07-76; 9. AGE 91

10. MARRIED; Name of Spouse Georgette Walker

11. USUAL OCCUPATION Porter

12. WAS DECEASED EVER IN U.S. ARMED FORCES? No

13. FATHER'S NAME D.K.

14. MOTHER'S MAIDEN NAME D.K.

BURIAL; DATE 1-23-68; NAME OF CEMETERY South View; LOCATION Atlanta Fulton Ga.

17. EMBALMER'S SIGNATURE J. M. Tucker; LICENSE NO. 2090

18. MORTICIAN Geneva Haugabrooks

19. MORTICIAN'S ADDRESS 364 Auburn Ave. N.E.

20. INFORMANT Mrs. Georgette Walker; Relationship Wife

21. INFORMANT'S ADDRESS 441 Felton Dr. N.E. #1

22. CAUSE OF DEATH PART I. DEATH WAS CAUSED BY: IMMEDIATE CAUSE (a) Cardiac Arrhythmia — minutes; DUE TO (b) Acute Myocardial Infarction — 1-2 days; DUE TO (c) Coronary Atherosclerosis — years

23. AUTOPSY? Yes ☐ No ☐

25. I hereby certify that I attended the deceased from 1-18-68 to 1-18-68, that I last saw the deceased alive on 1-18, and that death occurred at 5:15 p.m., from the causes and on the date stated above.

26. SIGNATURE SD Clement Jr. MD; ADDRESS Grady; DATE SIGNED 1-18-68

27. DATE REC'D BY LOCAL REG. 1-23-68; REGISTRAR'S SIGNATURE J. J. Hackney MD

Georgia Department of Public Health Vital Records Service

THIS IS TO CERTIFY THAT THE ABOVE IS A TRUE REPRODUCTION OF THE ORIGINAL RECORD ON FILE WITH VITAL RECORDS SERVICE, GEORGIA DEPARTMENT OF HUMAN RESOURCES. THIS CERTIFIED COPY IS ISSUED UNDER THE AUTHORITY OF CHAPTER 31-10, VITAL RECORDS, CODE OF GEORGIA.

DATE APR 15 1996

Michael R. Lavois
STATE REGISTRAR & CUSTODIAN
DIRECTOR, VITAL RECORDS SERVICE

(VOID WITHOUT IMPRESSED SEAL OR IF ALTERED OR COPIED)

**Death Certificate of Milous W. Walker, Sr.**

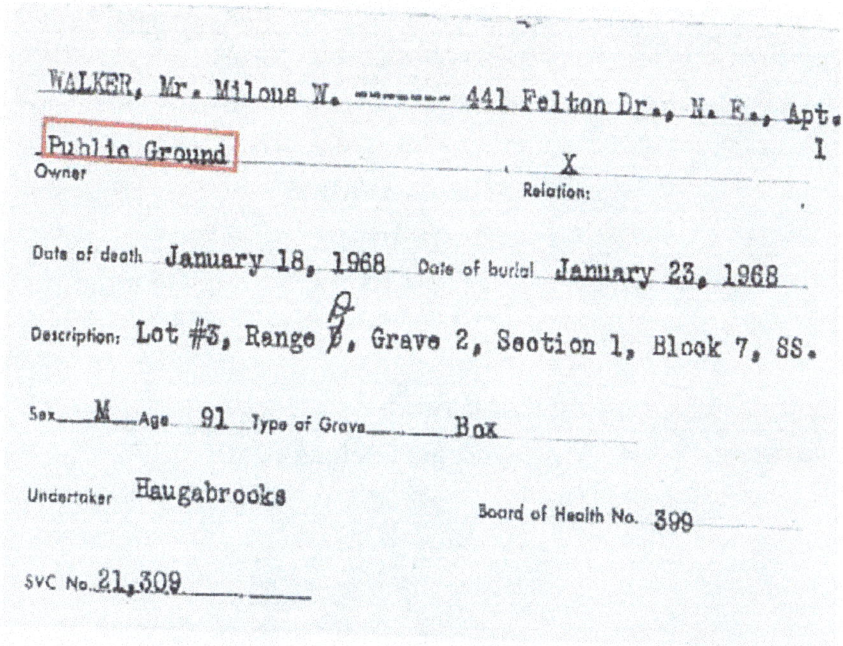

WALKER, Mr. Milous W. -------- 441 Felton Dr., N. E., Apt. I

Public Ground — X

Owner — Relation:

Date of death January 18, 1968 Date of burial January 23, 1968

Description: Lot #3, Range ~~D~~ Q, Grave 2, Section 1, Block 7, SS.

Sex M Age 91 Type of Grave Box

Undertaker Haugabrooks Board of Health No. 399

SVC No. 21,309

**Burial plot location of Milous W. Walker, Sr.**

**Milous Wilburn Walker, Sr. & his mother, Emma Felder Swift**

**Both are buried on PUBLIC GROUND . This is a section of the cemetery donated to families to bury their loved ones without any cost. The exception to this is that it is the responsibility of the families to remember the location and maintain the area. The cemetery charges a $20 per year fee if you are trying to locate the gravesite.**

**South View Cemetery Atlanta, Fulton Co., Georgia**

ancestry.com

## Social Security Death Index

| | |
|---|---|
| Name: | **Milous Walker** |
| SSN: | 252-01-4054 |
| Last Residence: | 30312 Atlanta, Fulton, Georgia, United States of America |
| Born: | 7 Jul 1876 |
| Died: | Jan 1968 |
| State (Year) SSN issued: | Georgia (Before 1951) |

**Source Citation:** Number: *252-01-4054*; Issue State: *Georgia*; Issue Date: *Before 1951*.

ancestry.com

## Georgia Deaths, 1919-98

| | |
|---|---|
| Name: | **Millous W Walker** |
| Death Date: | 18 Jan 1968 |
| County of Death: | Fulton |
| Gender: | M (Male) |
| Race: | Colored (Black) |
| Age: | 91 Years |
| County of Residence: | Fulton |
| Certificate: | 000951 |

**Source Citation:** Certificate Number: *000951*.

Father we thank thee for lesing us thee Milous Walker our brother.
Who's Christian witness helped us to grow more Christlibe toward one another,
We thank thee for his love of music, for his talent to play and to teach,
For his love of thy word the Bible, for his faith thy Heaven to reach,
We thank thee for his humility, for the child like quality of love, that indeared him to man kind below, and commend him to God above,
Thanks Father for Milous Walker, whose great tears unshamedly fell, when he told how Jesus Christ Gods Son, had died to save sinners from hell.

Mary Ruth T. King
Sunday School

The Family gratefully acknowledges all courtisies extended during the illness and passing of the late Mr. Milous W. Walker;

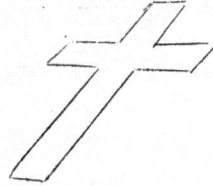

O B E S Q U I E S

F O R

MR. M I L O U S W. W A L K E R

JANUARY 23, 1960 — 2:P. M.
BIG BETHEL A. M. E. CHURCH
REV. REUBEN T. BUSSEY, PASTOR

HAUGABROOKS — MORTICIAN

THE OBITUARY

Mr. Milous W. Walker was born in Perry, Ge. Houston County, July 7, 1876. He was married to Miss Lula McCall and of this union four children were born, three girls and one boy. They moved to Atlanta while quite young. He became to member of Big Bethel A. M. E. Church and was very active in Sunday School and organized a Sunday School Orchestra that was still serving when he became too ill to attend. He was employed by the Sharp & Bohne Company for 42 years. He was married to Georgette Nalls who also survive him and his four children. Fifteen grand children, and 24 great grand children.

P R O G R A M

| | |
|---|---|
| ORGAN PRELUDE | |
| PROCESSIONAL | |
| SELECTION | What A Friend Choir |
| INVOCATION | Rev. E. B. Woods |
| SCRIPTURE | Rev. E. C. Brown |
| SOLO | Mr. H. J. Furlow |
| REMARKS | Mrs. Rosa B. Hanley<br>Fifty - Fifty Club<br>Mr. L. C. Mitchell<br>Sunday School<br>Selection of Sunday School<br>Rev. E. C. Brown<br>Class Leader |
| SELECTION | Sevant of God well Done<br>Choir |
| EULOGY | Rev. Reuben T. Bussey. |
| RECESSIONAL | |

INTERMENT — SOUTH VIEW CEMETARY

ancestry.com

## 1930 United States Federal Census

| | |
|---|---|
| Name: | **Annie L William** |
| Gender: | Female |
| Birth Year: | abt 1876 |
| Birthplace: | Georgia |
| Race: | Negro (Black) |
| Home in 1930: | Chicago, Cook, Illinois |
| Marital Status: | Married |
| Relation to Head of House: | Wife |
| Spouse's Name: | Oscar William |
| Father's Birthplace: | Virginia |
| Mother's Birthplace: | Georgia |

Household Members:

| Name | Age |
|---|---|
| Oscar William | 54 |
| Annie L William | 54 |

**Source Citation:** Year: *1930*; Census Place: *Chicago, Cook, Illinois*; Roll: *420*; Page: *6B*; Enumeration District: *139*; Image: *956.0*; FHL microfilm: *2340155*.

ancestry.com

## Illinois, Deaths and Stillbirths Index, 1916-1947

| | |
|---|---|
| Name: | **Oscar F. Williams** |
| Birth Date: | abt 1875 |
| Death Date: | 17 May 1944 |
| Death Place: | Chicago, Cook Co , Illinois |
| Burial Date: | 20 May 1944 |
| Burial Place: | Worth, Cook Co., Ill. |
| Death Age: | 69 |
| Gender: | Male |
| Father Name: | Columbus Williams |
| Spouse Name: | Annie L. |
| FHL Film Number: | 1983247 |

**Source Information:**
Ancestry.com. *Illinois, Deaths and Stillbirths Index, 1916-1947* [database on-line]. Provo, UT, USA: Ancestry.com Operations, Inc., 2011.

ancestry.com

## Cook County, Illinois Death Index, 1908-1988

| | |
|---|---|
| Name: | **Annie L Williams** |
| Death Date: | 5 Dec 1956 |
| Death Location: | Cook County, IL |
| File Number: | 88574 |
| Archive Collection Name: | Cook County (Deaths) |
| Archive repository location: | Chicago, IL |
| Archive repository name: | |

**Source Information:**

Ancestry.com. *Cook County, Illinois Death Index, 1908-1988* [database on-line]. Provo, UT, USA: Ancestry.com Operations Inc, 2008.

Original data: Cook County Clerk. *Cook County Clerk Genealogy* . Cook County Clerk's Office, Chicago, IL: Cook County Clerk, 2008.

**Lula Walker & granddaughter Julie Ann King**

JAN 05 1996

STATE OF ILLINOIS
County of Cook, } ss. DAVID D. ORR. County Clerk

I, DAVID D. ORR, County Clerk of the County of Cook, in the State aforesaid, and Keeper of the Records and Files of said County, do hereby certify that the attached is a true and correct copy of the original Record on file, all of which appears from the records and files in my office.

IN WITNESS WHEREOF, I have hereunto set my hand and affixed the Seal of the County of Cook, at my office in the City of Chicago, in said County.

David D. Orr
County Clerk

ORIGINAL 193

STATE OF ILLINOIS
MEDICAL CERTIFICATE OF DEATH

STATE FILE NUMBER 66662

DECEDENT'S BIRTH NO.

REGISTRATION DISTRICT NO. 16.10 REGISTERED NUMBER

1. PLACE OF DEATH a. COUNTY: COOK COUNTY, ILLINOIS

b. Death took place ☐ OUTSIDE city limits and in ... TOWNSHIP. ☒ INSIDE city limits and in the city, village, or town named at 1c

c. CITY, VILLAGE, OR TOWN: CHICAGO

d. LENGTH OF STAY IN 1b or 1c: 33 YRS

e. NAME OF HOSPITAL OR INSTITUTION (If not in hospital or institution, give street address): COOK COUNTY

f. LENGTH OF STAY (in 1e): 26 DAYS

2. USUAL RESIDENCE (Where deceased lived. If institution, residence before admission.) a. STATE: ILLINOIS b. COUNTY: COOK

c. Residence was ☐ OUTSIDE city limits and in ... TOWNSHIP. ☒ INSIDE city limits and in the city, village, or town named at 2d

d. CITY, VILLAGE, OR TOWN: CHICAGO

e. LENGTH OF RESIDENCE AT 2c or 2d: 32 YRS

f. STREET ADDRESS: 817 E 90th PL

g. Did decedent reside ON A FARM? YES ☐ NO ☒

3. NAME OF DECEASED a. (FIRST) LULA b. (MIDDLE) c. (LAST) WALKER

4. DATE OF DEATH (MONTH) (DAY) (YEAR): 9-27-60

5. SEX: FEMALE

6. RACE: NEGRO

7. MARRIED, NEVER MARRIED, WIDOWED, DIVORCED (specify): DIVORCED

8. DATE OF BIRTH: ESTIMATED

9. AGE (in years last birthday): 87

10a. USUAL OCCUPATION (Give kind of work done during most of working life, even if retired): TEACHER

10b. KIND OF BUSINESS OR INDUSTRY: PUBLIC SCHOOL

11. BIRTHPLACE (City and state or foreign country): DUBLIN GA.

12. Citizen of what country? USA

13. FATHER'S FULL NAME: JOHN STANLEY

14. MOTHER'S FULL MAIDEN NAME: UNKNOWN

15. Was deceased ever in U.S. Armed Forces? (Yes, no, or unknown) (If yes, give war or dates of service): NO

16. SOCIAL SECURITY NUMBER: UNKNOWN

17. INFORMANT a. SIGNATURE: MRS ANNE FORT

b. ADDRESS: 1310 W 64th ST

c. RELATIONSHIP TO DECEASED: DAUGHTER

18. CAUSE OF DEATH

PART I. DEATH WAS CAUSED BY: [Enter only one cause per line for (A), (B), and (C).]

IMMEDIATE CAUSE (A) PRIMARY BRONCHO PNEUMONIA

Conditions, if any, which gave rise to the above IMMEDIATE CAUSE (A), stating the UNDERLYING cause last. due to (B) ... due to (C) ...

INTERVAL BETWEEN ONSET AND DEATH

PART II. OTHER SIGNIFICANT CONDITIONS CONTRIBUTING TO DEATH BUT NOT RELATED TO THE TERMINAL CONDITION GIVEN IN PART I(A)

19. AUTOPSY? YES ☐ NO ☒

20. DESCRIBE CIRCUMSTANCES OF INJURY, IF ANY, WHOSE NATURE IS MENTIONED IN PART I OR PART II ABOVE.

21. I hereby certify that I attended the deceased from 9-2-1960, to 9-27-1960, that I last saw the deceased alive on 9-27-1960, and death occurred at 117 P M., from the causes and on the date stated above.

DATE 9/28/60 SIGNED Richard A. O'Connor M.D. ADDRESS COOK COUNTY HOSP PHONE SE-8-2500

MEDICAL CERTIFICATION — DR R O'CONNOR MD

22. DISPOSITION: BURIAL-REMOVAL-CREMATION (DATE) 10-1-60

CEMETERY: BURR OAK

LOCATION: WORTH ILL

23. FUNERAL DIRECTOR — FIRM NAME: MILLER & MAJOR

ADDRESS: 730 E 63 St CHICAGO 37 ILL

SIGNATURE: [signature] LICENSE NUMBER 5578

24. Received for filing SEP 28 1960 (Signed) Samuel L. Andelman M.D.

54 West Hubbard Street, Chicago 10
CHICAGO BOARD OF HEALTH LOCAL REGISTRAR

VS & R 200--BUREAU OF STATISTICS--ILLINOIS DEPARTMENT OF PUBLIC HEALTH--SPRINGFIELD

VS & R 200 U.S. Standard Certificate of Death

FILL IN WITH TYPEWRITER OR LEGIBLE PRINTING

**Death Certificate of Lula McCall Walker**

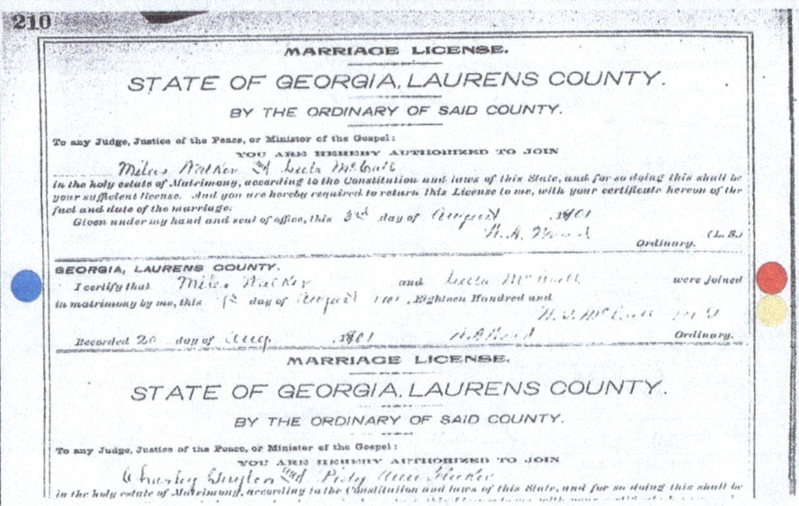

210

MARRIAGE LICENSE.

STATE OF GEORGIA, LAURENS COUNTY.

BY THE ORDINARY OF SAID COUNTY.

To any Judge, Justice of the Peace, or Minister of the Gospel:

YOU ARE HEREBY AUTHORIZED TO JOIN

Milous Walker and Lula McCall

*in the holy estate of Matrimony, according to the Constitution and laws of this State, and for so doing this shall be your sufficient license. And you are hereby required to return this License to me, with your certificate hereon of the fact and date of the marriage.*

*Given under my hand and seal of office, this* 3rd *day of* August 1901

H. A. Wood *Ordinary.* (L. S.)

GEORGIA, LAURENS COUNTY.

*I certify that* Milous Walker *and* Lula McCall *were joined in matrimony by me, this* 12 *day of* August 1901, *Eighteen Hundred and*

W. J. McCall M. G.

*Recorded* 20 *day of* Aug 1901 H. A. Wood *Ordinary.*

MARRIAGE LICENSE.

STATE OF GEORGIA, LAURENS COUNTY.

BY THE ORDINARY OF SAID COUNTY.

To any Judge, Justice of the Peace, or Minister of the Gospel:

YOU ARE HEREBY AUTHORIZED TO JOIN

Charley Guyton and Polly Ann Tucker

*in the holy estate of Matrimony, according to the Constitution and laws of this State, and for so doing this shall be*

**1901 Marriage of Milous W. Walker and Louisa 'Lula' Rebecca McCall**

## The Children of

## Louisa Rebecca (Lula) & Milous Wilburn Walker, Sr.

**Mattie (aka Mata) Annie Milous, Jr. Ethel**

Lula and Milous Wilburn Walker, Sr., have passed on a legacy of which their descendants should be proud. Out of their union, the occupations, careers, endeavors, and accomplishments of their generations of offspring, are innumerable, ranging from A-to-Z. These souls have been administrators, artists, athletes, authors, barbers, business owners, carpenters, cosmetologists, directors, doctors, educators, entrepreneurs, filmmakers, free-lancers, genealogists, gentlemen, homemakers, inspectors, jazz artists, journalists, kings, launderers, lawyers, linguists, managers, musicians, the musically-inclined, narrators, nurses, officers, orators, organizers, photographers, poets, producers, quality-controllers, queens, quick-thinkers, rappers, retailers, social workers, soldiers, translators, universalists, virtuosos, writers, existentialists, yogis, and zest-for-lifers.

An African adage states that those who boast of their ancestors, praise the merits of another. We, the current and future descendants of Louisa Rebecca McCall and Milous Wilburn Walker, are, and will be the embodiment of who they were. This privilege contains the spiritual, physical, and psychological aspects of life and living that will enable the success and survival of this family on the earth. It behooves us to seek to know from whence we came, so that the family legacy will be far more than just a story to be told.

It will be a beacon, a brilliant light for posterity, leading and guiding them into all truth.

*... And you shall know the truth,*
*and the truth shall make you free.*

*St. John 8:32*

# 100 SOULS

These stories, by Maurice Allen, Jr., of the Walker and McCall Families of Georgia are told in three chronicles: 1830-1870 / 1871-1900 / 1901-1940. The title represents an approximation of the number of descendants that have been born since the 1901 marriage of Milous Wilburn Walker and his bride, Louisa 'Lula' Rebecca McCall, the great-grandparents of the author.

There is an old adage that states:

"Don't judge a man until you've walked a mile in his shoes." The next page is a pictorial of 50 pairs of shoes of different styles, from different eras, worn by men, women, children and babies. This worthwhile journey is our walk through the life experiences of our ancestors, who were similarly shod with...

# 100 SOLES

# ACKNOWLEDGEMENTS

I would like to thank all of my family for their support, as I embarked on this worthwhile journey of finding our ancestors. My aunts, uncles, and cousins have all been very instrumental in this process of connecting to our past, and honoring our ancestors. I'd especially like to thank my parents, who are now with the ancestors. Their stories were the first wave of information that launched me into the world of genealogy.

Thank you to my friends and their families, who allowed me to assist them with their family history quests. The experience of helping others gave me the opportunity to hone valuable research skills that I use to this day.

Thank you, Houston, Texas, for embracing me during the 10 years I lived there. Organizations in Houston, that I would like to thank include The Clayton Library Center for Genealogical Research. Since 1995, their staff came to know me well, and I was able to benefit greatly from their helpfulness, and their expertise. The Julia C. Hester House and their staff were gracious to me as I discovered that Mrs. Hester and my paternal great-grandmother, Mrs. Louisa 'Lula' McCall Walker, were first cousins. I am grateful for the connection and the revelation.

Thank you, to the schools in Texas and Michigan, that contracted me to present my genealogy workshops to their students. The teaching experience was awesome.

| | |
|---|---|
| Betty Best Elementary School | - Houston/ Alief ISD |
| Klentzmann Middle School | - Houston/ Alief ISD |
| Atherton Elementary School | - Houston/ HISD |
| Jack Yates High School | - Houston/ HISD |
| Texas Southern University (TSU) | - Houston, TX |
| Southwestern Christian College | - Terrell, TX |
| The MS National Archives | - Jackson, MS |
| The MS Civil Rights Museum | - Jackson, MS |

21st Century After-School Program of Detroit

DPR Educational Services of Detroit

WEBSITES

fold3.com

ancestry.com

familysearch.org

heritagequestonline.com

www.ingramcontent.com/pod-product-compliance
Lightning Source LLC
Chambersburg PA
CBHW072121020426
42334CB00018B/1674
* 9 7 8 0 9 8 6 1 6 1 0 4 9 *